The Boundaries of Moral Discourse

Values and Ethics Series, Volume 8

The Boundaries of Moral Discourse

Mane Hajdin

Loyola University Press
Chicago

Loyola University Press
3441 North Ashland Avenue
Chicago, Illinois 60657

Cover design by Nancy Gruenke

Library of Congress Cataloging-in-Publication Data

Hajdin, Mane.
    The boundaries of moral discourse / Mane Hajdin.
        p.   cm. — (Values and ethics series; v. 8)
    Includes bibliographical references and index.
    ISBN 0-8294-0747-2
    1. Ethics. I. Title. II. Title: Moral discourse. III. Series:
Values & ethics series ; v. 8.
    BJ1031 .H3   1993
    170' .42—dc20
                                                        93-11148
                                                           CIP

Contents

Acknowledgments   ix

Introduction   xi

1. Morality vs. Other Types of Prescriptive Discourse   1
   1.1 Morality and Prudence   1
   1.2 Morality and Admirability   3
   1.3 Overridingness   7
   1.4 A Note on the Alleged Wider
      Sense of Morality   15
   1.5 Moral Sanctions   17

2. The Shoehorn Maneuver   21
   2.1 A Fresh Start   21
   2.2 The Shoehorn Maneuver and Universalizability 23
   2.3 Moral Discourse and the Shoehorn Maneuver   28
   2.4 The Designated Argument-Places in Moral and
      Prudential Claims   30
   2.5 Universalizability and the Designated
      Argument-Places   36

3. Agents and Patients   43
   3.1 Introduction   43
   3.2 Are There Any Multi-Agent and
      Multi-Patient Claims?   43
   3.3 Some Ambiguities   46
   3.4 The Standard Form of Moral Claims   48
   3.5 The Moral Community   49
   3.6 Moral Patients: Objections and Replies   56
   3.6.1 Duties to Oneself   56
   3.6.2 Deontological Ethics   57
   3.6.3 Impersonality   58
   3.6.4 Virtues   59
   3.7 Matters of Degree   62

4. Rights and Right-Holders   65
   4.1 Introduction: Correlativism vs. Anticorrelativism   65
   4.2 How to Talk about Rights   67
   4.3 Alleged Counterexamples to Correlativism   71
   4.3.1 Animals   72
   4.3.2 Charity   72
   4.3.3 Tax Evasion   75
   4.4 Refutations of Anticorrelativist Theories   76
   4.4.1 Limiting the Freedom of Others   76
   4.4.2 Claiming   79
   4.4.3 Waiving   83
   4.4.4 Protection of Liberties   83
   4.4.5 Rights as Grounds of Duties   85
   4.5 Dispensability of *Right*   86

5. Questions about Membership in the Moral Community 89
   5.1 The Independence of Questions about
       Membership in the Moral Community   89
   5.2 Membership in the Moral Community
       and Methods of Moral Argumentation   95
   5.3 An Alternative Way of Discussing
       Agency and Patiency?   99
   5.4 Applications   102
   5.4.1 Equality   103
   5.4.2 Equal Consideration   105
   5.4.3 Respect for Persons   107
   5.4.4 Everybody Should Count for One   111
   5.4.5 Value   112

6. Myself and Others   117
   6.1 Contingent Limitations on the Use of
       the Shoehorn Maneuver   117
   6.2 Essential Properties   122
   6.3 Conclusions about the Moral Community   127
   6.4 Personal Identity across Possible Worlds   130
   6.5 Transfer of Consciousness
       within a Single World   139

7. Consequences   145
  7.1 Relativism   145
  7.2 How to Argue with Radical Racists   146
  7.3 Stable and Unstable Membership in the Moral
      Community   150
  7.4 Applications   153
    7.4.1 Animals   154
    7.4.2 Inanimate Nature   157
    7.4.3 Fetuses   157
    7.4.4 Infants   158
    7.4.5 Members of Future Generations   160
    7.4.6 Computers   160
    7.4.7 Organizations and Groups   162
    7.4.8 Criminals   162
    7.4.9 The Insane and the Mentally Retarded   164

Notes   169

Bibliography   215

Index   227

Acknowledgments

The arguments presented here have been greatly improved as a result of Storrs McCall's patient and detailed criticisms of their numerous earlier versions. For stimulating discussion of these arguments I am also indebted to Jim Hankinson, Patricia Illingworth, Iddo Landau, and Bojana Mladenović. Section 1.5 originally appeared under the title "Sanctions and the Notion of Morality" in *Dialogue* 32 (1993): 757–60. It is reprinted here, with changes, by permission of the editor of *Dialogue*. Chapter 4 is reprinted, with changes, from Aleksandar Pavković, ed., *Contemporary Yugoslav Philosophy: The Analytic Approach* (Dordrecht, Netherlands: Kluwer Academic Publishers, 1988), 97–119, where it appeared under the title "A Defence of Rights-Duties Correlativism," © 1988 by Kluwer Academic Publishers. Reprinted by permission of Kluwer Academic Publishers.

Introduction

1

This book explores three different but interconnected kinds of boundaries of moral discourse.

First, it explores the boundaries that separate moral discourse from similar kinds of discourse (such as prudential discourse, the discourse of etiquette, and legal discourse). I argue that the understanding of these boundaries involves our understanding of the characteristic way in which moral discourse handles references to members of *the moral community*, that is those to whom moral precepts are addressed and those of whom it can be said that they are wronged when moral precepts are violated.

This exploration gives rise to the question as to what the boundaries of the moral community are. The boundaries of the moral community can be regarded, in a sense, as the boundaries of moral discourse, and constitute the second kind of boundaries of moral discourse that are explored in this book.

In giving my answer to the question about the boundaries of the moral community, I argue that the methods of argumentation that are normally used for resolving disputes within moral discourse are, in principle incapable of resolving disputes about the boundaries of the moral community. This conclusion implies that there are, in a sense, boundaries to what moral discourse can accomplish, and this is the third kind of boundaries of moral discourse that this book is about.

The book takes the work of R. M. Hare both as its main starting point and as its main target of criticism. Familiarity with the basic tenets of Hare's theory and arguments that support them is presupposed.

I need to emphasize that by "Hare's theory" I mean the theory presented and defended in *Freedom and Reason*[1] and *Moral Thinking*.[2] Experience shows that many people, including highly respected philosophers, hold very strong (usually unfavorable) views about Hare's philosophy that are based almost exclusively on his early book *The Language of Morals*.[3] The views expressed in that book have largely been incorporated into Hare's later theory, but they have been incorporated into it in a way that makes the book itself rather misleading if it is used as the principal source of information about Hare's current views.

Hare's theory is thus often summarily dismissed on the basis of arguments that may seem plausible when directed to the text of *The Language of Morals* but that have been either explicitly responded to or simply rendered obsolete by later developments of the theory. As Hare himself has put it:

> I still often meet philosophers who think that it is an argument against my views to show that what is right or wrong cannot depend on what somebody prescribes. I find it extraordinary that anybody should attribute to me the view that it so depends.[4]

Such views nevertheless continue to be attributed to Hare, usually on the basis of quotations from *The Language of Morals* that are, in the light of his later work, seriously misleading.[5]

Things are made even worse by the fact that Hare's theory is often carelessly lumped together with other forms of metaethical noncognitivism. As a consequence, the views toward his theory are often colored by its being associated with ideas such as those expressed in the (in)famous chapter on ethics in Ayer's *Language, Truth and Logic*.[6] This way of thinking perpetuates "the confusion of supposing that the only way to be a rationalist is to be a descriptivist. No progress can be made in moral philosophy by those who are the victims of this confusion."[7]

One can observe this confusion at work in the recent advent of moral realism. What attracts people to moral realism is the belief that defending moral realism is the only way to avoid moral relativism and nihilism. The option of combining noncognitivism (and thus antirealism) with antirelativism is not something that contemporary moral realists typically reject by argument: it simply does not occur to them that there is such an option. This, of course, is precisely the option developed in *Freedom and Reason* and *Moral Thinking*.

This book is not addressed to the victims of this confusion. It does nothing to dispel it because it assumes that its readers have already had it dispelled by reading Hare himself.

2

Hare has argued that the characteristics that distinguish moral discourse from other types of discourse are its prescriptivity, universalizability, and overridingness.

I treat his arguments in favor of the thesis of prescriptivity of moral discourse as conclusive and do not intend to challenge it in any way.

I also accept the thesis of universalizability of moral discourse. Yet, even though I accept the thesis itself, I criticize Hare's view about the importance of that thesis. What motivates this criticism is that Hare's treatment of universalizability leaves his readers with a puzzle that cannot be fully resolved within his theory. On the one hand, in order to convince his readers that moral discourse is universalizable, Hare argues that universalizability is not a feature that is peculiar to moral discourse. According to him, most of the types of discourse that we engage in (both prescriptive and nonprescriptive) are universalizable in exactly the same way. On the other hand, he argues that the universalizability of moral discourse has very important consequences, and no parallel consequences seem to follow from the universalizability of other types of discourse. It is puzzling how these two aspects of Hare's account of universalizability are supposed to fit together: if types of discourse other than moral are also universalizable, why is their universalizability not equally important?[8] I believe that the criticism of Hare's view of the implications of the thesis of universalizability that I propose in chapter 2 (while retaining the thesis itself) offers a way out of that puzzle.

Before embarking on that criticism, I reject, in chapter 1, the thesis that overridingness is what distinguishes moral discourse from other types of discourse that are also prescriptive and universalizable. The thesis is criticized in two different ways: first, assuming that overridingness could, in principle, be used to distinguish one type of prescriptive discourse from another, it is questionable whether moral discourse is the one that is overriding; and, second, it is in principle impossible to use overridingness to distinguish one type of prescriptive discourse from another, because all types of prescriptive discourse are bound to be on a par with respect to overridingness. At the end of chapter 1 I also briefly discuss and reject an alternative thesis, according to which the feature that distinguishes moral discourse from other types of prescriptive and universalizable discourse is that its prescriptions are backed up by "moral sanctions."

In chapter 2 I offer a solution to the question as to what distinguishes moral discourse from other types of prescriptive discourse.[9] As the starting point of this chapter I take the work of philosophers who pointed out the importance of arguments based on imaginatively putting oneself in the shoes of others ("the shoehorn maneuver" for short) in moral discourse. I first show that (contrary to Hare) the role that the shoehorn maneuver plays in moral discourse is not a consequence of its universalizability. I then show that we cannot distinguish moral discourse from other types of prescriptive discourse simply by saying that arguments based on the shoehorn maneuver are used in it, because such arguments are also used in prudential discourse. Finally, I show that we can distinguish the ways in which arguments based on the shoehorn maneuver are used in moral and in prudential discourse, and that we can therefore distinguish moral discourse from other types of prescriptive discourse by saying that arguments based on the shoehorn maneuver are used in moral discourse in a certain characteristic way. Arguments based on the shoehorn maneuver can be performed only on certain *designated argument-places*, and in moral claims argument-places of two different types are designated: those for moral agents and those for moral "patients" (those of whom it can be said that they are wronged when moral precepts are violated); while in prudential claims argument-places of only one type are designated: those for prudential agents.

Chapter 3 begins the discussion of moral agency and moral patiency from the perspective that is provided by the analysis of the notion of morality presented in chapter 2. It provides some additional clarification of the notions of moral agents and moral patients and the role that they play in our understanding of how moral discourse functions. Thus, it is shown there that the consequence of my analysis, according to which every moral claim must have (or be capable of being reformulated so as to have) a term for moral patients, is not without intuitive appeal and that this consequence is compatible with there being duties to oneself, with there being nonutilitarian ethics, with some of Parfit's suggestions about the "impersonality" of reasons for acting, and with the actual use of virtue-ascriptions. It is also shown that there are reasons for formulating all moral rules that one assents to so that variables for agents in all of them range over one and the same set (which we may call the set of moral agents) and so that the variables for patients in all of them range over one and the same set (which we may call the set of moral patients). In the final section of that chapter I argue that being a moral agent and/or patient is not a matter of degree.

In chapter 4 I argue that ascriptions of rights can always be replaced, without any loss, by ascriptions of duties—for example, the claim that "Paula has the right that Peter pay her five dollars" can always be replaced, without any loss, by the claim "Peter has the duty to Paula to pay her five dollars." The consequence of the rights-duties correlativism that I defend there is that there is no real difference between being a moral patient and being a right-holder (while moral agents are those that rights are held against). The rest of the book takes ascriptions of duties as the paradigm of moral claims and mentions only moral agents and moral patients as members of the "moral community." The role of this chapter is to justify the disregard for ascriptions of rights and for right-holders in the other parts of the book.

In chapter 5 I continue to investigate the functioning of terms for moral agents and moral patients by discussing the status of questions about membership in the sets of moral agents and moral patients. I argue that these questions are importantly different and relatively independent of questions about content of moral rules (where the content is expressed using individual variables). Answers to questions about membership in these two sets cannot be found by the application of arguments based on the shoehorn maneuver. This difference entails that Hare's refutation of moral relativism affects only relativism about the content of moral rules and leaves open the possibility of relativism about membership in the moral community. I then proceed to argue that, although the boundaries of the moral community cannot be discovered by the *application* of arguments based on the shoehorn maneuver, they can be discovered by studying the *limitations to the applicability* of such arguments. In this chapter I also show how the distinction between questions about membership in the moral community and questions about content of moral rules can help us avoid some of the problems that are routinely encountered with notions such as *equality, equal consideration,* and *respect for persons.*

In chapter 6 I offer an answer to the question as to what the boundaries of the moral community are. I first distinguish conceptual limitations to the applicability of arguments based on the shoehorn maneuver (which are relevant here) from merely practical limitations. I then argue that each participant in moral discourse regards certain properties as essential to being himself and that possession of these properties determines the boundaries of moral community for him. The second half of that chapter shows how my account of properties that are essential to one's being oneself can be related to some more technical accounts of the matter that have been offered in the literature.

The account of membership in the sets of moral agents and moral patients that I offer in chapter 6 constitutes a form of relativism about this membership. In chapter 7 I show that the consequences of this form of relativism are not as radical as they might seem to be. I first show that this form of relativism leaves considerable room for rational discussion about the membership. In the remainder of the chapter I spell out some of the consequences that the argument of this book might have for discussions regarding our treatment of animals, fetuses, infants, the mentally retarded, and similarly problematic classes of individuals. I try to show how, for at least some of them, especially for the mentally retarded, the difference between counting and not counting them as members of the moral community (although theoretically important) might not be of much practical importance.

This section has been the overview of the path that will be traversed in this book. In the remainder of this introduction I make explicit some of the methodological presuppositions of the book (section 3) and clarify some aspects of the terminology that I shall be using (section 4).

3

The criteria for evaluating a philosophical account of the functioning of any type of discourse, including moral discourse, I regard as analogous to the criteria that we use in evaluating an account of the grammar of a language.

The first criterion that we use in deciding whether to accept or reject something that is offered as an account of the grammar of, say, English is the criterion of correspondence with actual linguistic behavior. We certainly would not accept an account of English grammar that designates as correct English something that bears no resemblance to any of the ways in which English is actually spoken.

But we also do not expect the fit between an account of English grammar and the actual linguistic behavior of English speakers to be perfect. We can see that such a fit is not what is expected by simply reflecting on the obvious fact that what is currently accepted as the account of English grammar fits rather poorly the ways in which the majority of English speakers actually speak. This discrepancy suggests that we expect those who produce accounts of English grammar to do something different from simply reporting about the actual linguistic behavior of English speakers.

An account of English grammar that would at the same time capture the ways in which English is spoken in the slums of large United States cities and in Oxford lecture halls is logically possible, but it would have to be extremely complex. If such an account were offered, it would be rejected, as we do not want to accept anything that complex as the account of English grammar. A good account of grammar must have a certain kind of structure that can be characterized as *neat*; this is the second criterion for evaluating such accounts. (I am not going to undertake the task of providing a philosophical account of what *neatness* is since it is not necessary for my purposes here.)

However, we do not expect an account of English grammar to be so perfectly neat that it loses touch with actual linguistic behavior (an account that would disregard the existence of irregular verbs would certainly be neater than the account of

English grammar that is currently accepted, but it would depart from the actual use of the language too much). What we expect from an account of grammar is that it achieve equilibrium between neatness and correspondence with actual linguistic behavior.

But these two criteria are not the only ones that we use in assessing various systems of rules that could be proposed as rules of English grammar. There is a third. In creating and evaluating accounts of English grammar we tend to pay much more attention to the ways in which English is spoken by Oxford professors than by slum-dwellers, in spite of the fact that the latter are much more numerous. Some people may want to argue that this policy is nothing but a manifestation of some sort of class bias. But the policy may also be regarded as a manifestation of something more rational. Namely it is usually believed that the expressive power of what is spoken by Oxford professors is superior to the expressive power of what is spoken by average slum-dwellers. This belief may itself be a manifestation of some bias, but regardless of whether it is true, the fact that it is usually held by those who create and evaluate accounts of grammar, and that they would probably invoke it to justify their paying only limited attention to the uneducated, suggests that the third criterion for evaluating an account of grammar is that what the account designates as correct English should have as much expressive power as is compatible with respect for the other two criteria.

Needless to say, the three criteria listed here come into play only if what is offered as an account of grammar satisfies some basic requirements that any account of anything is supposed to satisfy, such as intelligibility and consistency. An account of grammar can always be dismissed for failing to satisfy such basic requirements, and failing to satisfy any of them cannot be compensated for by satisfying some other criterion well.

It does not seem unreasonable to take the three criteria used in evaluating an account of the grammar of a language as criteria for judging philosophical accounts of the functioning of a particular type or aspect of discourse. It seems that many contemporary philosophers are guided by these three criteria when they construct their theories or criticize theories that have been constructed by others.

As with grammar, we must bear in mind that all three criteria are relevant, and that none of them is decisive when taken in isolation. We also must bear in mind that no philosophical account can satisfy all three criteria perfectly. The account that we accept is one that receives, as it were, a higher total score on all three criteria taken together than any of the alternative accounts.

Such use of the three criteria means that pointing out that there is a gap between some philosophical account and the way people actually speak always counts against the account, but it rarely in itself amounts to a sufficient reason for rejecting it. Before we reject it we must see how large the gap is and whether the gap is compensated for by how the account fares on the remaining two criteria. In this respect, the philosophical method that is outlined here differs from the philosophical method that was popular during the fifties, in which pointing out that "people don't talk this way" was regarded as a knockdown argument against any philosophical account. Strict adherence to the latter method effectively prevents any interesting philosophical account from ever being accepted.

The resemblances between accounts of grammar and philosophical accounts of functioning of certain types or aspects of discourse do not end there. If a group of people accepts something as an account of the grammar of their language, they do not merely admire it as an intellectual achievement; they also modify their linguistic behavior somewhat in the light of the account. Such modifications make it possible for communication among them to proceed more smoothly and to be more fruitful, which in turn increases their well-being in various ways. A good account of grammar, therefore, must be such that speakers of the language can accept it, that they are relatively likely to accept it, and that its acceptance can be expected to produce some net increase in well-being of those who do accept it, through facilitating their communication. These features are, generally, possessed precisely by the accounts that satisfy the above three criteria.

There is no reason why one would not say the same about philosophical accounts of the functioning of certain aspects or types of discourse. We have probably all experienced that, once we accept some such account, our communication with others who accept it proceeds more smoothly and becomes more fruitful, thus increasing our well-being (in addition to any increase in well-being that comes from our simply enjoying discussions of various philosophical accounts). It happens that precisely the accounts that are selected by the three criteria are most likely to produce these beneficial consequences. I do not want to imply here that an increase in well-being must be regarded as the main reason for judging philosophical accounts by the three criteria, but it certainly can be regarded as a reason for doing so.

What I have presented in this section may remind some people of Rawls's idea of "reflective equilibrium." It is, however, important to note that Rawls's idea applies to a subject matter that is entirely different from what has been discussed above. The above criteria are the criteria for judging philosophical accounts of the functioning of various types of discourse: when applied within ethics, they become the criteria for judging philosophical accounts of moral discourse. They thus operate on the level of what is known as metaethics. Rawlsian reflective equilibrium, however, is to be established at the level of normative ethics: it involves balancing moral principles with specific moral intuitions. The application of the criteria discussed above to moral discourse, on the other hand, does not involve moral intuitions; the only intuitions that it might involve are linguistic intuitions.[10]

4

In examining the question as to what distinguishes moral discourse from other types of discourse, I shall assume that my readers are, at least in general, able to recognize instances of moral discourse, and that they agree that moral discourse seems to be a distinct type of discourse. The understanding of what the latter assumption involves may be facilitated if I say that what I call "a type of discourse" could also be called "a language-game." (The only reason for my generally avoiding the term *language-game* is that the use of that term is too strongly associated with the philosophy of the later Wittgenstein, while the general spirit of this book is very un-Wittgensteinian.)

Individuating types of discourse is analogous to individuating (types of) games. I expect that my readers have some inclination to say that moral discourse, prudential discourse, and aesthetic discourse are distinct types of discourse, just as, if I were writing about card playing, I would expect them to have some inclination to say that bridge, poker, and canasta are different games.

One thing that can certainly be said about moral discourse without giving rise to much controversy is that in moral discourse it is *moral claims* that we make, support, criticize, and so on. Moreover, when we engage in moral discourse, our aim is to arrive at moral claims that we will be able to accept. Within moral discourse we frequently make claims that are not themselves moral (such as factual ones), but we do that only when we need them in order to arrive at moral claims.

Philosophers who are interested in the topics that I discuss in this book speak about properties of moral claims more frequently than about properties of moral discourse. But the properties that are usually appealed to in various analyses of what makes something a moral claim rather than a claim of some other kind (e.g., universalizability) are relational rather than nonrelational properties. According to such analyses, in order to understand what makes something into a moral claim, we must understand how it is related to other claims, what proper reactions to it are, and so on. This can be expressed by saying that, according to these analyses, in order to understand what makes something into a moral claim we must understand the functioning of moral discourse (in spite of the fact that the term *discourse* is rarely used by the authors of these analyses).

Although what I mean by "moral claims" is in many respects analogous to statements and propositions (e.g., it can be said that an English and a French sentence express the same moral claim), I prefer the term *claim* in this context to terms like *statement* or *proposition* because the latter are suggestive of metaethical cognitivism, which is something that I do not want to endorse. Moreover, the term *proposition* is better reserved for something that constitutes a component of a claim, namely for what Hare would call its phrastic part. I use *moral claim* rather than *moral judgment* (which is what Hare normally uses), because the latter may be understood as referring to a mental entity, rather than a piece of moral discourse. (Within the discussion of Feinberg's account of rights, in subsection 4.4.2, the term *claim* will also appear in the sense in which Feinberg uses it, and the relation between this sense and the sense in which I am using it in the rest of the book will be examined.)

My use of the term *moral claim* is such that claims can be both singular (e.g., "Peter has a duty to Paula that ———") and universal (e.g., "Everyone has a duty to everyone that ———"). Universal moral claims I often call *moral rules*. More basic moral rules I sometimes call *moral principles* (I do not make a sharp distinction, such as the one made by Dworkin, between rules and principles). I sometimes call a set of moral claims that a given person assents to the person's *moral view*, or *moral system*.

A moral view or a moral claim can contradict another moral view or claim. I assume that this is currently regarded as uncontroversial: early versions of emotivism were abandoned precisely because they failed to acknowledge this. When we notice a contradiction in any context, we typically do not sit back and simply contemplate it: we try to eliminate it by engaging in a discussion of the appropriate type. This applies to contradictions between moral views and claims as well, and the type of discourse in which we try to eliminate such contradictions is, of course, moral discourse.

Thus, for example, the claim that the judge, morally speaking, ought to sentence a particular man to death, and the claim that the judge, morally speaking, ought not to sentence that man to death, contradict each other. But the latter claim does not contradict the claim that the judge, legally speaking, ought to sentence the man to death, because "morally speaking, ought" and "legally speaking, ought" are "operators" that belong to different types of discourse. It is not even appropriate to ask whether a moral claim contradicts a legal claim. Still there is obviously some sort of opposition between the claim that the judge, morally speaking, ought not to sentence the man to death, and the claim that the judge, legally speaking, ought to sentence the man to death. Namely, if what the judge actually does satisfies the moral claim then it will not satisfy the legal claim and vice versa. We can express this by saying that the moral claim *conflicts with* the legal claim.

It is important not to confuse cases where two views belonging to different types of discourse conflict with each other with cases where two views (belonging to the same type of discourse) contradict each other. Two contradictory moral views can be confronted within moral discourse, and two contradictory legal views can be confronted within legal discourse, but there is no type of discourse in which we could confront a legal view with a moral view. (We can do something else: we can confront a moral view that we, morally speaking, ought to do what the law requires with some moral claim that contradicts it.)

I occasionally say that in this study I analyze the notion of morality. By "analyzing the notion of morality" I do not mean anything different from investigating what makes something into a piece of moral discourse, that is, what distinguishes moral discourse from other types of discourse. The only reason that I use the phrase *analyzing the notion of morality* from time to time is that constant repetition of the words *moral discourse* could become tiresome.

Some philosophers who investigate topics that are basically of the same kind as those I discuss in this study say that they are investigating the *moral point of view*. I do not know what sort of thing the "moral point of view" is, but whatever it is, these philosophers seem to be concerned primarily with its manifestations in moral discourse. I do not know whether there is supposed to be some other way of investigating the moral point of view, but even if there is, these philosophers do not pursue it. I therefore prefer to say openly that what I am investigating here is simply moral discourse.

There is an ambiguity in the phrase *moral discourse* that needs to be clarified. One notion of moral discourse is such that moral discourse is differentiated from other types of discourse in terms of its internal features. One may call this the *analytic* notion of moral discourse. This notion is to be contrasted with what one may call the *anthropological* notion of moral discourse. The latter is such that moral discourse is differentiated from other types of discourse in terms of the role that it plays in the overall functioning of a society. We may discover that some different culture has a form of discourse that is, in terms of its internal features, completely unlike what we know as moral discourse in our culture, but that nevertheless plays a role in this other society similar to the role that our moral discourse plays in our society. Of such a type of discourse, we can say that it is moral discourse in the anthropological sense, but that it is not moral discourse in the analytic sense. The anthropological notion of moral discourse is such that it is very difficult to imagine a society that does not have moral discourse. The analytic notion is, on the other hand, such that it is quite possible that there are many societies that have no moral discourse. (Ambiguities analogous to the one between the analytic and anthropological notions of moral discourse can be found in some other terms, such as *science*: that is, of a radically different culture, we might say either that it has science vastly different from ours or that it has no science at all, but something else that performs a similar function.)

Both the analytic notion and the anthropological notion are useful notions, but they are useful for different purposes, and a great deal of confusion can be caused if they are not clearly distinguished. To avoid that confusion it needs to be understood that *moral discourse* is used in the analytic sense throughout this book. What I aim to capture are the internal workings of what we have known as moral discourse within the Western culture of the last couple of centuries. (More distant periods in the history of the Western world should be regarded as cultures different from ours, in the sense that is relevant here.) What I call moral discourse may turn out to exist outside these boundaries, but nothing that I say implies that it does.

It also needs to be emphasized that throughout this book *moral discourse* should be understood as referring primarily to the discourse that manifests what Hare calls moral thinking at the critical level. The theses that I advance in this book may have implications regarding the intuitive level of moral thinking, but the intuitive level is not the primary object of my investigation.

It is not the aim of this book to establish any specific moral rule. Various moral rules and moral arguments will appear in it as examples, but they should always be regarded merely as examples. It should be clear that my use of a particular rule or a particular argument as an example in no way implies my endorsement of that rule or argument.

Throughout this book, when the word *he* is used to refer to a definite person, its use, of course, implies that the person is male. However, when that word functions as an individual variable, it should be understood as ranging over individuals of both sexes. This is in accordance with what has long been accepted as the standard meaning of that word. Needless to say, I am aware that it is controversial whether such a use of the word *he* is justified. This is not the right place for entering into a discussion of the controversy, but merely for assuring my readers that my use of that word is not a result of either thoughtlessness or deliberate arrogance, but rather of my having carefully considered the arguments on both sides of the issue, and having, in good faith, concluded that the arguments against the traditional use of *he* do not outweigh the arguments that can be adduced in its defense.

Morality vs. Other Types of Prescriptive Discourse

1.1 Morality and Prudence

When Hare posed the question as to what distinguishes moral discourse from other types of prescriptive and universalizable discourse, he seemed to have thought that the main application of the answer to that question would be in distinguishing moral discourse from aesthetic discourse. In what follows, however, I largely ignore aesthetic discourse. A much better example of nonmoral discourse that is both prescriptive and universalizable and that consequently needs to be distinguished from moral discourse in terms of some third feature, is prudential discourse. Moral and prudential discourse are intuitively much closer than moral and aesthetic discourse and investigating the boundary between them is therefore a much more demanding test for any philosophical account of moral discourse that we might be tempted to accept.

At first glance, it seems doubtful whether prudential discourse is universalizable, because some sort of, what one might call, "egocentricity" seems to be an essential characteristic of that type of discourse. Hare sometimes speaks as if it were not universalizable and as if universalizability were sufficient to distinguish it from moral discourse.[1] However, this egocentricity is perfectly compatible with universalizability, in the sense in which universalizability is ascribed to moral discourse. Suppose that I assent to the prudential claim "Given that $10,000 would make me much better off, that I can easily embezzle $10,000, and that it is highly unlikely that such embezzlement would ever be discovered, prudentially speaking, I ought to embezzle $10,000." It is perfectly appropriate to say that this commits me to the universal prudential claim "Everyone who is in such a position that $10,000 would make him much better off, that he can easily embezzle $10,000, and that it is highly unlikely that such embezzlement would ever be discovered, prudentially speaking, ought to embezzle $10,000." If I "assented" to the prudential claim concerning my own situation without realizing that I would then be expected to assent to this (or some similar) universal prudential claim, then that would be a sign of my misunderstanding the nature of prudential discourse. This is aptly summarized by characterizing prudential discourse as universalizable.

Universal prudential claims, in their turn, commit me to certain prudential claims that concern behavior of specific other individuals in concrete situations. For example, someone who is in such a situation that he can easily, without being detected, embezzle $10,000 that would make him much better off, may come and ask me: "Should I embezzle $10,000? I know that it would be immoral, so please try not to give me any moral advice; what I wonder about is whether such a thing would be prudent of me." If I have already assented to the above universal claim, then I am committed to advising him that, prudentially speaking, he ought to embezzle the money. Incidentally, if there were no such thing as giving prudential advice to others, then we probably would not have *prudential discourse.*

At this point, while we are looking at moral and prudential discourse as two types of prescriptive and universalizable discourse that need to be distinguished, many people may be tempted to embrace Hare's solution and say that moral discourse is the overriding one, and they would probably be happy to stick to this solution if legal discourse and discourse about etiquette were brought under consideration and shown to be prescriptive and universalizable (which is somewhat doubtful).[2]

But suppose that the person to whom I have given the above advice about embezzlement takes my advice as overriding and acts on it. Many people would find it natural to describe the situation by saying that he has allowed prudential considerations to override moral ones. However, Hare is precluded from describing the situation in this natural way; what he must say is that, for the person in question, the considerations that we usually regard as prudential were in fact moral considerations.

Pointing out the oddness of this way of talking is, of course, not a very strong argument against Hare. This is because Hare makes it clear[3] that what he says about the meaning of *moral* is to a certain extent a matter of stipulation. He is not after an analysis of *moral* that would fit all the ways in which the word is actually used (it is used in too many radically different ways), but only after an analysis of one particular sense of the word. This is the sense that he considers the most important and on the whole the most useful, and he may therefore think it worthwhile to continue using the word in that sense, even if this sometimes leads to formulations that sound odd. There is nothing in his view that would necessarily commit him to being opposed to a suggestion such as the one that I am making at this point, namely that there is a sense in which the word *moral* is at least sometimes used, which is different from the one that he analyzes, but which is nevertheless useful and worthy of philosophical attention.

What I say in section 1.2 is also not in direct contradiction with Hare's theory because it merely points out the existence and importance of uses of the word *moral* that are such that overridingness is not a characteristic of the moral. I launch a more direct attack on the thesis that moral discourse is overriding in section 1.3.

1.2 Morality and Admirability

In an article published in 1982, Susan Wolf argued that people whose lives would be in perfect accordance with the requirements of morality would be rather unappealing people, and that people whom we find admirable and whose lives we take as models of what our lives ought to look like are usually people who do not satisfy the requirements of morality perfectly.[4]

She makes it clear that her view needs to be distinguished from the views of those who use similar arguments in order to attack a particular moral view; she insists that her argument that those who satisfy the requirements of morality perfectly have unappealing personalities is not tied to any precise content of these requirements: it applies, for example, to both perfect utilitarians and perfect Kantians.[5] In other words, if we accept her argument, then we have to agree not only that people are generally unappealing when they put too much effort into following perfectly the requirements of a morality that we do not endorse, but also that people are generally unappealing when they satisfy perfectly the requirements of the morality that we ourselves assent to.

Wolf's article also makes it clear that we cannot get around these conclusions by tinkering with the contents of our moral views. It is futile even to attempt constructing a system of *moral* requirements that would be better satisfied by Katharine Hepburn than by Mother Teresa.[6] Any argument that could be used for defending such requirements would either be grossly implausible or lack even the formal features of a moral argument.

Wolf's point is not only that there are considerations that can lead us to regard Katharine Hepburn or Jane Austen or . . . (pick your own example) as more admirable than Mother Teresa (while agreeing that Mother Teresa satisfies the requirements of morality more fully) and that such considerations guide behavior (because the lives of people that we consider admirable, in this sense, we typically regard as models of what our lives ought to look like) but also that we often regard considerations of this type as overriding the moral considerations.

For the purposes of my argument it is not important whether we would agree that lives that we ought to realize are lives that satisfy the requirements of morality less perfectly than the life of Mother Teresa. Some people might think that Mother Teresa is, after all, as admirable as she is moral. What is crucial is not so much the acceptability of what Wolf says about the unappealing character of morally perfect people, but its intelligibility. The intelligibility is sufficient to show that there is an important sense of *moral* such that moral considerations are not necessarily overriding.

As was explained in the preceding section, such considerations of the actual use of *moral* do not amount to a knockdown argument against Hare. He can still take the strategy of insisting that those who hold that Katharine Hepburn is more admirable than Mother Teresa and who regard these considerations of admirability as overriding moral considerations (in Wolf's and my sense of *moral*) in fact hold the moral view (in Hare's sense of *moral*) that one ought to lead a life similar to the life of Katharine Hepburn, rather than a life similar to the life of Mother Teresa. But the sense of *moral* that is put forward by this strategy not only fails to fit our ordinary use of the word, it also fails to fit very well many other things that Hare himself says about moral discourse (such as his discussion of "another's sorrow").

All of Wolf's examples of admirable people, of people that we take as models of what our lives should look like, are people who do not satisfy the requirements of morality perfectly but whose behavior does not depart very much from what would satisfy these requirements. Consequently, it is tempting to reply to her in the way that she has advised against, namely by attempting to construct a system of moral requirements that these people would satisfy. In order to discourage this line of reply completely I would like to point out that more radical examples could be found. Namely, it is possible to regard as admirable someone whose behavior is seriously immoral. It is moreover possible to find someone admirable precisely because his behavior is immoral.

Sometimes when we say that we admire someone who is immoral we mean that he is immoral by the standards of his society, but not by our own standards. However, it is also possible to admire the life of someone who is immoral by our own standards, and this is the case that I have in mind here.

Some people actually hold the view that immoral ways of life are admirable. Those of my readers who do not hold it should remember that they were at least tempted toward it while reading a novel or seeing a movie whose main heroes were pirates, highwaymen, well-organized bank robbers, or even murderers, who were highly intelligent and charming, who had exciting personalities, and who frequently outwitted the dumb law enforcers who were after them. We can admire such personalities without having the slightest doubt that murder or bank robbery is morally wrong and seriously so. What we admire in these characters may be inseparable from what makes their behavior immoral. And if we can understand the considerations that lead people to say that such immoral ways of life are admirable, then we can perhaps also understand that some people might regard such considerations as overriding the moral considerations, which may lead them to choose, say, the life of organized crime. There is certainly something wrong with such a choice, but I do not think that we can say that people who make this choice thereby commit a logical error or that they misunderstand the nature of moral discourse.

As before, the acceptability of the view that grossly immoral ways of life can be admirable is irrelevant for my argument. It is also irrelevant how many people think that it is acceptable. What is relevant is something much weaker, namely that it is an intelligible view.[7]

The discourse in which we make such claims about admirability of different lives is not only prescriptive, it is also universalizable. If someone says that Katharine Hepburn is admirable it does not seem improper to ask why he finds her admirable, and if he says that it is because she has the qualities *F*, *G*, and *H*, then he seems to be committed to the claim that others who have the qualities *F*, *G*, and *H* are (*ceteris paribus*) also admirable.[8]

The upshot of all this is that there is one more type of discourse, call it the discourse of admirability, that is prescriptive, universalizable, nonmoral, and such that we at least sometimes (and, if Wolf is right, very often) do not regard moral discourse as overriding it.

It is not my purpose here (nor elsewhere in this book) to provide a full account of the nature of the discourse of admirability. My main purpose here is to point out that it exists, because we need to take its existence into account if we want to construct an accurate characterization of moral discourse.

It needs to be noted however, that the discourse of admirability is also distinct from prudential discourse.[9] People who lead lives that we consider admirable are frequently dissatisfied and might have been much better off if they had led other, less admirable, lives. If we think that the life of some great revolutionary or artist was admirable, then we usually will not be led to revise our assessment of it if we learn that throughout most of that person's life he was intensely unhappy because of poverty or sexual frustration or frequent migraines, and that this was ultimately a consequence of the very same things that made us consider his life admirable.

On the other hand, it is quite plausible to argue that, for many people, uneventful family life in some quiet suburb is, in the long run, the option that would satisfy them most, but it would be difficult to argue that this is the most admirable form of life that we can imagine. It may be suggested that some such option would have been most satisfying even for some of those people whose lives turned out to be admirable because they actually took a different path. Such suggestions might or might not be justified; what is important to notice now is that while we are engaged in the discourse of admirability, they are typically irrelevant.

1.3   Overridingness

So far I have been assuming that it is perfectly clear to all of us what it means for a type of prescriptive discourse to be overriding and have argued (under that assumption) that it is dubious whether it is a feature of moral discourse that it is necessarily overriding. In this section I criticize the notion of overridingness itself.

In section 9.3 of *Freedom and Reason*, where he introduces the idea of one prescriptive claim overriding another prescriptive claim, Hare writes, "I interpret this term as meaning, not only that we in fact act on the one and not the other, but that we think that we *ought* to act on one even though it involves disregarding the other."[10]

Now the crucial term *ought* is somewhat ambiguous. When we encounter this word, we know that we are dealing with a claim that belongs to some type of prescriptive discourse, but we do not know which one. The *ought* in question may be a moral *ought* or a prudential *ought* or an *ought* of admirability or conceivably of some other sort.

So, if we follow Hare and interpret "Which type of prescriptive discourse is overriding?" as "The claims of which type of prescriptive discourse ought we to follow?" then we have to interpret the latter formulation as a question that belongs to moral discourse or a question that belongs to the discourse of admirability or prudential discourse or legal discourse or . . . As all these questions that can be expressed by that formulation are in fact different questions, it is only to be expected that the answers to them will be different.

Now, I submit that if we attempt to find answers to all these questions, we shall eventually be faced with the result that each type of prescriptive discourse claims of itself that it is overriding. If someone asks, "Ought I, morally speaking, to follow moral prescriptions or prescriptions of some other sort (that might conflict with moral prescriptions)?" then the only tenable answer is "Morally speaking, you ought to follow moral prescriptions. You ought to violate the prescriptions of this other sort whenever they conflict with moral prescriptions." This answer is unavoidable, because it is merely a reformulation of the irrefutable claim that one morally ought to do whatever one morally ought to do.

The overridingness of moral discourse is therefore very easy to establish within moral discourse, but impossible to establish outside it. For example, it is impossible to establish it in prudential discourse, because within prudential discourse we shall encounter the same pattern of reasoning as above, which will this time inevitably lead us to the conclusion that prudentially speaking we ought to violate the requirements of morality whenever they conflict with those of prudence.

This point does not preclude the possibility of one type of prescriptive discourse delegating its "authority" to another. For example, investigation, within prudential discourse, of "Prisoner's Dilemma" situations may lead us to conclude that, under certain conditions, for each of us, the best way of satisfying the requirements of prudence is by accepting and following the requirements of morality.[11] The possibility of our reaching such a conclusion has nothing to do with the above discussion of overridingness, because it would be misleading to express the conclusion by saying that moral discourse overrides prudential discourse. If we accept this conclusion and always act on it, then we shall never be violating the requirements of prudence. Rather, we shall always be following the requirements of prudence by following the requirements of morality. If anything gets overridden by moral claims in this example, this will be only some prima facie prudential claims.

Note that such delegation of the authority of prudential discourse to moral discourse is an outcome of a complex prudential argument; it is not a direct consequence of the formal features of prudential discourse. Those who endorse this argument would say that, if it somehow turned out that the argument were wrong, then prudence would require us to violate morality whenever morality and prudence conflict. This means that even people who endorse the argument regard prudential discourse as, prudentially speaking, overriding moral discourse; but (because they endorse this argument) they believe that there is no opportunity for this overridingness to make much difference.

It is also possible to claim within discourse of one type that some other type of discourse is relatively overriding, that is, that it overrides some third type of discourse. This is, in fact, a corollary to the possibility of delegation of authority as it amounts to the first type of discourse delegating its authority to the second but declining to delegate it to the third. Although we can claim such relative overridingness for the second type of discourse within the first one, the above argument still applies, and within discourse of the first type, we are still committed to regarding it (the first type) as overriding both the second and the third and indeed as being the absolutely overriding one. Within moral discourse we might, for example, say that legal discourse overrides prudential discourse, but in saying that we would be committed to regarding moral discourse as overriding both legal and prudential discourse.

By *delegation of authority* between types of prescriptive discourse one can mean two different things that are not distinguished with sufficient clarity by contemporary authors in the field, and it may be worthwhile to digress for a moment to clarify the matter.

That one type of prescriptive discourse, say prudential, delegates its authority to another, say moral, can mean that within
prudential discourse we have assented to the prescription (*a*)
"One ought to behave in ways that would satisfy the moral prescriptions that one would assent to if one engaged in moral
discourse" or it can mean that within prudential discourse we
have assented to the prescription (*b*) "One ought to engage in
moral discourse."[12] How does one go about following (*a*)? One
pretends that one engages in moral discourse, and one thereby
sees to what conclusions the rules of moral argumentation lead.
One then constructs a simple prudential argument that takes as
its premises (*a*) and "If I engaged in moral discourse I would
assent to ——— ." The conclusion of this prudential argument
then guides one's behavior. In following this line of reasoning
one never really engages in moral discourse but merely pretends to do so because one never takes moral claims to be
behavior-guiding in themselves while it is part of their meaning
that they are behavior-guiding in themselves (i.e., prescriptive).

On the other hand, how does one go about following (*b*)?
One simply engages in moral discourse. The conclusions that
one reaches within moral discourse then guide one's behavior
(simply because of the prescriptivity of moral discourse).

If one follows (*a*) then the whole procedure is firmly
anchored in prudential discourse. This means that, if at any
point one starts having doubts about acceptability of the prudential claim (*a*), one can go back and review the prudential
arguments that led one to accept (*a*). If the review shows these
arguments to be defective one can replace (*a*) by some different prudential claim and then go on to follow this new claim.

On the other hand, (*b*) is a one-way ticket.[13] If one follows
(*b*) one makes a leap into moral discourse, and after that one
simply gets carried by the prescriptivity of moral discourse.
After the leap is made one makes no further reference to
either (*b*) or anything else in prudential discourse. At the
point of reaching moral conclusions and acting on them one
may even forget that one has ever assented to anything like
(*b*). In the case of (*b*) one cannot go back and review the arguments that led one to the acceptance of (*b*) as easily as one
could in the case of (*a*), because moral discourse in which one

finds oneself after the leap may generate prescriptions about engaging in other types of discourse and these prescriptions could conceivably restrict or prohibit one's engaging in prudential discourse.[14]

The overriding authority of a type of prescriptive discourse is always, as it were, self-proclaimed. Delegation of authority is, from the standpoint of the delegating type of discourse, merely a further affirmation of its own supreme authority. Metaphorically speaking, a type of discourse could not delegate its authority unless it regarded itself as having it in the first place.

Now, if my argument is correct, then all types of prescriptive discourse are necessarily on a par so far as overridingness is concerned. This means that when we are engaged in building a philosophical theory about these types of discourse, it is misguided even to attempt to use overridingness as a feature that would distinguish one of them from the others.

This result may leave some people dissatisfied. They would probably express their dissatisfaction by saying something like the following: "We can see from your arguments that each type of prescriptive discourse *claims* of itself that it is overriding. But which one is *really* overriding?" These people seem to be dissatisfied with my allowing the question of overridingness to be asked only within the competing types of discourse themselves; what they would like to have is some sort of Archimedean point that is outside all types of prescriptive discourse that we are looking at and from which we could move one of them to the privileged position of "real" overridingness. My answer to that is that there cannot be such an Archimedean point (as is usually the fate of Archimedean points).

Suppose that we discover or invent some new type of discourse that is neither moral nor prudential nor of any other type that we have mentioned so far and that this is the type of discourse in which it is possible to say without any bias which one of the types of discourse that we have been discussing is "really" overriding. As the concept of overridingness has an *ought* built into it, this new type of discourse will be able to handle the concept of overridingness only if it is itself prescriptive. We have already seen that it is perfectly possible for one type of prescriptive discourse to claim relative overridingness for some other type of prescriptive discourse, so there is no obstacle in principle to our reaching, within the new type of discourse, the conclusion that, for example, moral discourse overrides prudential discourse (or vice versa).

But is it possible, within this new discourse, to claim absolute overridingness for, say, moral discourse (i.e., to claim that moral prescriptions always override prescriptions of any other kind)? It is not. It is not possible because the new type of discourse is itself prescriptive, and the argument that I have formulated above applies to any type of prescriptive discourse: this includes the new one. As any other type of prescriptive discourse, it must claim absolute overridingness for itself.

An attempt to find a source of ultimate authority that would resolve which type of prescriptive discourse is "really" overriding is therefore bound to result merely in adding another member to the family of prescriptive discourse in which every member claims of itself that it is overriding. No matter how many new members we keep adding to the family, we shall not succeed in establishing an objective hierarchical structure to it. Giving a high-sounding name, such as "the discourse of practical rationality" or "the second-order prescriptive discourse" to a newly invented type of discourse cannot protect it from the force of this argument. (That new type of discourse would, of course, be second-order prescriptive discourse insofar as it delegates or declines to delegate its authority to other types of prescriptive discourse. However, any type of prescriptive discourse could be called second-order prescriptive discourse on that ground; consequently none of them deserves to be called *the* second-order prescriptive discourse.)[15]

The gist of the argument that I have just presented is basically the same as what Kelsen expressed by saying[16] that "there is no third point of view" from which we could resolve (what we normally call) conflicts between positive law and morality.

That the world of prescriptive discourse is not perfectly harmonious and free of conflicts should not surprise us if we reflect on the fact that various types of prescriptive discourse came into existence independently and more or less spontaneously. Their existence is not a result of some overall plan.[17]

Now, my argument may lead one to expect that the world of prescriptive discourse (considered as a whole) would be full of strife and disorder (no matter how much order there is within each type of prescriptive discourse). However, when one looks around one sees some, but not too many, obvious manifestations of that disorder.

The experience of being fully aware that one's behavior cannot satisfy the prescriptions that one has assented to while engaging in prescriptive discourse of different types (e.g., being simultaneously aware that a certain course of action would be morally wrong and that it would make one's life admirable) can be a highly tormenting one. Disastrous consequences could follow if such experiences were frequent, but fortunately they are not. The question therefore arises: why are such situations not more frequent (as one may expect them to be on the basis of my argument)?

Several factors contribute to that fortunate result. Some of them are related to certain facts of human psychology and are independent of the content of prescriptions that we assent to; others are related to the actual content of our moral, prudential, and other kinds of views.

First, in most situations it simply happens that we direct our thoughts to prescriptive considerations of only one type. For example, it may be that I have engaged in an argument that belongs to the discourse of admirability, that as a result of that argument I have reached the conclusion that I ought to do such and such a thing, and that I have then done that thing. If someone had made me enter a moral discussion about the same matter I would have reached the conclusion that I ought not to do that thing, and I might have ended up in a situation of conflict. But luckily (or perhaps unluckily) no one provoked such a moral discussion, so I never considered this act of mine within moral discourse, and I did not end up in a situation of conflict. In short, we often avoid situations of conflict simply by not considering every possible action in every type of prescriptive discourse in which it could be considered.

Second, even if I consider some possible act of mine in two different types of discourse, and reach conclusions that cannot both be satisfied, it is still possible that when the time for acting comes I shall conveniently forget one of the results and so act on the other without experiencing any conflict.

Leaving such human weaknesses aside, we should also note that within each type of prescriptive discourse, the most popular views happen to be those that do not provide excessive opportunity for conflict with other types of prescriptive discourse.

First, in all types of prescriptive discourse, views that are widely accepted contain claims that in many situations it is indifferent whether we behave in some way or not (although views that would make everything either required or prohibited are possible in principle), and this reduces the probability of conflicts. Widely accepted moral systems, for example, claim that many kinds of behavior are morally indifferent and thus leave considerable room for one's following the requirements of prudence or admirability without being immoral. Second, it often happens that the behavior that is required by prescriptions of one type of discourse is also behavior that is required by prescriptions of some other type of discourse, although the grounds for those prescriptions are totally independent. The views that people widely accept are such that this occurs much more often than one would expect it to occur if selection of views were random. Finally, as we have already seen, it is possible to reach, within prescriptive discourse of one type, a conclusion that would delegate the authority of that type of prescriptive discourse to another type of prescriptive discourse.

Strong arguments often compel us to accept the views that, as it turns out, have these features that restrict the opportunity for conflict with the prescriptions of other types. One might speculate whether we are, perhaps, in situations where the relevant arguments are not so strong, inclined to accept the views that have these features precisely because we subconsciously dread the experience of conflict.[18]

1.4   A Note on the Alleged Wider Sense of Morality

The view that I defended in the preceding section can be clarified further by being contrasted with the somewhat similar view expressed by Frankena:

> We sometimes think that the requirements of morality and those of prudence or self-interest may conflict. Now suppose we ask, "When they conflict, what should one do? Which takes precedence, morality or prudence?" It then seems natural to say that this is a moral question. But, if we say this, then it appears that morality comes in in two places, once as one of the rival claimants, and again as the final court of appeal that judges between them.[19]

Now, I do not find it especially natural to say that the question about the conflict between morality and prudence is a moral question. Nor is my only disagreement with what Frankena says in this passage about how *the* question should be characterized, because I do not think (as Frankena seems to think) that there is one and only one question here that merely waits to be characterized in some way or the other. I think that the formulation that we have here is ambiguous and that we may interpret it as a formulation of a moral question. But we may equally well interpret it as a formulation of a question of some other sort, say prudential. Different interpretations of this formulation yield different questions, and there is no question to deal with prior to some such interpretation. Which of these interpretations will be the most "natural" depends on the context; none of them is in itself more natural than the others.

Moreover, I believe that if this formulation is interpreted as a formulation of a moral question, then it must be a formulation of a trivial moral question ("Ought one, morally speaking, to follow moral prescriptions or prudential prescriptions?") to which the answer is obvious.

Immediately after the passage quoted above, however, Frankena goes on to distinguish two senses of *moral* and *morality:*

a "wider" one, in which moral discourse would be "the final court of appeal" among various types of prescriptive discourse, and a "narrower" one, in which morality is "one of the rival claimants." He then proceeds to argue that it is better to use the words *moral* and *morality* in the narrower sense, which is congenial to my view. However, in arguing that, he never seems to doubt that the so-called "wider" sense does make sense, and that we could use the words *moral* and *morality* in that sense. On the other hand, my view is that the "wider" sense of *morality* is incoherent: it is a consequence of the argument of the preceding section that, even if there were a type of discourse that would be prescriptive and neither moral in the narrower sense nor prudential nor . . . it still could not do the job of "the final court of appeal" because it would necessarily be one more of "the rival claimants."

Frankena also seems to suggest that if requirements of morality and prudence coincide, then it is possible to combine the narrower and "wider" conceptions of morality.[20] Now, if I set aside my belief that there is nothing to combine here, because the "wider" conception is incoherent, I would still object to this argument of Frankena's for at least two reasons. First, the argument seems to assume that morality in the narrower sense and prudence are the only "rival claimants" that morality in the "wider" sense (if there could be such a thing) would have to adjudicate between. But, in fact there are other "rival claimants" such as the discourse of admirability, legal discourse, and the discourse of etiquette. Second, Frankena seems to forget that requirements of various types of prescriptive discourse coincide or fail to coincide because of what goes on within each of these types of discourse. Even if what goes on within each of two types of prescriptive discourse, say moral and prudential, turns out to be such that their requirements coincide, they still remain distinct types of prescriptive discourse. When they do not actually conflict, distinct types of discourse, such as morality in Frankena's narrower sense and prudence, still remain potential sources of conflict because the convergence of their requirements is dependent on specific arguments within them, and these arguments may turn out to be wrong. As Frankena's distinction between "wider" and narrower senses of morality seems to be based on the *possibility* of conflict between morality in the narrower sense and other types of prescriptive discourse, the distinction would still remain with us even if it turned out that requirements of morality and other types of prescriptive discourse do coincide (assuming here for the sake of argument that the distinction otherwise makes sense). Finally, if one attempted to build it into the concepts of prudence or morality that their requirements coincide, then one would merely generate confusion and would soon find oneself in the situation in which it would be necessary to invent some new terms for what we now call *morality* and *prudence.*

1.5 Moral Sanctions

If the above criticism of the notion of overridingness is correct, then we are now left with a gap that needs to be filled: we need to find something else as a feature that distinguishes moral discourse from other types of prescriptive and universalizable discourse. At this point some people may be tempted to suggest that it is a feature of moral discourse that its prescriptions are backed up by sanctions of some special sort and that this is precisely the feature that we are looking for. In this section I explain briefly why this will not do.

This view is sometimes explicitly argued for, as by T. L. S. Sprigge,[21] and sometimes appears in the background of discussions that are centered around other issues, as in Narveson's *The Libertarian Idea.*[22]

The first problem that any such attempt must face is that of providing an independent specification of the precise sort of sanctions that would be characteristic of morality. Narveson says that morality is enforced by " 'informal' means" and that "verbal means are preeminent among these: we shout at miscreants, we prod and natter and nag both ourselves and others."[23] Sprigge suggests "withdrawal of liking" as the most general characterization of typically moral sanctions, and *social censure, ostracism,* and *boycott* are other terms that readily come to mind in this context. The main problem with these terms is not that they are vague, but that what they pick out, upon reflection, turns out not to be related to moral discourse any more closely than to some other types of prescriptive discourse.

It does not take much observation to notice that expressions of dislike, social censure, and other alleged moral sanctions are in fact distributed in a way that suggests that the basis for their distribution is not moral wrongness (as perceived by those who distribute the sanctions), but something different. As McCloskey has remarked in an article published two years before Sprigge's:

> Social censure is not punishment; it is an arbitrary thing which does not relate peculiarly to moral offences as such. It tends to be directed towards 'bad form' and anti-social behaviour, and against morality more usually when it is also bad form.[24]

Reflections on the results of section 1.2 would probably tend to reinforce this point. Whether we are going to like or dislike someone, seek or avoid his company, seems to be much more closely related to the evaluations that we accept within the discourse of admirability than to how his behavior fares within moral discourse.

But suppose that we can somehow overcome this difficulty and that by introducing some subtle distinctions we can succeed in producing a specification of some sort of sanctions that would be peculiar to morality. Let us call them sanctions of the sort *S*. It might seem that we could then try to argue that it is a feature of moral discourse that its prescriptions are backed up by sanctions of the sort *S*.

The analysis would then have to face another difficulty; that of unpacking the notion of *backed up*.[25] That a prescription is moral only if it is backed up by a sanction of the sort *S* obviously cannot mean that it is moral only if those who assent to it *actually* apply a sanction of the sort *S* to everyone who has ever violated the prescription. The counterexamples to any such analysis would be all too easy to find.

Nor is wishing that a sanction of the sort *S* be applied to those who violate a prescription either a necessary or a sufficient condition for regarding that prescription as moral. I may acknowledge that someone I love has violated a moral rule, and at the same time most intensely wish that he not be subjected to any sanction, including a sanction of the sort *S*. A spiteful person, on the other hand, could conceivably wish that someone be subjected to a sanction of the sort *S*, while being fully aware that the person has not violated any moral prescription.

The only connection that could, with some reason, be said to obtain between moral prescriptions and sanctions of the sort *S* is that those who assent to a prescription and regard it as moral also regard sanctions of the sort *S* as something that *ought*[26] to be implemented whenever the prescription is violated.[27] The question now arises as to what sort of *ought* this is. If we say that it is moral, then we are in trouble: on the analysis that we are considering, something is a moral prescription only if it is backed up by sanctions of the sort *S*, which means that those who assent to the original prescription must agree not only that some sanctions of the sort *S* ought to be applied to those who violate it, but also that there are some other sanctions (also of the sort *S*) that ought to be applied against those who fail to apply the first set of sanctions against the violators of the original prescription. And the last clause would, on the analysis proposed, mean that there is a third set of sanctions that ought to be applied against those who fail to apply the second set of sanctions, and so on.[28] We can avoid this infinite regress only if we say that the prescriptions that regulate the application of the sanctions of the sort *S* are not themselves moral prescriptions. But to say that it is part of the analysis of the notion of morality that a prescription belongs to moral discourse only if there is a prescription that belongs to some sort of nonmoral discourse that requires that sanctions of the sort *S* be implemented whenever the first prescription is violated, seems to be grossly implausible regardless of which type of nonmoral prescriptive discourse we have in mind (legal, prudential, etc.).[29]

Moreover, suppose that contrary to what has just been said there is a type of prescriptive nonmoral discourse *D* such that it seems plausible that it is part of the analysis of the notion of morality that a prescription is moral only if there is a prescription belonging to D that requires implementation of sanctions of the sort S whenever the first prescription is violated. There would still be a problem. Moral prescriptions are reached by techniques of moral argumentation while prescriptions belonging to D are presumably reached by techniques of argumentation characteristic of D. If the two are distinct types of discourse (as we have assumed) then we have to count on the possibility that moral arguments will at least sometimes lead us to adopt a certain prescription, while arguments in D will not lead us to adopt the prescription that sanctions be applied whenever the first prescription is violated. When that happens we can do one of the following:

1. Try to save the proposed analysis by insisting that the first prescription is not an acceptable moral prescription after all.
2. Try to save the proposed analysis by insisting that there simply must be a prescription in D that requires that sanctions be applied whenever the moral prescription is violated.
3. Give up the analysis of morality in terms of sanctions.

If we choose the first option, then we are disregarding (what appeared to be) moral arguments and are taking arguments from D as deciding whether a moral prescription is acceptable or not. This amounts to saying that moral discourse is not an independent type of discourse at all, but merely a way of presenting the results of D.[30] On the other hand, the second option disregards the arguments in D, which amounts to a merging of D with moral discourse in a way that is similar to the first option. This leaves us with the third option as the most plausible.

2

The Shoehorn Maneuver

2.1 A Fresh Start

In the previous chapter, I started the investigation of what distinguishes moral discourse from other types of prescriptive and universalizable discourse by considering two answers to that question (in terms of overridingness and in terms of moral sanctions) that have already been developed in philosophical literature, and I provided reasons for not accepting either of them. In this chapter I shall offer a different answer to that question.

The answer that I shall offer takes as its starting point the fact that in moral discussions we often ask our interlocutors to put themselves in the shoes of someone else, and we are often asked by them to put ourselves in the shoes of someone else, that is, to imagine ourselves as having properties that we do not actually have[1] but that are relevant to the moral claim under consideration. This technique has been dubbed "the shoehorn maneuver."[2]

The importance of the shoehorn maneuver in moral discussions has been pointed out by many philosophers including C. I. Lewis[3] and, more recently, Thomas Nagel,[4] Zeno Vendler,[5] John Harsanyi,[6] and Mary Bittner Wiseman,[7] as well as Hare. I shall take it for granted here that these philosophers were basically right in pointing out the importance of the shoehorn maneuver in moral discourse. I shall assume that it has been established that we often use the arguments that involve the maneuver in our moral discussions, and that the use of such arguments often plays a crucial role in these discussions.

What I shall be concerned with here is whether the problem of what distinguishes moral discourse from other types of prescriptive and universalizable discourse could be resolved by pointing out that in moral discourse we use arguments that involve the shoehorn maneuver and making that into a part of our analysis of the concept of morality. In section 2.3 I argue that a bare appeal to the fact that we use arguments based on the shoehorn maneuver in moral discussions is not sufficient to distinguish moral discourse from all other types of prescriptive and universalizable discourse, because such arguments are also used in prudential discourse.

However, I also argue that there is an important difference between the ways in which arguments based on the shoehorn maneuver are used in moral discourse and the ways in which they are used in prudential discourse, and that we can therefore distinguish moral discourse from all other forms of prescriptive discourse by incorporating reference to the way in which such arguments are used in it into our analysis of the notion of morality. I first appeal to the reader's linguistic intuitions in order to establish that there is a difference between the use of arguments based on the shoehorn maneuver in prudence and in morality, and I then (in section 2.4) proceed to articulate what precisely that intuitively felt difference is. In the process of articulating it, it will be necessary to introduce the notions of a *designated argument-place,* a *moral agent,* and a *moral patient.* These notions make it possible to characterize moral discourse as prescriptive discourse in which two types of argument-places are designated for performance of arguments based on the shoehorn maneuver: those for moral agents and those for moral patients.

But before I proceed to discuss the suggestion that an appeal to the notion of the shoehorn maneuver can help us in analyzing the notion of morality I must deal, in section 2.2, with one preliminary objection, which stems from Hare's writings and which would make this suggestion a nonstarter. Namely, Hare seems to think that the role of the shoehorn maneuver in moral discourse is a consequence of its universalizability. Given that we have already included universalizability in our analysis of the notion of morality, it would be, on this view, simply redundant to make a separate reference to the shoehorn maneuver within the analysis.

2.2   The Shoehorn Maneuver and Universalizability

In order to see whether the importance of the shoehorn maneuver is really a consequence of the universalizability of moral discourse, we may want to have a closer look at the structure of moral arguments that involve the shoehorn maneuver. Suppose that someone made a moral claim that under the given circumstances it was morally permissible for John to treat Mary in a particular way and that we want to challenge that claim by such an argument. We would then say something like the following:

Example 1

1. You said that under the given circumstances it was morally permissible for John to treat Mary in this way. But this commits you to saying that under such circumstances it is morally permissible for anyone who finds himself in the position in which John was to treat in this way anyone who is in the position in which Mary was.
2. This commits you to saying that, under these circumstances, it could be morally permissible for someone to treat you in this way, should you find yourself in the position in which Mary was.
3. Now please try to imagine very vividly that you are in this position and that you are treated in that way.
4. Do you still think that it was morally permissible for John to treat Mary in that way?

In this argument, stage 1 invokes universalizability of moral discourse, stage 2 is an uncontroversial application of the universalized claim to our interlocutor, stage 3 is the request that the shoehorn maneuver be performed, and stage 4 is the final request to our interlocutor to draw a moral conclusion from the whole procedure. Typically when we employ such an argument we expect that our interlocutor will not like what he "sees" while performing the shoehorn maneuver and that he will therefore revise the moral claim he has made.

Now if the role of the shoehorn maneuver in moral discourse were a consequence of its universalizability, then one could not consistently think that moral discourse is universalizable and that arguments of the above form are not proper moral arguments. But notice that if these four stages correctly represent the structure of arguments that involve the shoehorn maneuver, then only the first stage involves universalizing.

If someone challenged the appropriateness of stage 1 and insisted that a singular moral claim does not commit him to any universal claims, then we could accuse him of not understanding that moral discourse is universalizable. But it is logically possible to understand fully that moral discourse is universalizable and therefore accept stage 1 as well as the uncontroversial stage 2 and still think that stages 3 and/or 4 do not belong to a proper moral argument. One could thus accept the universalizability of moral discourse and still deny that arguments of this sort have any role (certainly not an important role) to play in moral discourse.

For example, one could say: "I understand that the claim that I have made about John's treatment of Mary commits me to the claim that it would be permissible for someone to treat me in the same way if the circumstances and our respective positions were relevantly similar to John's and Mary's. But I simply refuse to engage in any vivid imagining of that situation."

One could respond to that by saying that one cannot fully understand the content of stage 2 unless one performs some such thought-experiment. This response would be controversial, but even if we assume that it would not, there is still a possibility[8] of someone's going through stages 1, 2 *and* 3, performing the shoehorn maneuver, and then, at stage 4, saying: "Yes, I have very vividly imagined that I was in the position in which Mary was and that I was treated in the way in which she was treated, and I can say that I would not at all like to be treated in that way. I acknowledge, in other words, that I would not like it if the moral claim that has been obtained by universalization of my original claim were always obeyed. But what does all this have to do with the acceptability of either the universal claim or my original claim?" This response seems inappropriate but it does not seem to be inconsistent with the person's understanding that universalizability is a feature of moral discourse. If we want to say that there is something inappropriate about this response we must invoke some feature of moral discourse other than its universalizability. No amount of unpacking of the notion of universalizability will tell us that this response is inappropriate.

Nothing in the argument that I have just made hinges on whether we accept or reject Hare's view that has been the subject of much debate,[9] that whenever one vividly imagines being in a certain position, which includes imagining that one has certain preferences, one thereby acquires *actual* preferences for that hypothetical situation. One may accept that view and still say: "I have imagined very vividly that I was in the situation in which Mary was, which included my imagining that I had the preferences that Mary had, and that I was treated in the way in which she was treated, and I realize that in such a hypothetical situation I would strongly prefer not to be treated in that way. Moreover, through that thought-experiment, I have acquired strong actual preference not to be so treated in such a hypothetical situation. In other words, I now have a preference that the claim obtained by universalizability of my initial claim not be obeyed in all cases. But what does this preference of mine have to do with the acceptability of either the universal claim or my initial claim?"

The significance of divorcing the use of the shoehorn maneuver that is peculiar to moral discourse from its universalizability can be further appreciated if we compare the case of moral discourse with that of prudential discourse.

Let us consider again the example from section 1.1, of my saying that, under certain circumstances I, prudentially speaking, ought to embezzle $10,000. We have already seen that such a singular prudential claim commits me to a universal prudential claim, which in turn commits me to singular claims that concern behavior of individuals other than myself. Now, suppose that someone attempts to argue in the following way:

Example 2

1. You said that you, prudentially speaking, ought to embezzle $10,000 (that belongs to someone else),

given that $10,000 would make you much better off, that you can easily embezzle $10,000, and that it is highly unlikely that you will be caught. But this commits you to saying anyone who finds himself in such circumstances, prudentially speaking, ought to embezzle $10,000 (that belongs to anyone else).

2. This commits you to saying that someone who is in a position such that embezzling $10,000 that belongs to you would make him much better off, that he can easily embezzle the money, and that it is highly unlikely that he will be caught, prudentially speaking, ought to embezzle your $10,000.

3. Now please try to imagine very vividly that your own $10,000 has been embezzled.

4. Do you still think that, prudentially speaking, you ought to embezzle the money?

The obvious response here is that I would intensely dislike someone's embezzling my $10,000, but that this has nothing to do with the acceptability of the prudential claims that I have made or am committed to. If someone insisted that I have to reconsider my prudential claims, because I would not like others to follow them at my expense, he would simply show that he does not understand what prudential discourse is. That I would not like other people to behave in certain ways does not constitute a challenge to the claim that it would be prudent of them to behave in these ways.

Of course, I may often have good reasons not to give others prudential advice that I would not like them to follow. That would not be prudent of me. But the prudence of uttering a certain prudential claim is separate from its acceptability. The question of whether one ought, prudentially speaking, to behave in a certain way is different from the question as to whether, prudentially speaking, one ought to say that one ought, prudentially speaking, to behave in that way.

These remarks about prudential discourse reinforce the claim that the use of the shoehorn maneuver in morality is not a consequence of its universalizability, because they show that not only is it logically possible that there be a type of discourse that is universalizable and in which the shoehorn maneuver would not be used in the way in which it is used in moral discourse, but that there actually is such a type of discourse.

Admittedly, Hare says at one point[10] that applicability of arguments of the form that I have outlined ("golden-rule" arguments, as he calls them) in moral discourse is not a consequence of its universalizability alone, but rather of its universalizability taken together with the fact that what moral discourse is about impinges on our interests.[11] The remarks about prudential discourse that I have just made show that this will not do. Behavior that constitutes one's following or violating the prescriptions of prudential discourse also impinges on the interests of others, but this does not seem to have any consequences for how prudential disputes are resolved.

The result of this subsection is that neither universalizability of a particular type of discourse nor its universalizability together with impingement on interests is a sufficient condition for the applicability of the arguments (involving the shoehorn maneuver) of the sort that we use in moral discourse. This means that saying that it is a part of the notion of morality that moral claims are subject to such arguments would constitute a nontrivial addition to the analysis in terms of prescriptivity and universalizability. The presence of universalizability within the analysis does not make such an addition redundant.

If universalizability is not a sufficient condition for applicability of arguments based on the shoehorn maneuver, is it at least a necessary one? One is tempted to say that it is, because arguments of the form that has been discussed in this section would be impossible without stage 1, and stage 1 would be impossible without universalizability. However, one needs to go through all four stages of the procedure only if the claim that one wants to criticize is not itself universal. Sometimes moral discussions begin by someone's putting forward a moral claim that is already universal. In dealing with such a claim it would be pointless to invoke universalizability: as it is already universal, there is nothing to universalize. If we want to criticize such a claim on the basis of the shoehorn maneuver, we can dispense with stage 1, which is the only stage that involves universalizability, and begin our argument at stage 2. This shows that universalizability is necessary only for applying arguments based on the shoehorn maneuver to singular claims. This connection between universalizability and the shoehorn maneuver is important, but it does not amount to universalizability being a necessary condition for application of arguments that involve the shoehorn maneuver.

2.3   Moral Discourse and the Shoehorn Maneuver

Let us now consider a possible analysis of the notion of morality according to which the feature that distinguishes moral discourse from other types of prescriptive discourse is precisely that moral claims are subject to arguments that involve the shoehorn maneuver. Could this feature fill in the gap that was left by our dismissal of overridingness as a feature of moral discourse?

One may be inclined to say that it could, because no other type of prescriptive discourse that we are familiar with at first sight appears to share this feature. However this initial appearance will turn out to be deceptive.

The claims of admirability obviously are not subject to arguments based on the shoehorn maneuver. We noticed in 1.2 that we can regard the lives of pirates, highwaymen, and well-organized bank-robbers as admirable, and someone's pointing out that we would not at all like to be in the shoes of their victims does not constitute a step toward showing that they are not admirable (although it would constitute a step toward showing that they are immoral). Moreover, even our putting ourselves in the shoes of those whose lives we are evaluating is not relevant for discussions within the discourse of admirability, as we have also noticed in 1.2 that it is possible to consider a person's life admirable even if the person is dissatisfied with it.

Legal discourse and the discourse of etiquette are obviously not serious candidates for discourse in which arguments involving the shoehorn maneuver would be applicable, which seems to leave us with prudential discourse as discourse that needs to be examined in this respect. And have we not just shown, in the preceding section, that arguments that involve the shoehorn maneuver are not legitimate within prudential discourse?

The answer is no. What has been shown there is something much weaker. In the preceding section I have first given an example of a moral argument involving the shoehorn maneuver (Example 1), and have then given an example of an unlikely attempt at a prudential argument (Example 2) that was a close imitation of that moral argument. It turned out that the latter was obviously out of place in prudential discourse. However, that arguments of this particular sort are out of place in prudential discourse does not entail that any argument involving the shoehorn maneuver must be out of place there.

Suppose that I have made the claim that under the given circumstances John, prudentially speaking, ought to behave in a certain way. Suppose that, as my partner in the prudential discussion, you want to criticize that claim of mine. You could quite naturally say something like the following:

Example 3

1. You said that under the given circumstances John, prudentially speaking, ought to behave in a certain way. But this commits you to saying that anyone who finds himself in the circumstances of this sort, prudentially speaking, ought to behave in this way.
2. This commits you to saying that under the circumstances of this sort you, prudentially speaking, ought to behave in this way.
3. Now please try to imagine very vividly that you are in the circumstances of this sort and that you behave in this way.
4. Do you still think that John, prudentially speaking, ought to behave in this way?

This argument seems perfectly appropriate for prudential discourse, and it does involve the shoehorn maneuver. What I find out while imagining that I am in the circumstances in which John is and that I pursue the proposed course of behavior is certainly relevant for deciding whether such behavior would be prudent of John. If the thought-experiment made me see that the proposed course of behavior would leave me dissatisfied, this insight would lead me to revise the universal claim obtained at stage 1 and my initial claim about John.

The appropriateness of the argument of Example 3 shows that mere applicability of arguments that involve the shoehorn maneuver is not peculiar to moral discourse. The analysis of the notion of morality that was proposed at the beginning of this section therefore fails. Still, this analysis was a step in the right direction.

Arguments based on the shoehorn maneuver are used in both moral and prudential discourse, but the ways in which they are used are not exactly parallel, as was shown in 2.2. The next section (2.4) will try to articulate the differences, hinted at in 2.2, between the ways in which the arguments based on the shoehorn maneuver are used in moral and in prudential discourse. This will serve as the basis for an analysis of the notion of morality that will provide a better account of the difference between moral discourse and other types of prescriptive discourse than the analyses that we have considered in chapter 1.

2.4   The Designated Argument-Places in Moral and Prudential Claims

What exactly is the crucial difference between Example 2 and Example 3? In both of them a prudential claim, made by an interlocutor, was universalized (stage 1) and applied to him (stage 2). He was then asked to perform the shoehorn maneuver (stage 3) and his initial claim was finally challenged on the basis of the results of that maneuver (stage 4). Yet, the "argument" of Example 2 was grossly out of place while the argument of Example 3 was perfectly legitimate. Why ?

In order to answer this question let us first look at what we do at stage 1 of the four-stage procedure. This stage aims at our finding a universal claim that is such that the original claim is derivable from it by a process of derivation that includes universal instantiation. Stage 1 consists in our reconstructing that derivation, starting with the original claim made by our interlocutor, and then proceeding backward toward the appropriate universal claim. Universalizing, in the narrow sense,[12] is nothing but reconstructing the universal instantiation that is part of that derivation.[13] In other words, in universalizing a claim we produce a claim that is exactly like it, except that an individual constant that occurred at a certain argument-place(s) is replaced by an individual variable and that a suitably placed universal quantifier is supplied to bind that variable.

Usually, however, this replacement and introduction of the universal quantifier is not the only thing that we do at stage 1, since most claims that are made in everyday discussions are formulated in ways that preclude us from regarding them as straightforward conclusions of universal instantiation. We often need to reformulate and disambiguate the claim made by our interlocutor (or, as is probably better, ask him to do that) and reconstruct, with his help, other parts of the derivation that links the original claim with the suitable universal claim.

In particular, we should note that universalizing, being a reconstruction of universal instantiation, is always a procedure that is performed on certain argument-places. Given that many locutions that we use in everyday discussions do not make their logical form obvious, we may often need to do some work before we arrive at an expression that will clearly display the argument-places on which universalization may be performed. In the process, we may need to resolve which of the ordinary language terms occurring in the claim under consideration were intended as individual constants, which is often problematic.[14]

At stage 2 we derive, by universal instantiation, a claim that refers to our interlocutor from the claim obtained at stage 1. This is again an operation that is performed on certain argument-places, and within the same argument the argument-places on which stage 2 is performed are the same as those on which stage 1 has been performed. (If they were different there would not be any reason to consider them as two stages of the same argument.)

Given that what happens at stages 1 and 2 determines the content of the thought-experiment that our interlocutor will be asked to perform at stage 3, which is, in turn, supposed to determine the reply that we are going to get at stage 4 and so the outcome of the whole argument, and that what happens at stages 1 and 2 must be characterized as a procedure that is performed on certain argument-places of the claim that is under consideration, we can regard each argument that is based on the shoehorn maneuver as a procedure that is performed on these argument-places.[15] This entails, among other things, that the claims to which such arguments are to be applied must display the relevant argument-places or be capable of reformulation that would display them.

Now, in Example 3, the argument that involved the shoehorn maneuver was applied to the claim that John, prudentially speaking, ought to behave in a certain way, and it was performed on the argument-place that was occupied by the name *John* in this claim. *John* was the term that referred to the individual to whom this claim was, in a sense, addressed,[16] to the individual of whom it would be possible to say that he satisfied (followed) or violated it. Moreover, one would not fully understand the claim under consideration if one did not know that the word *John* in it refers precisely to the individual of whom it could be said that he followed or violated it. Every prudential claim must contain such a term. If the claim is singular, then the term will be an individual constant referring to some definite individual; if the claim is universal then the term will be a variable (bound by a suitably placed universal quantifier) ranging over individuals to whom the claim is, in this sense, addressed, that is, the individuals of whom it can be meaningfully said that they satisfy (follow) or violate it. Let us call such individuals *prudential agents*, and let us call an argument-place (within a prudential claim) that is intended[17] for a term that represents them an *argument-place for prudential agents*. For example, everyone who understands the open claim "———— ought, prudentially speaking, to behave in such and such way" must understand that the term that comes to fill "————" will be a term that refers to someone to whom this claim is addressed, someone of whom it can be meaningfully said that he follows or violates it.

We can therefore say that in Example 3 an argument involving the shoehorn maneuver was performed on the argument-place for prudential agents. We have seen that the argument was a perfectly appropriate one, and it is indeed a feature of prudential discourse that we can always (try to) criticize a prudential claim by performing such an argument on its argument-place for prudential agents.

But it is also a feature of prudential discourse that the arguments involving the shoehorn maneuver are improper if performed on any other argument-place. Saying that this is a feature of prudential discourse captures our feeling that there was something very odd about Example 2. In that example an attempt has been made to perform an argument involving the shoehorn maneuver not on the argument-place for the prudential agent (in that example the prospective embezzler was the prudential agent), but rather on the argument-place that was filled by a term that referred to someone who was affected by the behavior of the prudential agent (namely the owner of the money that was to be embezzled). That turned out to be a clear violation of the rules of prudential discourse.

We can summarize this by saying that the fact that a certain piece of discourse is prudential *designates* certain argument-places in it as the argument-places on which it is legitimate to perform arguments involving the shoehorn maneuver, and that the argument-places that are so designated are the argument-places for prudential agents. Within prudential discourse, such arguments cannot be properly performed on any other argument-places as no other places in prudential claims are designated for that purpose.

When I want to say that a certain argument-place is designated as an argument-place on which arguments involving the shoehorn maneuver may be performed, I will usually say simply that it is "designated."

Let us now apply this pattern of reasoning to moral discourse. Every moral claim must also contain either an individual constant referring to the individual to whom the claim is, as it were, addressed, of whom it can be meaningfully said that he obeys (follows, satisfies) or disobeys (breaks, violates) the claim (or its negation)[18] or an individual variable ranging over such individuals. Following a well-established practice we may call these individuals *moral agents*. Moreover, a person who formulates a moral claim has to intend that a particular place within it be filled by a term that represents moral agents.[19] This place we can call the *argument-place for moral agents*. Moral claims that do not display that structure must be capable of being reformulated so as to display it.

Now, Example 1 was an example of a perfectly legitimate moral argument, although it was not performed on the argument-place for the moral agent. In that example, the claim under criticism was the claim that it was permissible for John to treat Mary in a particular way. The argument was performed on the argument-place that contained the name *Mary* in the original claim, and that was certainly not the name of the moral agent in that example: the moral agent was John.

We can now articulate the insight that we reached at the end of section 2.3, and say that although in both moral and prudential discourse we employ arguments based on the shoehorn maneuver, the difference between the two types of discourse is that in the prudential the only argument-places designated for performance of such arguments are the argument-places for prudential agents, while the application of such arguments in moral discourse is not similarly restricted (i.e., we cannot say that the only designated argument-places in moral discourse are the argument-places for moral agents).

However, we still need to provide a more positive account of the designated argument-places in moral discourse.

Let us begin by noting that not all argument-places in moral claims that can be occupied by individual variables or constants are designated: in morality, as in prudence, there are some such argument-places on which it would be inappropriate to perform arguments based on the shoehorn maneuver. For example, in any moral discussion that we might have about the claim that, morally speaking, John ought not to use any weapon in dealing with Mary, it would certainly not be a legitimate move to say: "Please imagine that you are in the position of the weapon." We understand that such an argument would be inappropriate simply in virtue of understanding the claim under consideration.[20]

The second thing that we should note is that, although places for moral agents are not the only designated argument-places in moral claims, they are among the designated places. A shoehorn maneuver that is required by a moral argument that is performed on the argument-place for moral agents can be called an *agent-oriented* maneuver. That there are moral arguments that hinge on agent-oriented maneuvers is worth emphasizing because they are usually neglected in the literature:[21] most examples of the maneuver that are discussed by philosophers are of the same sort as Example 1, that is, not agent-oriented.

We would typically use a moral argument that involves an agent-oriented maneuver, when the claim that we want to criticize strikes us as too restrictive or too demanding. Suppose for example that someone claims that Sally ought to give 90% of her salary to the first beggar she happens to see on her payday. It would be quite natural to argue against him by pointing out that he is committed to the universal claim that everyone who finds himself in the position in which Sally is, ought to do so, which in turn entails that he, himself, ought to do so, if he finds himself in such a position, and then asking him to imagine that he is in such a position and is parting with 90% of his salary, as his rule requires.

Given that we have by now concluded that in moral discourse there are argument-places that are not designated, that the places for moral agents are designated, and that there are designated places other than those for moral agents, what remains to be done now is to somehow characterize those other designated places, such as the place occupied by the name *Mary* in Example 1. The terms that appear in those other designated argument-places of moral claims are either constants that refer to individuals of whom it can be meaningfully said that they are wronged (or perhaps even victimized) if the claim (or its negation)[22] is violated, or variables ranging over such individuals. Moreover, an argument-place in which such a term occurs will be designated only if it is intended[23] for a term that refers to (or ranges over) individual(s) of whom it can be meaningfully said that they are wronged if the claim is violated. Let us call such individuals *moral patients*,[24] and let us call the argument-places that are intended for terms that represent them the *argument-places for moral patients.* Shoehorn maneuvers that are required by arguments performed on these argument-places may be called *patient-oriented* maneuvers. We would typically use a patient-oriented maneuver in order to criticize a moral claim that strikes us as too lenient.

The conceptual apparatus that has been introduced in this section enables us to say that it is a feature of moral discourse that a moral claim has two types of argument-places on which arguments involving the shoehorn maneuver may be performed: places for moral agents and places for moral patients. This feature distinguishes moral claims from prudential ones, because in the latter we can find only one type of designated argument-place: the argument-place for prudential agents.

An alternative way of making the same point is to say that it is a feature of moral discourse that we employ in it both arguments based on agent-oriented shoehorn maneuvers and arguments based on patient-oriented shoehorn maneuvers.

As this feature does not seem to be a contingent one, we can say that its presence (together with prescriptivity) is precisely what makes something into a piece of moral discourse, rather than discourse of some other sort. We have thus, by improving on the suggestion that moral discourse is the prescriptive discourse in which arguments based on the shoehorn maneuver are used, so as to avoid the problem of 2.3, arrived at the analysis of the notion of morality that successfully differentiates moral discourse from other types of prescriptive discourse.[25] The account of the presence of two types of designated argument-places in moral claims fills the gap that was left open by our dismissal of the overridingness of moral claims.

2.5 Universalizability and the Designated Argument-Places

The analysis of the notion of morality that I have just presented may seem to involve a considerable departure from Hare's own analysis, and in some respects it is indeed rather different from his. However, in view of the argument presented in 2.2, precisely a departure of this kind is necessary in order to preserve a very important part of Hare's theory about the functioning of moral discourse. The important part that I have in mind is of course his account of the role of the shoehorn maneuver in our moral discussions. He believed that this account follows from the universalizability of moral discourse, but the considerations adduced in subsection 2.2 show that this is not so. Therefore, one can continue to regard the bulk of Hare's characterization of how our moral discussions proceed as a consequence of the analysis of the notion of morality only if one replaces his analysis of that notion with an analysis that would go along the lines that I have advocated.

Such an analysis also eliminates the puzzle, which was presented in the Introduction, as to why the universalizability of moral discourse is, according to Hare, so important when there are, in his own view, many other types of universalizable discourse, whose universalizability is not that important. The answer is that universalizability per se is not very important; the universalizability of moral discourse appears to be more important than it is because of its connection with the applicability of the shoehorn maneuver, which is the really important feature of that discourse. The shoehorn maneuver, in its turn, has such importance in moral discourse because the places for moral patients, as well as the places for moral agents, are designated.

According to my account, moral claims, both singular and universal, are moral by virtue of being subject to arguments based on agent-oriented and patient-oriented maneuvers. When such arguments are applied to singular claims they have to start with stage 1, which involves universalizability; the applicability of such arguments therefore entails that moral claims are subject to universalization on the argument-places for moral agents and the argument-places for moral patients. So far as the universalizability on the argument-places of these two types is concerned, one need not mention it as a separate feature within an analysis of the notion of morality. What about other argument-places that might be filled by individual constants? Is it a feature of moral discourse that moral claims are subject to universalization on these other places? If it is not, then the whole of universalizability can be regarded as included in the applicability of arguments based on the shoehorn maneuver; if it is, the universalizability must be regarded as an additional feature of moral discourse.

Consider, for example, the claim that King Arthur did something morally wrong in using Excalibur against Sir Lancelot. If the person who makes this claim is prepared to elaborate by saying, "Given that King Arthur possessed property F, he did something morally wrong in using Excalibur against Sir Lancelot, who possessed property G" and if he regards *King Arthur* as the name of the moral agent and *Sir Lancelot* as the name of the moral patient, then he certainly must be ready to universalize on the places occupied by these two names and agree to something like: "Anyone who has the property F would do something wrong in using Excalibur against someone who has the property G." If he refused to universalize in that way, it would indeed be appropriate to accuse him of not understanding what moral discourse is. The question is whether he needs to deal with the name *Excalibur* in the same way. Thus, if he refused to replace *Excalibur* by something like "anything that has the property H" (where H is some property that Excalibur has), would that show that he does not understand what moral discourse is?

Hare would probably say that the name *Excalibur* must be dealt with in the same way as the other two names we encountered in this claim, as he seems to think that it is a feature of moral discourse that we must be ready to perform universalization on any and every argument-place that we find occupied by an individual constant.[26] However, if my interlocutor fully appreciated the prescriptivity of his claim about King Arthur, if he were prepared to relate it to other moral claims that he makes and to put himself in the shoes of various individuals who have the property F and the shoes of individuals who have the property G and to draw conclusions from these thought-experiments, I would be reluctant to accuse him of not understanding what moral discourse is on the sole ground of his refusal to eliminate the name *Excalibur* from the claim.

We should note that while we cannot even begin to engage in anything that would resemble moral discussion with someone who would refuse to universalize on the places for moral agents and moral patients, we can have quite a long and meaningful discussion with someone who would refuse to universalize on the place of *Excalibur* in the above example. This discussion would certainly resemble typical examples of moral discussions very closely, and I find this resemblance close enough to say that it would be a moral discussion, while Hare is committed to insisting that it is, in spite of that resemblance, a discussion of some other, nonmoral, sort.

Not much hinges on whether one agrees with Hare's or with my view on this particular matter. However, this itself counts in favor of my view, because it provides for a simpler analysis of the notion of morality.[27]

There are, however, some cases where something of significance may, at first, appear to hinge on whether we treat the requirement of universalizability as applying to argument-places other than those for agents and patients. "It is usually held that spatial and temporal properties do not count (because they cannot be defined without reference to an individual point of origin of the coordinate system),"[28] in other words, that dates and spatial locations cannot be morally relevant as such (i.e., independently of what happened on them). This is surely a very significant principle, and it does seem to imply that the requirement of universalizability applies to places occupied by spatial and temporal coordinates.

Thus suppose that someone says that everyone has a duty to treat everyone else in a certain way, as long as they both find themselves at the spatio-temporal location l, but that there is no such duty at any location distinct from l (even if it is similar to l in every respect). We certainly want a theory that will enable us to say that there is something seriously problematic about this claim. Hare's theory enables us to say this by summarily dismissing the claim on the ground that it fails the requirement of universalizability. According to Hare's theory this claim is therefore not a genuine moral claim at all.

If we restrict the requirement of universalizability to places for agents and places for patients, then we are precluded from dismissing the claim on the ground that it fails the requirement of universalizability, as it satisfies the restricted requirement perfectly. However, we are still able to say that it is seriously problematic. We only need to ask the person who put forward the claim to put himself in the shoes of the relevant agents and patients who find themselves at *l*, and then to put himself in the shoes of the relevant agents and patients at a location other than *l*, keeping everything the same except the location. This will undoubtedly lead him to conclude either that people have the duty in question both at *l* and at other locations similar to *l*, or that they do not have it at all. His original claim will thus be rejected. Admitting claims that contain ineliminable spatio-temporal coordinates as genuine moral claims therefore does not make much difference, because, once admitted, they are bound to be refuted by substantive moral reasoning.

No moral claim containing ineliminable spatio-temporal coordinates can survive such scrutiny. The important thesis that spatial and temporal locations are, as such, morally irrelevant can thus be accommodated within a theory that restricts the requirement of universalizability to argument-places for agents and argument-places for patients.

I will therefore treat only universalizability on the places for agents and patients as a feature that a claim has simply in virtue of being moral. This makes it unnecessary to treat universalizability as a separate element in my analysis of the notion of morality, as universalizability on the places of these two types is entailed by their being designated.

Any analysis of the notion of morality that, like Hare's, insists on universalizability on every argument-place that may be occupied by an individual constant faces an important problem. It is an important advantage of analyses that restrict the requirement of universalizability to specific argument-places (as does the analysis that is advocated here) that they avoid that problem. The problem stems from the fact that moral claims as we formulate them in everyday situations do not readily display individual constants, variables, predicates, quantifiers, and so on. Thus, as we have already noticed, it is often necessary to reformulate everyday moral claims in order to make them display the structure about which the questions of universalizability can be profitably asked.

Now, if universalizability as a necessary condition for a claim being moral consists merely in the requirement that it be universalizable on certain argument-places (as in my analysis), then we can have a fairly straightforward test for whether this condition is satisfied. The test consists in reformulating the original claim so that it displays these argument-places and then checking whether the person who put forward the claim is ready to universalize on them. In reformulating the claim in this procedure, we know exactly what to look for.

On the other hand, if the necessary condition is that the person who put forward the claim be ready to universalize on all argument-places that may be occupied by individual constants, then the procedure is not so straightforward and may even be indecisive. We may reach some reformulation of the original claim, and the person may be ready to universalize on all argument-places occupied by individual constants in that reformulation, but there will always be a nagging doubt that there could be some other reformulation that would display some argument-place on which the person would not be ready to universalize.

For example, our first reformulation may contain a predicate that at first sight appears perfectly innocent. However, if we try to analyze its meaning, we may discover an individual constant somewhere in its analysans. If we now replace the predicate with its analysans, we shall get a new reformulation that, because of the presence of that constant, might not satisfy the requirement even if the first one did.

No matter how carefully we reformulate the claim, there is no guarantee that further analytic efforts and more careful reformulation will not reveal a hidden individual constant somewhere in the claim. Searching for individual constants that may be hidden anywhere in any acceptable reformulation of the claim may therefore be an endless task. On the other hand, the task of searching for hidden individual constants at certain specific argument-places is a manageable one.

Agents and Patients

3.1 Introduction

The answer to the question of what distinguishes moral discourse from other types of prescriptive and universalizable discourse that I have offered in chapter 2 avoids the problems into which other answers to that question have run (discussed in chapter 1). However, in order to show that the answer is really acceptable, it needs to be spelled out in more detail what it implies and what it does not imply. Moreover, it needs to be shown that what the answer does imply is not implausible. This chapter and the following one are devoted to this task. The remainder of the book is devoted to dealing with an important further problem that opens itself up once we accept the analysis of the notion of morality outlined in the preceding chapter.

3.2 Are There Any Multi-Agent and Multi-Patient Claims?

Moral claims typically have several argument-places for moral agents and several argument-places for moral patients. For example, in the claim

> For every x and for every y, x has a duty to y that x stand in the relation R_1 to y, whenever x has the property F and y has the property G, unless y stands in relation R_2 to x

all argument-places occupied by the variable x are the argument-places for moral agents, and all occurrences of the variable y are in the argument-places for moral patients.

In this example, all argument-places for moral agents were occupied by the same variable. We can think of many other examples that share this feature as well as many examples of singular moral claims where all argument-places for moral agents would be occupied by the same individual constant. This raises the question as to whether there are any situations where the argument-places for moral agents are occupied by different terms within the same claim.

A possible example of such a claim could be the claim that it was morally wrong of Susie and Sally to jointly attack and injure Tom. It seems that in that example, both the name *Susie* and the name *Sally* were intended as the names of moral agents.

But such a claim can always be regarded as an amalgamation of two claims that can be considered separately, in our example the claim that Susie did something morally wrong in attacking Tom and contributing to his injury, and the claim that Sally did something morally wrong in attacking Tom and contributing to his injury. We may therefore, for most ends and purposes, disregard such cases and proceed as if all argument-places for moral agents within a single claim were always to be occupied by the same term. The same holds for the places for patients.

Moreover, there is a reason for treating claims about Susie's and Sally's contributions to their joint venture as more basic than the claim about the joint venture itself. The reason is based on the fact that we feel that there is an important connection between the claim that it was morally wrong of Susie and Sally to jointly attack and injure Tom and the claim that it would be morally wrong of Susie, Sally, and Samantha to jointly attack and injure Tom. Namely, we think that there is an underlying moral rule from which both these claims can be derived. The way of analyzing these claims that I have suggested above is in accordance with that belief. If we analyze them in that way, then they can both be derived from the claim that it would be morally wrong of anyone to attack anyone and contribute to his injury (or something similar). On the other hand, if we rejected this analysis and insisted on leaving these claims as they are, then we would be forced to regard them as belonging to separate segments of morality, which seems implausible.

There are, however, some cases where the pattern of analysis that I have offered for the case of Susie and Sally may, at first, appear to be inapplicable. Suppose it is said that it was morally wrong that Philippa, Phillida, Philomena, and Phyllis gave the same advice to Ronald, because receiving the same advice four times was a very humiliating experience for him. Suppose it is also said that if only one or two of them had given him the advice, that would have been a morally good thing, because Ronald was badly in need of that advice. (The cause of his humiliation was not the content of the advice but its repetition.) Here the outcome is not a result of a straightforward adding up of individual contributions in the way in which Tom's injury was a result of straightforward adding up of Susie's and Sally's contributions, because in this case the same individual contributions would have led to a very different result if fewer people had joined.

Nevertheless, it is still possible to analyze the content of the claim about the way Ronald was treated in terms of individual contributions to that treatment. We can for example say that it was morally wrong for Philomena to give that advice to Ronald, given that the advice had already been given to him two times. That claim has only one argument-place for a moral agent, namely the one occupied by the name *Philomena.* The allusion to other advice-givers at the end of the claim does not create a designated argument-place. We can also say that it was morally wrong for Phyllis to give that advice to Ronald, given that the advice had already been given to him (more than) two times. We can universalize this by saying that it is morally wrong for anyone to give that advice to Ronald if the advice has already been given to him two times (or more). By following this pattern we can say everything there is to say in such cases without resorting to multi-agent claims.

Incidentally, we should note that, if the original claim were not analyzable in the way suggested here, it would be incapable of guiding anyone's behavior: if Philomena is to adjust her behavior to the requirements of morality, then she needs to be able to derive from them a claim that is addressed to her (rather than to her-together-with-others).

Mutatis mutandis, the same questions can be raised and the same answers given about the argument-places for moral patients.

3.3   Some Ambiguities

It is a consequence of my account that in order to engage profitably in moral discussions we need to be able to reformulate our moral claims in a manner that will make them display terms for moral agents and moral patients. This may strike some people as unnatural. After all, we say things like "Rape is wrong" or "Adultery is immoral" and even though these statements do not contain any terms that would represent moral agents and moral patients, they seem perfectly intelligible as they are.

It may, therefore, be useful to see that this requirement is not here merely because such reformulations suit my theory, but that it has some intuitive support.

For example, consider the fact that throughout the centuries most people have been prepared to say that rape is wrong. This may seem like a case of remarkable continuity in agreeing to the same moral claim. However, if we look at how saying that rape is wrong was justified at different times, we shall see that the continuity is only apparent. Today most people presumably view rape of a woman as something that is directed against the woman who is subjected to it. What happens to the woman is viewed as being directly relevant for the moral evaluation of the act. But rape of a woman can be, and in the past often was, viewed as primarily an affront to the dignity of the woman's husband or, if she was unmarried, to the dignity of the head of her family. The way in which rape affects these males can be regarded as directly relevant, and the woman can be regarded as merely a medium through which the rapist causes certain important consequences in these males. These two moral outlooks are so radically different that it seems quite natural to say that we are here dealing with two different moral claims, and that it is an unfortunate ambiguity that the same sequence of words ("Rape is wrong") is used to express both of them. This ambiguity can easily be removed if we reformulate the claim that rape is wrong so as to make it clear who is intended as the moral patient. If we think that it is desirable that such an ambiguity be removed, then we have a reason for accepting the requirement that our moral claims be reformulated so as to make reference to moral agents and moral patients explicit.

Similarly, many people say that adultery is wrong, but if we ask them why they think it is wrong, we will quickly discover that they have quite different things in mind. Some will regard adultery as an instance of deception or as a breaking of the trust (or something similar) between the spouses. They would blame the adulterous spouse for treating the nonadulterous spouse in this way and would leave the extra-marital partner alone. Others might regard adultery as akin to theft and would blame the extra-marital partner as the one who has wronged the nonadulterous spouse.[1] Here again we have an ambiguity that we would intuitively regard as undesirable. By following the requirement of explicit reference to moral agents and moral patients and making it clear who is intended as the moral agent this ambiguity can be easily removed.

Sometimes ambiguities of this sort are made worse by the fact that a certain term within a moral claim, as initially formulated, may appear to refer to a particular individual as moral agent or patient, but further questioning of the person who formulated the claim can reveal that this is not what he intended, that he had in mind someone else as the moral agent (or patient). "It would be morally wrong to torture this cat" appears to take the cat as the moral patient, but further questioning may reveal that the person who made this statement thought that the reason it would be wrong is that some humans might be adversely affected by seeing the torture, and so intended them as moral patients. Similarly, "This child shouldn't do such things" may appear to take the child as the moral agent, but further discussion may reveal that what was meant is that the child's guardian should see to it that the child does not do these things, that is, that the guardian was intended as the moral agent.

Many more examples of this sort could be cited, but the above ones should be sufficient to establish that there are important ambiguities in many of the everyday formulations of moral claims and that we can remove these ambiguities by making it explicit who was intended as the moral agent and who was intended as the moral patient. The requirement that such reformulations of ordinary moral claims be provided is therefore intuitively acceptable independently of the theoretical arguments of the first two chapters.

3.4   The Standard Form of Moral Claims

Moral claims can be formulated by means of a large number of different words such as *moral value, (morally) good, (morally) bad, immoral, (moral) duty, ought* (in its moral sense), *(moral) obligation, (morally) right, (morally) permissible,* and so forth.

However, as all these words are interdefinable,[2] most of the philosophical investigation of moral discourse can proceed by concentrating on one of them.

Of all these words, the best one to concentrate on is the word *duty* because its use provides us with a natural tool for removing most of the ambiguities about which terms within the moral claim are intended to be terms for moral agents and which are intended to be terms for moral patients.

Namely, whenever we see something of the form

$$\xi \text{ has a duty to } \chi \text{ that } \xi\Phi\chi.$$

it seems fairly straightforward that the place of ξ is intended for the term for moral agent(s) while the place of χ is intended for the term for moral patient(s).[3]

In a moral claim that has the form "ξ has a duty to χ that $\xi\Phi\chi$," whatever stands at the place of $\xi\Phi\chi$ specifies the content of the duty, that is, the conditions under which the claim is satisfied (obeyed) and hence the conditions under which it would be violated.[4] Of course, the fact that I am using a single character Φ here (which is a metalinguistic "dummy" for a relation symbol) should not be taken to imply that the content of a duty will always (or even typically) be a simple, unanalyzable, binary relation between ξ and χ. What is abbreviated by Φ here will often have a highly complex logical structure. For example, the content of some duty that we have may be a conditional[5] that has as its antecedent a complex disjunction of complex conjunctions, and so on.[6]

What I have said so far about moral agents and moral patients has the important consequence that in order to understand a moral claim it is not sufficient to understand its illocutionary force (in the terminology of Hare's *The Language of Morals*: its neustic part), that is, to know that it is a moral claim and not a claim of some other sort and to know its propositional content (in Hare's terminology, its phrastic part), that is, to know its conditions of satisfaction.[7] In addition to these two things, one must know which terms occurring in the claim were intended to represent moral agent(s) and which were intended to represent moral patient(s).

For example, the claim that Paula has a moral duty to Peter's wife, Petra, not to have an affair with Peter, and the claim that Peter has a duty to his wife, Petra, not to have an affair with Paula have the same illocutionary force (namely, they are both ascriptions of moral duties) and the same propositional content (namely, both of them would be violated just in case Peter and Paula have an affair and obeyed just in case they do not). Still they are obviously different moral claims, and one's understanding of them is obviously not complete without an understanding of what makes them different, that is, without an understanding of who is intended as the moral agent. Someone who failed to see this difference would be likely to make highly inappropriate moves in a moral discussion that might arise about these claims.

3.5   The Moral Community

In moral arguments we are typically required to link moral claims in which moral agents and patients are represented by individual constants with the more basic moral claims in which they are represented by individual variables bound by universal quantifiers.[8] Each of these variables, like any other individual variable, needs to be regarded as ranging over a certain set of individuals, that is, over a certain domain.

Moreover, individual variables that occupy argument-places for moral agents and variables that occupy places for moral patients range over different, and often narrower, domains than other individual variables that we use, including variables that appear within moral claims but do not occupy argument-places of these two types. (No confusion arises from the fact that within a single moral claim we may have individual variables ranging over different domains precisely because argument-places for moral agents and patients are designated.)

If one assented to something like "For every *x* and for every *y*, *x* has a duty to *y* that *x* does not strike *y*," one would probably regard that as entailing that Paula has a duty not to strike Peter, but one certainly would not intend that to entail that lightning has a duty not to strike trees. One would not intend *x* as ranging over a set that includes lightning, nor *y* as ranging over a set that includes trees.[9]

The question now arises as to whether I have to regard variables for moral agents in all claims that I assent to as ranging over one and the same domain. In other words, do I have an option of regarding the variable for moral agents in a certain claim that I assent to as ranging over one set and the variable for moral agents in some other claim that I assent to as ranging over some different set? The same question can be asked about moral patients. My answer to this question will use the same general strategy that was already used in section 3.2.

At first sight it may appear plausible to say that different branches of morality involve different sets of agents and patients. For example, it can be argued that rules of medical ethics take medical practitioners as moral agents and their patients (in the ordinary sense of the word) as moral patients, while agents and patients of the rules of sexual morality are actual or potential sexual partners and so on. When the matter is looked at in this way, then the corresponding sets in different branches of ethics may turn out to be different.

It is indeed possible to formulate a rule of, say, medical ethics by saying something like the following:

For every *x* and for every *y*, *x* has a duty to *y* to keep the facts about *y*'s health to himself and then adding *in a metalanguage* that the above rule belongs to medical ethics and that the variable *x* in it ranges over the domain of medical practitioners while the variable *y* ranges over the domain of medical patients.

However, the information that was, in this example, provided in the metalinguistic explanation about the rule, can be incorporated into the rule itself. We can say

> For every *x* and for every *y*, *x* has a duty to *y* to keep facts about *y*'s health to himself if *x* is a medical practitioner and *y* is a patient.

Having this longer rule amounts to the same thing as having the shorter rule together with the metalinguistic explanation that it applies only to medical practitioners and their patients. In the longer rule, variables *x* and *y* range over wider domains. The longer rule is, in a sense, addressed even to those of us who are not medical practitioners, but its application to such agents is uninteresting as they always obey that rule in a trivial way.[10] When rules of various specialized branches of ethics are formulated in this way, we can both regard the variables for agents in all of them as ranging over one and the same domain, which is the same as the domain for variables for agents in the most basic moral principles, and the variables for patients in all of them as ranging over one and the same domain, which is the same as the domain for variables for patients in the most basic moral principles. We can regard these two sets as *the* domain of moral agents and *the* domain of moral patients, respectively.

Now, it seems possible to formulate rules of a particular branch of ethics in both these ways. In some cases the first way may have certain practical advantages. However, the second way (the one in which variables for agents in all moral claims to which one assents range over one and the same set and so do variables for patients) enjoys a special sort of priority.

Neither medical ethics nor sexual ethics nor any other branch of ethics can stand on its own. The rules belonging to each of them need to be related to general moral principles. Rules of medical ethics will typically be justified by being derived from some general moral principles together with empirical facts about the practice of medicine. Variables for agents in these general moral principles range over the whole domain of moral agents and variables for patients range over the whole domain of moral patients. In order to investigate logical relations between the rules of medical ethics and these general principles we must take variables for agents and patients in the rules of medical ethics to range over the same wide domains. That is why the second way of formulating rules of medical ethics (or any branch of ethics) has priority over the first: it provides the link with general moral principles and (via these general principles) with other branches of ethics. The first way of formulating these rules, although sometimes natural, obscures the connections among the various branches of ethics.[11] From now on I shall therefore disregard the possibility of formulating the rules of specialized branches of ethics in the first way.

Now suppose that someone were to reply to all this that although he is interested in medical ethics, he simply does not care to investigate logical relations between the rules of medical ethics and general moral principles (nor between medical ethics and other specialized branches of ethics). He would need to be reminded that the logical relations between these claims may turn out to be such that they are inconsistent: the only way to ensure that the claims are consistent is to investigate the relations between them. If he were to respond to that by saying that inconsistencies are fine with him, then I would not have any further arguments to offer against him, except that of pointing out that striving after consistency seems to be a general feature of all types of discourse that we engage in.

A more sophisticated version of the above reply to my argument would consist in saying that the discourse of medical ethics is a type of discourse in its own right, separate from moral discourse. But, first, it does not seem that this is how most people normally think of medical ethics. We do not think that the fact that medical ethics is called ethics manifests some ambiguity in the word *ethics*. Second, it is not clear what reasons anyone would have for engaging in this special discourse.[12]

The argument of this section I believe, dismisses the suggestion made by N. Fotion,[13] that morality consists of rules of two different types: "action-rules" and "range-rules." In our example about confidentiality in medicine, the rule in its shorter formulation (or something like it) is what Fotion would call an action-rule, while the rule saying that all and only medical practitioners are bound by such rules of medical ethics would be called a range-rule[14] by him. Fotion allows that ordinary moral discourse may often combine what he calls a range-rule and what he calls an action-rule in a single sentence, but he regards such sentences as mixtures of two originally distinct elements. What Fotion's proposal amounts to is that the way of formulating moral rules that was exemplified in my first version of the rule about confidentiality should be considered paradigmatic. But if morality is regarded as consisting of two fundamentally different types of rules, as Fotion suggests, then it becomes impossible to survey relations between the more and less general moral rules.

The argument that I have used in this section to deal with the specialized branches of morality such as medical ethics can also be applied to moral systems of societies divided into castes. Behavior that such a system requires of or toward members of a higher caste may be drastically different from what it requires of or toward members of a lower caste. Still, existence of castes does not affect the unity of the set of moral agents nor the unity of the set of moral patients: each of them must encompass all the castes. The moral system of such a society will normally provide some reasons for different treatment of different castes. In order to provide such reasons it must contain some very basic moral principles in which variables for moral agents range over members of all castes and from which more specific rules can be derived. In order to make these derivations possible, we need to present all rules of the system in a form that makes the relevant variables range over the same wide sets.

I also believe that the argument of this section cannot be refuted by considerations that Michael Tooley presents in *Abortion and Infanticide*.[15] He claims there that cats cannot be intended as moral patients in moral claims regarding access to university education, in exactly the same way as newspapers (in the sense of physical objects) cannot be intended as moral patients in any meaningful moral claims, and that this is so even if we assume that cats can be intended as moral patients in some moral claims (e.g., in prohibitions of torture). What the example is supposed to illustrate is that for some individuals (e.g., cats) it can be conceptually impossible to be intended as moral patients in *some* universal moral claims in exactly the same way in which it is conceptually impossible for some other individuals (e.g., newspapers) to be intended as moral patients in any moral claim. For Tooley, the proper procedure for dealing with questions about moral patiency is to take one specific topic of moral discourse at a time and consider what the possible moral patients for that topic are.[16] He does not think that there is an important unity to the set of all moral patients.

Tooley's only argument for this view is that it is as difficult to imagine a serious moral dispute about university education of cats as it is to imagine a serious moral dispute that would take newspapers as moral patients. The reason that I am not persuaded by Tooley's argument, although I agree that both types of dispute are difficult to imagine, is that I think that they are difficult to imagine for different reasons.

A serious moral dispute about university education of cats is difficult to imagine because such a dispute would violate a general requirement for any type of rational communication, namely the requirement that we should say only things that are, in one way or other, interesting. We normally do not argue about university education of cats because it is totally uninteresting: nothing hinges on it, as cats are unable to register for university education anyway. The uninterestingness of this topic is sufficient to explain why there are no disputes about it, and Tooley is not justified in concluding that it is defective in any other way (if we grant, for the sake of argument, that cats are capable of being moral patients). Moreover, in the unlikely case of someone insisting on having a moral discussion about university education of cats, those of us who think that cats are capable of being moral patients could enter into such a discussion, that is, they could produce moral arguments about university education of cats, arguments that would connect (uninteresting, but still meaningful) moral claims about university education of cats with the more basic moral claims.

On the other hand, no one would have any idea how to react to someone's insistence on having a moral discussion that involves newspapers as moral patients. A proposal for such a discussion would not be merely uninteresting, it would be defective in some more fundamental way. We would not have any idea how to go about connecting putative moral claims about newspapers with more basic moral claims, because none of us regards variables for moral patients in any of his moral claims as ranging over newspapers. That is why it is difficult to imagine a serious moral dispute that involves newspapers as moral patients. As this reason is very different from the reason for there being no moral disputes about university education of cats, it seems that these examples of Tooley's fail to support the policy of considering questions of moral patiency separately for different topics of moral discourse.

In this section I have argued that each participant in moral discourse is committed to formulating all moral rules that he assents to in such a way that variables for agents in all of them range over one and the same set and that variables for patients in all of them range over one and the same set. It should be noted that I have not said anything about the relation between these two sets. Since we regard most normal human adults as being both moral agents and moral patients, we may, I think, safely assume (without waiting for any further arguments) that there is at least some overlap between the two sets. It seems much less clear whether there can be any individuals who belong to one of those domains without belonging to the other. Is the set of moral agents a subset of the set of moral patients? Is it perhaps the other way around? Could the two be coextensive? These questions still remain open, and will be discussed in chapter 6. Nevertheless, it may be useful to have a term for the union of the two sets. At this point I am therefore introducing the term *moral community* for that union.[17]

3.6   Moral Patients: Objections and Replies

It is a consequence of my analysis of the notion of morality that every moral claim must contain (or be capable of a reformulation that contains) a term for moral patient(s): otherwise, on my account, we would not have any ground for saying that the claim is moral rather than a claim of some other sort. This may be a cause of some resistance to the account, and this section will be devoted to anticipating and answering some objections that concern the role that my account gives to moral patients. It is, by the way, interesting to note that no similar resistance is likely to be caused by the role that I have assigned to moral agents.

3.6.1   Duties to Oneself

Some readers might be under the impression that my account, because of the role that it assigns to moral patients, precludes the possibility of there being duties to oneself. But that would be a misunderstanding, as nothing that I have said so far precludes the possibility of terms for agents and patients, within the same claim, referring to the same individual, or even the possibility of their being one and the same term (that simply recurs at argument-places of both types). Moreover, nothing that I have said precludes the possibility of there being moral claims of the form

> For every x and for every y, x has a duty to y that, if
> $x=y$, then ———

which may also be used to express duties to oneself.

Duties to oneself can therefore easily fit the framework in which moral claims are regarded as having argument-places for moral agents and argument-places for moral patients. But one might now ask why one should bother to make them fit my framework: why should one insist on regarding an individual that has a duty to himself as playing two distinct roles rather than only one (which might appear to be more natural)? The reason is, again, that formulating claims that express duties to oneself so that they exhibit argument-places for moral agents and argument-places for moral patients enables us to relate these claims to other moral claims. On the other hand, if one is not interested in relating claims that express duties to oneself to other moral claims, then one indeed has no reason to formulate them in this way, but then one also has no reason to regard them as moral claims. If one tries to imagine a moral discussion that would deal exclusively with duties to oneself, one sees that it would be indistinguishable from a prudential discussion. We can thus say that what makes claims that express duties to oneself *moral* is their being regarded as parts of a system that expresses duties to others as well.

3.6.2 Deontological Ethics

Another objection that can be made against the view that moral patients need to be represented in every moral claim is that this view has a built-in bias for consequentialism, which casts doubt on its metaethical status. This objection interprets the requirement that every moral claim point to some individual(s) who would be wronged if the claim were violated, as a requirement that the propositional content of moral claims involve some consequences for moral patients of the behavior of moral agents.

However, this objection is based on the wrong assumption that it is accurate to describe the dispute between those who were traditionally considered to be consequentialists (e.g., utilitarians) and the proponents of what is called *deontological ethics* (e.g., Kantians) as a dispute between those who take the consequences of behavior into account when they morally evaluate it and those who refuse to take the consequences into account. Although Kantians say that they do not take the consequences of behavior into account when they morally evaluate it, they in fact do. No theory can afford to refuse to take consequences into account because some consequences must be considered in order to describe behavior in a relevant way. If deontological ethics really did not take the consequences into consideration it could never contain the prohibition of killing, for in order to describe something as killing we must know that someone's death was among its consequences. There is no fact of the matter as to where the act itself ends and its consequences begin; we can place the boundary wherever we like.[18] That is why we should not regard deontological ethics as ethics in which consequences of our acts are not considered. Disputes that went on between Kantians and utilitarians were not really disputes as to whether we should take the consequences into account, but rather as to which consequences contribute to the rightness or wrongness of behavior: only consequences within certain narrow limits as proposed by Kantians, or consequences belonging to a much wider range, as suggested by utilitarians. Once we perceive deontological ethics in that light, we see that the way in which I introduced the notion of moral patient is in no way hostile to it.

Finally, we only need to inspect some system of deontological ethics to see that its claims in fact contain terms for moral patients. Kant, to take the best-known example, makes it clear that what the categorical imperative requires us to do is to treat certain individuals in a particular way, the individuals in question being, in his view, all and only rational beings.

3.6.3 Impersonality

Derek Parfit has argued that "our reasons for acting should become *more impersonal.*"[19] It is important to examine whether the "impersonality" that Parfit has in mind is in conflict with the view that moral claims always involve moral patients.

One aspect of that impersonality is that the consequences of our behavior may often be so diffused and mixed with the consequences of the behavior of other moral agents that considerable harm is done, although we cannot say of any of the moral agents involved that he has affected any single moral patient in any perceptible way.[20] But even in situations of this sort, harm that is done is not somehow free-floating; it is harm that is done to moral patients. Moreover, we can say that everyone has a duty to everyone else not to *contribute* to any perceptible harm to him (even if the contribution would, in itself, be imperceptible);[21] and that the harm in situations of this sort results from violations of this rule. That we must endorse some such rule may be a very important substantive moral conclusion, but it in no way conflicts with analyzing morality in terms of moral agents and moral patients.

Another aspect of "impersonality" that Parfit has in mind involves his theory of personal identity over time. His theory of personal identity may be very important for the question as to how one should individuate members of the moral community but, again, it does not conflict with regarding moral claims as having argument-places for moral agents and argument-places for moral patients.

Finally, Parfit has argued that certain paradoxes related to future generations cannot be resolved by appealing to any "person-affecting" principles. This may amount to an important objection to the role that I have assigned to moral patients. However, this argument of Parfit's is heavily dependent on his views on personal identity across possible worlds, which are effectively the same as Kripke's and are thus subject to criticisms presented in section 6.4.

3.6.4   Virtues

We sometimes say things like "John is courageous" or "John is honest." These claims belong to moral discourse as well, and they do not seem to make any reference to moral patients. It could therefore be objected that my analysis of the notion of morality is incapable of accounting for such claims' belonging to moral discourse. My first answer to this objection is to reaffirm what one may call the standard view on the matter, namely the view that ascriptions of virtues, that is, moral claims that are about character traits of moral agents, need to be analyzed in terms of moral claims about behavior associated with these character traits, behavior that in some way or other involves moral patients. A claim that ascribes a certain virtue to John is thus to be understood as meaning that John's character is such that he has a steady tendency to fulfill moral duties of a certain kind. On this analysis we cannot assent to any moral claims about character traits without assenting to some moral claims that express duties.

Some philosophers dismiss this standard view and insist that this is not a correct and complete analysis of the meaning of moral claims about character traits (virtue-ascriptions) or at least that it is not a correct and complete analysis of what some people have in mind when they make such claims. A whole philosophical industry sprang into existence around that dismissal of the standard view, under the name *virtue-ethics*.

Virtue-ethicists' dismissal of the standard view is sometimes a result of a misunderstanding of what the standard view involves. For example, it is often suggested that the standard view does not fully accommodate the importance of the role that virtues play in our lives. But saying that virtue-ascriptions are to be analyzed in terms of duties, which is what the standard view claims, is perfectly compatible with acknowledging that, in our day-to-day lives, spontaneous exhibitions of virtue are much more frequent than behavior directly prompted by conscious thinking about duties. Every proponent of the standard view would happily acknowledge that. (This is analogous to the compatibility of the thesis that medical theories should be ultimately analyzed in terms of the concepts of biology and chemistry with the acknowledgment that medicine has much more direct impact on people's lives than fundamental biology and chemistry.)

It is also sometimes said that the standard view cannot accommodate the fact that examples of virtuous individuals (supplied by, say, literature or religious traditions) play a far more prominent role in moral education than any explicit discussion of moral duties. But the standard view is perfectly compatible with the acknowledgment of that fact. The standard view is not trying to be a theory about moral education and implies nothing whatsoever about it. Education, in general, does not always mirror the logical structure of its subject matter. Explicit instruction in the rules of grammar is not normally the central part of teaching foreign languages to beginners, but that in no way proves that the enterprise of grammar is somehow misguided.

But suppose that all such points of misunderstanding have been clarified and that my opponent still insists that at least some people have intended by ascriptions of virtues something different from what the standard view allows.

My strategy for dealing with this objection would be to acknowledge that it is probably true that some people have intended something different by such claims. However, I would also say that insofar as they have intended something different by such claims, it is not clear why one should regard their claims as moral claims. If certain ascriptions of virtues are not analyzable in terms of ascriptions of duties, then they will have to be supported and criticized in some way that is different from the way in which we support and criticize ascriptions of duties. But if certain claims are always to be discussed separately, then there is no reason to regard them as belonging to the same type of discourse.[22] (It may, by the way, easily turn out that those who understand virtue-ascriptions in some such way in fact regard them as belonging to what I have called the discourse of admirability.)

The next move that my opponent could make would be to say that my removing these virtue-ascriptions from moral discourse cannot be justified, because there is a long tradition, going back to ancient Greek philosophy, of regarding claims of precisely that sort as paradigms of moral claims. That there is such a tradition seems true, but it is questionable what that proves.[23] If the question is about which of the two types of discourse (the one in which we discuss such virtue-ascriptions or the one in which we discuss duty-ascriptions) should be labeled moral, then it seems much more relevant to observe how the term *moral* is used today as opposed to how it (or a corresponding term in another language) was used a long time ago. But insofar as the issue is purely terminological, it is not terribly important: if someone really wanted to call the type of discourse in which we discuss virtue-ascriptions (that are not analyzable in terms of duty-ascriptions) *moral* discourse I would not mind too much inventing some other term for what I have been calling *moral*. Or we could use the word *moral* for both, provided that we make it clear that it is ambiguous and that these are two distinct types of discourse (and that this book is about one of them only).

What one certainly cannot conclude from the fact that there is a long tradition of using the word *moral* for virtue-ascriptions that are not analyzable in terms of duty-ascriptions is that they must belong to the same type of discourse as one in which we discuss duty-ascriptions, which is also called *moral.* This would be like arguing that because there is a long tradition of calling a certain game that is popular in Europe *football,* it must be the same game as what is called *football* in North America. We know very well that bringing together a European football team and a North American football team and telling them to "play football" would result only in chaos: there is no game that they could play together. Exactly the same happens if one brings together a virtue-ethicist and someone who understands the word *moral* along the lines that I am trying to articulate in this book, and instructs them to have "a moral discussion."[24]

3.7 Matters of Degree

So far I have simply assumed that membership in the sets of moral agents and/or moral patients is not itself a matter of degree: an individual either is or is not a member. After all, membership in these particular sets is only a specific type of set membership, and it is a feature of the notion of set membership that it does not admit of degrees.

Some philosophers seem to disagree,[25] and I therefore want to emphasize why matters of degree in morality are always to be treated as aspects of the contents of the relevant moral claims and not as affecting membership in the moral community and why, even in a moral system in which interests or needs (or whatever) of certain moral patients were systematically discounted, it would be improper to say that they have a lesser degree of moral patiency.

Suppose that moral agency and moral patiency were matters of degree. One could then say, for example, that someone has full (100%) moral patiency while someone else has only 70% of moral patiency.

The first problem with this claim is that its meaning is unclear. We may suppose it means that if we have a certain duty that we can satisfy, in respect of a "full" moral patient, by doing such and such a thing, then we can satisfy that same duty with respect to a 70% moral patient by doing only 70% of that thing. But contents of many of our duties are such that it would be very difficult to articulate what it means to perform 70% of that content.

Suppose now that we somehow manage to overcome the first difficulty and that we are able to make sense of performing 70% of any duty that we might have. We then must face the second difficulty. If someone is a 70% patient, then presumably any duty can be satisfied with respect to him by performing only 70% of what we would be required to perform with respect to a 100% moral patient. But it is highly unlikely that anyone has ever held or that anyone will ever hold the view according to which, with respect to certain individuals, all duties are to be "discounted" by the same percentage. One might think that requirements of just distribution are satisfied if individuals belonging to a certain group have only 70% of the income or leisure that, other things being equal, belongs to "full" moral patients, but it is unlikely that he will then also think that each of them should be given 70% of a vote in public elections. A sexist may think that a woman should receive only 70% of the income that a man would, other things being equal, receive, but when considering the question of voting he may conclude that women should have full votes or no votes at all or perhaps votes that are worth only 39% of a male vote: it is unlikely that he would settle for 70% again (and if he would, it is unlikely that he would keep settling for 70% in considering all other moral questions). It is tempting to say that women or members of certain races or of certain social groups were, in certain periods, regarded as having "a lower degree" of membership in the set of moral patients (and/or the set of moral agents), but as soon as we try to make this way of talking more precise by asking "Which degree?" we see that it is impossible to make it precise.

The third difficulty is that for some systems of rules it is not only implausible but also impossible to apply all rules of the system with the same rate of "discounting." Suppose we have a system of rules that includes (1) a rule as to how much influence on public decisions we should give to everyone, (2) a rule about access to the voting procedure, and (3) a rule about voting itself, telling us how to count votes. We cannot take this system as a whole and apply all three rules with the same rate of discount. If someone's vote is to be worth only

70% of a "full member's" vote and if his chances to participate in voting are only 70% of a "full member's" chances to participate, then his chances to influence public decisions by voting must be 49%, and not 70%, of a "full member's" chances to influence them.

For these reasons it is better to treat matters of degree in morality as part of the content of moral claims and to treat membership in the sets of moral agents and moral patients as a yes-or-no matter. This means that instead of saying that someone assents to the rule

> For every x and for every y, x has a duty to y that, if x
> has the property F and y has the property G, then x
> provides income I to y

and that he regards the variable y as ranging over the set that has both "full members" and 70% members (to which the rule is applied differently so that they end up with lower income) we should say that he assents to the following rule:

> For every x and for every y, x has a duty to y that, if x
> has the property F and y has the properties G and H,
> then x provides income I to y, and, if x has the prop
> erty F and y has the property G but does not have
> the property H, then x provides 70% of the income
> I to y

where y simply ranges over a set in which there are no degrees of membership. As before, we should note that keeping the discounting within the content of moral rules also has the advantage of making it possible to relate any questions that might arise about it to other moral questions.

4

Rights and Right-Holders

4.1 Introduction: Correlativism vs. Anticorrelativism

A significant part of moral discourse consists in defending and criticizing moral claims that ascribe rights. The account of morality that I have been defending so far can therefore be regarded as acceptable only if it is capable of accommodating right-ascriptions. This chapter shows that the account is capable of accommodating them.

We often make and criticize both ascriptions of rights and ascriptions of duties within the same moral discussion, and in doing so we assume that they stand in some logical relation to each other (although it might not always be clear what precisely the relation is). We therefore must treat ascriptions of moral rights as belonging to the same type of discourse as claims that express moral duties; we cannot relegate right-ascriptions to a type of discourse of their own.

Each right-ascription ascribes a right *to* someone, that is, it contains an individual constant referring to the individual who has the right or an individual variable ranging over such individuals. These individuals can be called *right-holders*. An explanation of how ascriptions of rights fit the framework of my analysis must provide an explanation of how the notion of a right-holder is related to the notions of a moral agent and a moral patient.

The view I defend in this chapter is a view that once seemed uncontroversial to many moral philosophers but that is currently decidedly out of fashion. This is the view that

χ has a right (against ξ) that $\xi\Phi\chi$

can be regarded as equivalent to

ξ has a duty to χ that $\xi\Phi\chi$. [1]

I shall be referring to this view as *correlativism* and to the contradictory view as *anticorrelativism*.[2]

It is a consequence of correlativism that being a right-holder is nothing but being a moral patient. The defense of correlativism presented in this chapter will thus be a justification of the disregard for right-ascriptions and right-holders in the rest of this book.

The majority of anticorrelativists concede that an ascription of a right commits one to the ascription of the correlative duty, but deny the converse because according to them the meaning of the word *right* is such that the content of an ascription of a right is richer than the content of the ascription of the corresponding duty.

I take it for granted here that we can move from right-ascriptions to duty-ascriptions and concentrate on showing that we can equally well move from duty-ascriptions to right-ascriptions (or, in other words, that replacing a right-ascription by a suitable duty-ascription does not involve any loss in meaning). I do not attempt to argue directly with the minority of anticorrelativists who would deny that there is implication in either direction between right-ascriptions and duty-ascriptions.[3] However, some of the points that I make (especially in section 4.2) have obvious implications that cast a doubt on this view.

According to correlativism, as I have presented it here, being a moral patient for a particular duty is both necessary and sufficient for having the correlative right, and it is not a feature of the concept of a moral patient that the duties that are owed to them are *necessarily* beneficial to them (although, as a matter of fact, they usually are). Correlativism therefore differs from Bentham's theory of rights (although both theories spring from similar theoretical motivation) in one respect: a correlativist, unlike Bentham, does not claim that respect for a right is necessarily beneficial to the holder of that right. In this way correlativism avoids some of the objections that were raised to the theory according to which being a right-holder is just being a beneficiary of a duty.[4]

Needless to say, if we choose to qualify our duty-ascriptions as prima facie or *sans phrase* (all things considered) then we must qualify the right-ascriptions in the same way; and we should expect a duty-ascription that is qualified in some such way to be equivalent only to a right-ascription that is qualified in the same way.

It should perhaps also be mentioned that both correlativism and various versions of anticorrelativism apply to only one of different senses that the noun *right* has in moral contexts. In particular, we should note that there is another, perfectly legitimate, sense of the word such that saying that someone has a moral right in that sense to do something is equivalent to saying that he does not have a duty not to do it. In order to avoid confusion, I shall follow the practice of using the expression *liberty-right* when I need to invoke that notion (rather than simply *right*). Being a holder of a liberty-right is then obviously nothing but being a moral agent.

4.2 How to Talk about Rights

It may now be objected that my formulation of the issue between correlativism and anticorrelativism does not do justice to what various philosophers who hold these views have in mind because they are interested in providing a general account of right-ascriptions as we find them in actual moral discourse and the form in which I have presented right-ascriptions does not do justice to many of the right-ascriptions that we encounter every day.

At first glance it really does not seem that the noun *right* is, in virtue of its meaning, restricted to contexts of the form

$$\chi \text{ has a right (against } \xi) \text{ that } \xi \Phi \chi$$

Some uses of the noun *right* may fit the model easily (e.g., "Paula has a right that Peter pay her five dollars") but many seem to be quite different. For example, we often speak about having rights to life, liberty, property, free speech, education, travel, and so on.

I want to claim that each such expression, insofar as it has any definite meaning at all, can be replaced without loss by an expression of the form just mentioned. Moreover, I want to claim that, for the purposes of a serious and fruitful philosophical discussion of rights, each of them should be so replaced.

In order to support these claims, I now put forward the following principle: we do not understand the meaning of an ascription of a certain right to someone unless we know what counts as violating (infringing) the right (and so what counts as respecting it). (In other words, in order to know what a particular right is all about, we must know what is the case when it is respected [or violated].)[5]

This principle merely applies to right-ascriptions the same idea that can be encountered in the well-known principles that one cannot understand an assertion without knowing what is the case when it is confirmed or falsified, that a necessary condition for understanding an order is to know what constitutes obedience or disobedience to it, that a promise cannot be understood without knowing what counts as keeping or breaking it, or that in order to understand a duty-ascription one must know what constitutes following or violating it.

When a right is ascribed to someone by an expression of the form "χ has a right (against ξ) that $\xi\Phi\chi$," then it is very easy to see what its conditions of being respected are, and so what the whole ascription means. Obviously such a right is respected just in case the relation that is designated by what we put at the place of Φ obtains between the appropriate individuals; otherwise it is violated. If someone says, "Paula has a right that Peter pay her five dollars by Wednesday," then we understand immediately that a part of his meaning is that the right would be respected just in case that Peter does pay five dollars to Paula by Wednesday and that it would be violated if Peter does not pay five dollars to Paula by Wednesday.

How do rights to life, education, and so on, fare in the light of our principle about conditions of being respected? What must be the case for my right to life to be respected? When is that right violated?

Could it be that someone's right to life is respected just in case he lives, and is violated otherwise? If he is about to die would that in and of itself constitute a violation of his right to life? Hardly. I do not know anyone who speaks English correctly who means *that* when he says that someone has a right to life. Deaths of incurable illnesses are not counted as violations of the right to life (at least in the absence of some special explanation), while clear-cut cases of murder usually are.

Similarly, it is obvious that the right to travel does not have as its condition of being respected that its holder actually travels. This is not what we mean by the "right to travel." Very many people have their right to travel respected without ever traveling anywhere.

It seems that we can speak about a violation of a right only when someone is somehow responsible for it. Saying that a right has been violated invites not only the question, Whose right it is? but also the question, Who violated it? An aspect of the conditions that make the right violated is that *someone* has violated it.[6] When we say that a right has been violated we do not need to be able to identify the violator immediately, but we are implying that there is a violator and that he is identifiable in principle.

If violation of a right is always a violation of someone's right by someone, then the violation itself can be described as failure of a certain relation to obtain between the two. And if this is what the condition of violation of the right is, then its condition of being respected consists in that same relation obtaining between the two individuals.

Thus, for any right, regardless of the linguistic form that we might have initially chosen for ascription of that right, the conditions of being respected always have the form of a certain relation obtaining between someone (bearer of the correlative duty) and the right-holder.

Now, suppose we take an ascription of a right to χ which does not embody the form "χ has a right (against ξ) that $\xi\Phi\chi$," and we analyze its meaning in terms of the conditions of being respected. By the above reasoning we shall come up with something that can be stated in the form "that $\xi\Phi\chi$" as the condition of being respected for that right. We can then try to formulate an ascription of a right that would be different in form from the original one but would give the same condition of being respected to the right it ascribes. Whatever other results this exercise might have, there will always be one formulation that will immediately suggest itself, and it will be of the form "χ has a right (against ξ) that $\xi\Phi\chi$." This formulation is as much an ascription of a right as the original one: they both ascribe the right to the individual that is referred to by the expression that we put at the place of χ and they both have the same condition of being respected ("that $\xi\Phi\chi$"). Therefore, they are for most ends and purposes interchangeable.

The preceding paragraph has provided us with a recipe for replacing all ascriptions of rights that are not of the form "χ has a right (against ξ) that $\xi\Phi\chi$" with ascriptions that have that form. What has been said in the preceding section can now be applied to all the ascriptions of rights that may result out of applications of this recipe.

Readers should note that I am not asking them to replace the formulations that they are used to with the ones that I am proposing in order that my analysis may be applied to them. There are quite independent reasons for preferring my "canonical" form of right-ascriptions.

Ascriptions of that form make it more obvious what their conditions of being respected are. Their meaning is therefore much clearer. Moreover, ascriptions of rights that do not have this form tend to be highly ambiguous[7] and these ambiguities have proven to be pernicious to moral argumentation.

Take, for example, the claim that we all have the "right to life." What does it mean? What are its conditions of being respected? To begin with, most people would agree that at least a part of these conditions is that others abstain from murdering us. But what else is included? Do the conditions include others' helping those of us whose lives are in danger? Do they include providing us with everything we need to sustain life, or even someone's doing everything that is necessary to minimize the risks to our lives? Does the right to life entail the right to medical care (and if it does, what type and what amount of medical care)? Is the right to life not already respected if the state takes some reasonable steps toward achieving some (or all) of the above conditions (e.g., by enacting appropriate laws and providing institutions that will enforce them)?

The above questions have no determinate answers. Everyone who uses the phrase "right to life" must determine for himself and tell us what he means by "right to life."

Trying to figure out what "right to life" *really* means is a pointless exercise. It can mean any or all of the above things and perhaps many more. It just happens to be highly ambiguous, and the same holds for all the other phrases that involve rights without following the form that I have advocated.

One might try to patch the things up by distinguishing three or four or seven different senses of such a phrase, but new ambiguities will keep popping up. Moreover, a classification of senses of one such phrase would be of little general use, as the ambiguities in the meaning of, say, "right to travel" or "right to education" will not follow the same pattern as the ambiguities in "right to life." The only way to get rid of such ambiguities once and for all is to put all our ascriptions of rights in the form "χ has the right (against ξ) that $\xi\Phi\chi$."

Phrases, like "right to life," that can be used to express very different claims about rights are pernicious because they often lead us to forget that each of the different claims (different in the sense of having different conditions of being respected) that they can be used to express needs to be defended (or attacked) by different arguments.[8]

4.3 Alleged Counterexamples to Correlativism

Having justified the specific form in which I present all claims involving rights, I can now go back to the dispute between correlativism and anticorrelativism.

Given that the anticorrelativist believes that the implication between rights and duties holds in one direction only, the most straightforward argument for his position would consist in finding a counterexample to its converse, that is, an example in which "χ has a right (against ξ) that $\xi\Phi\chi$" does not hold, although "ξ has a duty to χ that $\xi\Phi\chi$" holds.

In this section I discuss three putative examples of the kind that have been invoked in support of anticorrelativism.

4.3.1 Animals

The first example concerns our duties to animals. It has been alleged that we have some duties to animals, but that the animals do not have the corresponding rights.[9]

Both elements of that alleged counterexample are in fact far from obvious, indeed much less obvious than the thesis (correlativism) that the example is intended to refute. Careful investigation seems to be necessary in order to ascertain whether we have any duties in which animals can be moral patients. Maybe we do not. Maybe all our seeming duties to animals are in fact duties to someone else, as was held by many respectable people, including Kant.[10] In that case animals not having rights is not a counterexample to correlativism, and it may well be that someone else who is the real moral patient of our duties concerning animals has the corresponding rights.[11]

Equally careful investigation is necessary to ascertain whether animals have rights: many contemporary philosophers have presented arguments to the effect that they do. Given that both animal rights and duties to animals are controversial, it seems quite possible that they will stand or fall together, which would support correlativism.

In fact it seems that the only people who firmly believe that animals do not have rights, although we have duties to them, are precisely those people who have already accepted a certain anticorrelativist conception of rights (which is such that it makes it impossible for animals to have rights). That is why the example of animals cannot be of much use in converting anyone to anticorrelativism.

4.3.2 Charity

The second, much more powerful example is that of charity. Many people hold that there is a duty of charity although the potential recipients of charity do not have the right to receive it.

To fill in the details of the example, suppose that by charity we mean simply almsgiving, and that alms are typically given by individual donors directly to individual recipients (i.e., that there is no centralized system for distribution of charity). Suppose, moreover, that there is no problem with distinguishing those who are really in need of charity from those who would fraudulently present themselves as such.

In that case it seems reasonable to say that an individual beggar who approaches you asking for money really has no right to your money, although you might still have the duty to provide charity and your giving money to him would count toward satisfaction of your duty of charity.

In order to see whether this is really a counterexample to the rights-duties correlativism, we must see what exactly is the content of your duty of charity. The duty of charity is such that we cannot ascertain whether you are satisfying or violating it just by looking at what you are doing at some specific occasion. The duty of charity does not require that you give money to some particular beggar at a specific time. If I see you refusing to give anything to a particular beggar at a particular time, I am not entitled to conclude that you are neglecting your duty of charity. For all I know you might have given considerable amounts of money to several beggars the day before. Nor can I conclude that you are discharging your duty of charity simply on the basis of seeing you give something to a particular beggar on a particular occasion. Maybe that is the only time in your entire life that you did such a thing. No particular instance of your giving alms constitutes the satisfaction of your duty of charity, although each such case counts toward satisfaction of that duty. It is only by observing your behavior over a longer period of time and computing the total amount that you have given in alms over the period that I can conclude whether you have neglected your duty of charity or not.

It is logically possible to discharge the duty of charity by giving a very small amount of money (perhaps less than a cent) to every beggar you see, or even every beggar you know about. It is even possible to imagine a system of almsgiving that would require every donor to do precisely that. Such a system would, however, be unreasonable because the costs of performing such numerous transactions, to both donors and recipients, would be excessive. That is why the duty of charity has the form it has, namely the form that allows you to satisfy it by giving alms only to some, randomly chosen beggars on some, randomly chosen occasions. This enables donors to give a more reasonable amount of charity in each individual transaction (without affecting the total amount given over a period of time), and thereby reduces the total costs of performing the almsgiving transactions. Note that, if the selection of occasions on which alms are given is really random and if the frequency of giving and the amounts given are properly adjusted, then each beggar ends up receiving approximately the same amount as he would under a system that would require each donor to give alms to every beggar.

The result of this discussion is that you are following your duty of charity if you are performing acts of almsgiving on randomly chosen occasions but with the right frequency. This is the content of the duty of charity. That a particular beggar who approaches you on a given occasion does not have the right that you give him anything on that occasion is, therefore, not a counterexample to the rights-duties correlativism, as you do not have a duty that would correspond to *it*, namely the duty to give him something on that occasion.

Still, if correlativism holds, then we must be able to formulate an ascription of some other right that exists if and only if the duty of charity, as described above, exists. I am going to claim that indeed there is such a right.

In order to discover what the right is, let us first ask ourselves who is the moral patient of the duty of charity. One possible answer is that it is a duty owed to the poor, taken together, as a group. If we conceive it in that way, then I do not see anything odd with saying that the poor as a group have the right to receive alms. On this account, no particular member of that group has such a right, but the group as a whole has the right to receive a certain portion of the income of each person who is reasonably well-off (the distribution of that amount on particular members of the group being random). However, the tenability of this line of argument is conditional upon it being possible for groups to be moral patients in the strict sense, which seems questionable.

Fortunately, the duty of charity can be redescribed as a duty owed to particular beggars. What do you owe a particular beggar who approaches you? What relation must hold between you and him if you are not to violate your duty of charity? It cannot be the relation of giving him a certain amount of money, as the duty of charity involves randomness. But you do have a duty to include him in the domain over which you randomly distribute your donations. You do not owe him a donation, but you owe him a chance of a donation. Another way of putting it is to say that the relation that must obtain between you and him is the relation of giving-a-certain-amount-of-money-with-a-certain-probability. And again, I do not see anything odd with saying that as much as you have a duty to stand in that relation to him, he has the right that you stand in that relation to him. The claim that a poor person has the right to a certain probability of receiving a charitable donation seems quite reasonable.

The rights that correspond to the duty of charity are on my account very similar to the rights of lottery players. Buying a lottery ticket clearly gives you certain rights (both moral and legal). Your rights are not violated when you lose (this is a normal feature of a lottery), but they would be violated if the design of the machine used in drawing numbers made it impossible for your number to win. In other words, as a participant in a lottery you do not have the right to win the prize, but you do have the right to a certain chance of winning the prize.

4.3.3 Tax Evasion

The third alleged counterexample to correlativism are the duties to abstain from "free riding," and perhaps the best example of "free riding" is tax evasion. This example has been discussed by Hart[12] and by Lyons,[13] and they failed to find rights correlated with this duty because they were looking in the wrong direction. They assumed that the candidates for holders of rights correlated with the duty to pay taxes are the recipients of various tax-funded services and then went on to point out that they either have no right to such services or that, when they do, the connection between the right and the duty turns out to be dubious. But it is quite possible to conceive the duty to pay taxes as a moral duty in which the relevant moral patients are not the beneficiaries of the tax-funded services but other taxpayers.

Every act of tax evasion diminishes the budget of the state and thereby contributes to creating the need that more taxes be collected in the next round of tax collection. This means that the honest taxpayers are likely to end up paying more taxes than they would if there were no tax evasion. This reasoning applies to every society that has taxes and in which the government is not likely to be indifferent to the total amount of taxes that it succeeds in collecting. It is independent of the uses to which the budget is put and of whether the government has any rationale for maintaining the budget on one level rather than another.

Once tax evasion is viewed that way, it does not seem unreasonable to say that every taxpayer has the right that everyone else pays his fair share of taxes (because that ensures that he will not be required to pay more than his fair share of taxes). This right can be viewed as the correlative of the duty to pay taxes (the duty to abstain from tax evasion).

4.4   Refutations of Anticorrelativist Theories

The alleged counterexamples to correlativism that I have discussed above (section 4.3) were intended to appeal to the intuitions about the concept of rights that we have prior to accepting any particular analysis of it. I hope to have shown that the appeal was unsuccessful and that these examples do not compel us to reject correlativism. In this section I examine some specific suggestions for an analysis of the meaning of the noun *right* to see whether any of them presents a real threat to correlativism.

4.4.1   Limiting the Freedom of Others

In 1955 H. L. A. Hart published an article entitled "Are There Any Natural Rights?"[14] and in the first part of the article he presented his anticorrelativist account of rights.

Crucial to his argument is the distinction between the duties that can be properly described as duties *to* someone (or obligations)[15] and duties that cannot be so described. He seems[16] to be willing to concede to the correlativist that duties of the first kind (duties-to) imply rights, but he also believes that there are duties of the second kind.

From what I said in earlier chapters, the reader can easily conclude that I believe all duties are duties-to. If someone were to refute this view he would have to be able to produce a counterexample: an example of a duty that is not a duty-to. Hart however does not provide any such example. He mentions the duties concerning the treatment of animals and babies, but not in a way that would amount to such a counterexample.

For the sake of argument we may grant him his assumption that duties to treat animals and babies in a certain way are not duties to animals or babies, but that still would not entail that they are not duties-to at all. It may well be proper to describe them as duties to someone else, and Hart does not investigate that possibility at all.[17] The only thing that Hart was entitled to conclude from his treatment of the animals/babies example is that the way in which we formulate our claims about duties often fails to make it obvious to whom these duties are owed (who the moral patients are) and sometimes even misleads us about that. When a given claim about duties makes it difficult to figure out who is intended as the moral patient, then it will also be difficult to formulate the equivalent claim about rights. But although it can be difficult, I do not see any reason to believe that it will ever be impossible.

If we leave this difficulty in Hart's argument aside and concentrate on the outcome of his analysis of rights, we shall see that he says that having "a right entails having a moral justification for limiting the freedom of another person and for determining how he should act."[18] What he means is presumably that the holder of a right is morally justified in limiting the freedom of others in certain specific ways, namely the ways that are aimed at ensuring that the right is not violated. In other words, he seems to hold the view that "χ has a right (against ξ) that $\xi\Phi\chi$" is equivalent to the following:

ξ has a duty to χ that $\xi\Phi\chi$ and χ is morally justified in limiting ξ's freedom so as to ensure that $\xi\Phi\chi$.

This analysis may seem plausible when we look at examples of some duties that are indeed accompanied by such justification. For instance, you have a duty to abstain from murdering me,

and if you attempted to violate that duty of yours I would be justified in doing many things that are otherwise wrong in order to
ensure that you comply with it. It is then tempting to say that
both these elements constitute my right not to be murdered.

But if we look at some other examples, the analysis starts to
lose its plausibility. If you borrowed five dollars from me and
promised to return it, then I have a right to receive five dollars
from you. But if you then threaten to violate that right there
are very few things that I am morally justified in doing in
order to ensure your compliance. I would be justified in
reminding you of your promise, commenting on your unrelia-
bility, and after a while perhaps insisting that you pay.
Grabbing a valuable piece of your property, capturing and
then torturing you, abducting your children or threatening to
do any of these things would all greatly increase my chances of
exacting five dollars from you, but I would not be morally justified in doing anything like that.

So Hart obviously could not have meant that a particular
right that I possess gives me moral justification to do anything
that might prevent its violation. What I am morally justified in
doing varies from case to case, and no amount of thinking
about the *concept* of a right, or about the contents of the
proposition that replaces $\xi\Phi\chi$ in the particular case, will tell us
what it is. In order to decide what the morally appropriate
reactions to possible or actual violations of our rights (or
duties) are, we need to bring in moral principles, arguments,
and considerations that were not pertinent to deciding
whether the right (or duty) in question really is a moral right
(or duty). These are two totally different moral questions.

Someone might acknowledge that there are ways of limiting
freedom of others that are justified in the cases of some rights
that I possess and not justified in others, but still claim that there
is a certain minimal reaction to an attempted or actual violation
of my right that is justified in the case of every right that I possess. I doubt that those who attempt this line of argument will
ever be able to describe what that minimal reaction is.[19]

There is admittedly one trivial way in which χ's having a
right that $\xi\Phi\chi$ (and not having waived it) limits ξ's freedom. It
makes it impossible for ξ to behave morally while not $\xi\Phi\chi$. But
any duty that ξ has is sufficient to limit ξ's freedom in that way.

If that is all that is meant, then the second conjunct of Hart's analysis (as I represented it) becomes redundant, and the whole analysis collapses into correlativism.

My argument against Hart can now be summarized in the following way. He says that it is part of the meaning of the noun *right* that the right-holder is morally justified in limiting freedom of others. This can mean that every right justifies limiting freedom of others in (*a*) all possible ways that could reduce the probability of a violation of the right, (*b*) certain specified ways, or (*c*) at least one way. Interpretation (*a*) is highly implausible; I do not see how (*b*) could be made sufficiently specific (while still remaining a part of the analysis of the concept of a right); and (*c*) is in danger of collapsing into correlativism.

The popularity of theories like Hart's seems to be a result of the fact that the term *right* in the sense of a moral right is very frequently used in arguments in favor of introducing the corresponding legal rights [20] and that legal rights typically provide legal justification for certain forms of coercion. The frequency with which moral rights are mentioned in such contexts makes it understandable how it could appear plausible that the moral justification of coercion is somehow part of the meaning of *moral right*.

4.4.2 Claiming

Another popular analysis of rights is Feinberg's,[21] according to which "χ has a right (against ξ) that $\xi\Phi\chi$" is equivalent to the following:

> ξ has a duty to χ that $\xi\Phi\chi$ and χ is in a position to make (valid) claims concerning $\xi\Phi\chi$.

A powerful criticism of Feinberg's account has been provided in William Nelson's article "On the Alleged Importance of Moral Rights"[22] that frequently gets overlooked by admirers of Feinberg's analysis. Most of what I am going to say in this subsection can be regarded as a restatement or elaboration of Nelson's criticisms.

Making a claim in the particular sense of the word *claim* that Feinberg is interested in is supposed to be something different from making a claim in the sense in which I have been using the word in this book. The difference can be illustrated by comparing Peter's claiming in some casual conversation that a particular lost object that he has seen in the lost-and-found office is Paula's and should be returned to her (this is already an instance of claiming in the wide sense in which I have been using the word) with Paula's coming to the lost-and-found office and claiming the object back (this is claiming in the sense that Feinberg is interested in).

To understand Feinberg's analysis it is important to notice that he conceives the activity of making claims as an activity governed by constitutive rules. That someone has made a claim is for him an institutional fact. It can be understood only when viewed within the framework of the institution of claiming, just as the fact that a batter is out can be understood only within the framework of the institution of baseball. Feinberg seems to think that there is a rule to the effect that right-holders (and right-holders only) are in a position to make claims (in the second sense of the word) in morality and that this is the same sort of rule as the rule that only an umpire can pronounce a batter out.

Someone other than an umpire may attempt to go through the motions of pronouncing a batter out, but according to the rules of the game of baseball, that simply does not count as pronouncing him out. According to Feinberg's analysis (as I have presented it), someone may go through the motions of making a moral claim but fail to make a valid claim either because (1) there is no regulative moral rule imposing the appropriate duty on the appropriate individual; or (2) he is not in the right position to make a claim, that is, he is not a right-holder in this particular case, either because someone else is a right-holder or because no rights are involved; or perhaps because (3) he violated some other constitutive rule of the institution of claiming.[23]

It seems obvious that Feinberg's vision of claiming (and so of rights) in morality is heavily influenced by the paradigm of legal claiming. In legal contexts there is indeed a clear difference between the two senses of claiming that were illustrated by the example of the lost object; and claiming in the second sense is indeed a complex institution governed by all sorts of constitutive rules. It may well be that the notion of legal rights should be analyzed in terms of that institution. Constitutive rules of legal claiming (in the strict sense) specify who will be recognized as a claimant for certain types of cases, what the deadlines for making claims are, who will hear the claims, and even what size of paper is to be used for making claims. If your purported claim violates any of these rules, then from the point of view of the law it is null and void, that is, it is not a legal claim at all. If Peter has broken a contract that he had made with Paula, and if John is merely a busybody in no way related to Paula, then Paula can sue Peter (i.e., make a legal claim) for breach of contract, while John cannot. Nothing that John can do counts as making a legal claim in that matter.

Feinberg's analysis assumes that in morality there is also a difference between the two senses of *claiming* and that there is an institution of moral claiming in the strict sense which is roughly similar to the institution of legal claiming. Is there such an institution?

Suppose Peter is about to violate some moral right of Paula's. John, the busybody, enters the scene and starts reminding Peter of his duties to Paula, pointing out the immorality of his intended conduct, and exhorting him to respect Paula's rights. John's conduct in this example might have been wrong in many different ways, it might have been rude and even immoral, it might have violated many regulative rules, but we cannot say that it violated any constitutive rules. We cannot say that what he did does not *count* as pointing out the immorality of Peter's intended conduct or as exhorting Peter to respect Paula's rights. And it does not seem that Paula herself could do anything more than that. As has been remarked by Jan Narveson,[24] it is not clear how making a claim that one's moral rights be respected could amount to anything more than pointing out the immorality of the conduct that would violate them.

In short, Feinberg has not provided us with any reasons to regard claiming in morality as an institution similar to legal claiming. To be sure, moral claiming can be regarded as an institution in the way in which any form of speech act can be regarded as an institution, but it is not an institution with as stringent constitutive rules as are necessary for the success of Feinberg's analysis. In particular it does not have constitutive rules that would restrict the class of possible claimants in any interesting way. This means that the second conjunct of Feinberg's analysis of rights (as I have reconstructed it) will always hold, which means that the analysis will collapse into correlativism. It also means that morality is unlike law in that there is no substantial difference between making a moral claim in Feinberg's purportedly stricter sense and making a moral claim in my loose sense of the word.

I would now like to reinforce this argument by pointing out that not only is it a fact that the institution of moral claiming, as Feinberg conceives it, does not exist but that it is also quite natural that it does not exist, as such an institution would have no point.

A rationale for having an institution can be either that its operations are fun in themselves or that it enables us to achieve, in a more orderly fashion, something that is itself outside the institution. Examples of the former are various games; examples of the latter are legal institutions (including the institution of legal claiming). Constitutive rules of legal claiming determine what counts as a valid claim, just as constitutive rules of a game determine what counts as scoring a point. But making a valid legal claim is not merely like scoring a point; it has important further consequences. Only if I am in the position to make a valid legal claim (in the strict sense) will I be able to set in motion the system of legal coercion. The institution of legal claiming is normally used as means to that end. That is the point of having it.

What would be the point of having an institution of moral claiming as Feinberg conceives it? It is unlikely that such claiming would be great fun in itself. But in morality there is no system (analogous to the system of legal coercion) that one could set in motion by making moral claims (or fail to set in motion because one failed to satisfy all the constitutive rules of the institution). Therefore I do not see any further purpose that Feinberg's institution of moral claiming could serve. And if there is no such purpose, then my ability or inability to make valid claims in it would not make any difference. This pointlessness of moral claiming (when conceived in Feinberg's way) makes it quite unsurprising that there is in fact no such institution.

4.4.3 Waiving

It may seem to some people that the right-holder's power to waive his rights is an essential feature of the concept of right and that it is left out in the correlativist account.[25] Two replies can be made to that suggestion.

First, it is not entirely obvious that every moral right involves such a power of waiver. In law there are rights that cannot be waived, and it is not clear that morality should be different in that respect. To be sure, there may be good moral reasons for attaching such a power to every right, but I do not see why there should be anything conceptually wrong with a right that cannot be waived.

Second, what we call the "power to waive a right" can be redescribed without the use of the word *right*. To have a power to waive a certain right is to be in a situation to perform a speech act that changes the moral aspects of the situation in such a way that something that previously would have counted as a violation of a right does not count as a violation anymore. Something that would have counted as immoral in the absence of that speech act is not immoral after it has been performed. Now, moral patients often have the power to change the moral aspects of the situation in exactly the same way, and this power of theirs is totally independent of whether they will also be described as holders of rights or not. A moral patient often has an option to perform the act of *permitting* the relevant moral agent to behave toward him in a way that would otherwise be wrong. A right-holder's waiving his right amounts to the same thing as a moral patient's permitting a moral agent to behave contrary to what would otherwise be his duty. The idea that the rights can be waived is therefore perfectly compatible with the correlativist account of rights.

4.4.4 Protection of Liberties

Rights, if respected, usually make it easier for us to do certain things that we have a liberty-right to do. If I have a right that others abstain from forcibly preventing me from speaking publicly, and if others respect that right, then speaking publicly is likely to be an easier task for me than it would be otherwise. Moreover, I have a liberty-right to speak publicly.

This might be viewed as suggesting that there is some conceptual connection between rights and liberty-rights. An analysis of rights that would attempt to incorporate this suggestion would have to say that "χ has a right (against ξ) that $\xi\Phi\chi$" is, in virtue of the meaning of the noun *right*, equivalent to

ξ has a duty to χ that $\xi\Phi\chi$ and χ has a liberty-right that $\chi\Psi\zeta$ and $\xi\Phi\chi$ facilitates $\chi\Psi\zeta$

where ζ is a place-holder for a term that refers to some moral patient(s) and Ψ for the description of the way in which there is a liberty-right to behave toward these patients.

The casual and imprecise way of talking about rights that was criticized in section 4.2 promotes this line of analysis. In everyday moral discourse rights are frequently referred to in terms of the activities that are facilitated when their conditions of being respected are met (rather than in terms of these conditions themselves). For example, my right that others abstain from forcibly preventing me from speaking publicly is often referred to as my "right to speak publicly" and this promotes the idea that there is some sort of conceptual connection between that right and my liberty-right to speak publicly.

The way of talking about rights that I have advocated in section 4.2 has already greatly reduced the plausibility of this line of analysis, but there are two more arguments against it.

The first is that it can be argued convincingly that there are situations in which we have a right, the respect for which facilitates our doing something that we do not have a liberty-right to do (something that is wrong for us to do). For example, it may be argued that I have a right that others abstain from forcibly preventing me from speaking publicly even in a situation where respect for that right facilitates my speaking publicly in a manner that promotes racism, which is something that I do not have a liberty-right to do.[26]

One may reply to this argument by saying that although respect for my right can sometimes facilitate my doing wrong things, it will always facilitate at least one thing that I have a liberty-right to do. This may be a sound reply to my first argument, but it paves the way to my second argument.

Namely, whenever someone has a duty to me I can find some trivial activity that I have a liberty-right to perform and that would be facilitated by respect for that duty. For example, a great number of duties that others have to me in some way facilitate my scratching my ear, and scratching my ear is something that I almost always have a liberty-right to do. Some such trivial activity will make the last two conjuncts of the proposed analysis true in the case of any duty. This trivializes the whole analysis, and makes it for most ends and purposes collapse into correlativism.

4.4.5 Rights as Grounds of Duties

It is sometimes suggested that there is an asymmetry between rights and duties because rights are grounds of duties, that is, that they are somehow prior to duties.

One possible meaning for this suggestion is that rights are somehow ontologically prior to duties. This is sometimes on the minds of people who speak about "natural rights." This naive idea of rights as something like an aura that surrounds human beings seems to be implicit in much of the popular, nonphilosophical thinking about rights. However, it is too obviously defective to be worth attacking.

Another way in which rights could be prior to duties is *ordo cognoscendi*, that is, it could be argued that we become acquainted with claims about rights first and that we then derive claims about duties from them. This is often true. For example, I found out about my right that others abstain from injuring me long before I found out about John Smith's duty to abstain from injuring me (and long before I found out about John Smith's existence). If John Smith asks me why he should abstain from injuring me I would quite naturally answer, "Because I have a right that others abstain from injuring me." In that case it is indeed quite appropriate to say that my right is the ground of his duty and not the other way around.

However, such examples do not establish any general point about rights. In this example, the ascription of a right involved an element of universality that was absent from the claim about the duty, and that element of universality is responsible for the asymmetry rather than the fact one claim involves the word *right* and the other the word *duty*. The content of the right was that *others* (i.e., everyone else) behaves to me in a certain way, while the content of the duty was that John Smith (i.e., a specific individual) behaves to me in that way. I often find it convenient to express the moral norm requiring everyone to behave toward me in a certain way by saying that I have a right to it, but I could express it in terms of duties and nothing would be lost: the duty of everyone to behave in such and such a way toward me is prior to John Smith's duty to behave in such and such a way toward me in exactly the same way in which my right that everyone behaves in such and such a way toward me is prior to John Smith's duty.

4.5   Dispensability of *Right*

If correlativism is correct, then the noun *right* is dispensable: we could live without it. It could be eliminated from our moral language without any loss to its expressive power.

This does not mean that the correlativists claim that the notion of duty must be regarded as prior to the notion of right. If correlativism is correct, then the term *duty* is as dispensable as the term *right*: talking about duties can always be replaced by talking about rights, without any loss.

Correlativists are likely to be accused of not "taking rights seriously," but that accusation would be unjust: they can take rights very seriously, as seriously as they take morality itself. What they do not take too seriously is only the term *right,* as they believe that this term is neither more nor less important to morality than *duty* or *ought* or *good* or *morally prohibited.*

Although having any one of these terms (without the others) would be sufficient for having a moral language as expressive as the present one, having all of them is still useful. Having the term *right* in addition to *duty* in our moral language is useful in exactly the same way in which having the term *moral prohibition* is: although none of them is logically indispensable, they enable us to say things that we want to say in a less cumbersome way. Moreover, in some moral discussions we may want to focus our attention on the moral patient rather than on the moral agent, and use of the word *right* (rather than *duty*) enables us to do that. Use of the word *right* also gives us the dubious benefit of being able to achieve rhetorical effects that could not be achieved otherwise.

In a language that contains both the word *right* and the word *duty* we can either take *duty* as more basic and define *right* in terms of it, or take *right* as more basic and define *duty* in terms of *right*. It is a matter of choice and nothing hinges upon which option we choose.

Some moral positions might be easier to formulate in terms of rights and some in terms of duties. However, if correlativism is correct, then any moral position can be formulated in terms of rights and no moral position must be so formulated. This implication of correlativism has an important further consequence in that it is misleading to describe some disputes in contemporary normative ethics as disputes over "right-based morality."

If *right-based morality* is to be understood as referring to a system of normative ethics in which principles involving rights are taken as basic, then the label is totally uninformative, as any moral principles can be formulated so as to include the word *right*. If *right-based morality* is to be understood as referring to a system of normative ethics formulated in the language that takes the noun *right* as a primitive term, then the label is again uninformative, as that language is equivalent to the language that takes *duty* as a primitive term.

The only sense that we can make of the phrase *right-based morality* that would be consistent with there being a dispute between its proponents and proponents of other normative-ethical views is that the phrase refers to a system of ethics that takes as its basic principles some principles that are easier to formulate in terms of rights than in some other terms. "Easier to formulate" is, however, very vague, which is why I think that the use of the label *right-based morality* only confuses the issues to which it is applied. It is, by the way, interesting to note that many philosophers have engaged in the discussion over *right-based morality* without attempting to specify what exactly is supposed to be covered by the label.

If the notion of a right (and hence the notion of a right-holder) is dispensable in this way, then it is permissible to concentrate on duty-ascriptions and notions of a moral agent and a moral patient in the rest of our investigation of moral discourse and the moral community.

Questions about Membership in the Moral Community

5.1 The Independence of Questions about Membership in the Moral Community

The failure of different analyses of the notion of morality to account successfully for the differences between moral discourse and other types of prescriptive discourse (discussed in chapter 1) has led us to analyze the notion of morality in terms of argument-places for moral agents and argument-places for moral patients as designated argument-places in moral claims (chapter 2). Realizing that the presence of argument-places of these two types in moral claims is precisely what makes them moral led us to investigate them further, and this resulted in our introducing (in chapter 3) the notion of the moral community, which consists of the set of moral agents and the set of moral patients. The latter set turned out, in chapter 4, to be the same one as the set of right-holders.

The question that arises quite naturally, once the notion of moral community has been introduced is, Which individuals belong to the set of moral agents and/or the set of moral patients? or in other words, Who are the members of the moral community? The remainder of this book is devoted to that question.[1] This chapter discusses the status of this and similar questions without attempting to answer them. The answer is offered in chapter 6, and the implications of that answer are explored in chapter 7.

It hardly needs to be pointed out that our answer to the question about boundaries of moral community has important practical consequences. One who does not regard human fetuses as members of the community is obviously not going to have any moral qualms about having or performing an abortion (except perhaps because of its side effects). If one regards animals as moral patients one is not likely to become a butcher. Whether we count Martians as members of the moral community may determine (in the words of John Harris) whether we shall "have them for dinner in one sense or in the other."[2] Most of the consequences have to do with membership in the set of moral patients, but what we think about membership in the set of moral agents has consequences of its own. If we regard Martians as moral agents we may morally criticize their decision to exterminate us; otherwise, we can only look at it as some sort of natural disaster.

It also hardly needs to be pointed out that most of the available answers to the question about membership in the moral community are controversial. People disagree as to whether all human fetuses or no fetuses at all or only some fetuses belong to the moral community, and the same holds of animals, comatose humans, and various sorts of possible extraterrestrial beings. It is also notable that the focus of such controversies changes. A century ago it was uncontroversial within the Western world that animals do not belong to the moral community: today it has become controversial. On the other hand, it is uncontroversial today that at least normal human adults are members of the moral community, but we can easily imagine that at the time of the first contacts between different races it may have been genuinely controversial, within each of the groups that came into contact, whether the individuals of the other race belonged to the moral community.

A feature of questions about membership in the moral community that needs to be pointed out, however, is their relative independence of questions that concern the content of our moral rules. Suppose, for example, that we are discussing the wrongfulness of lying, that is, that we are discussing whether to accept or reject something like "For every x and for every y, x has a duty to y that x does not lie to y." If someone challenges such a rule, the standard procedure is to ask him how he would like it if someone were to lie to him, that is, to ask him to perform a patient-oriented shoehorn maneuver. Of course, the discussion usually does not end here: at further steps of such a discussion various modifications in some such rule may be proposed and examined so as to ensure its consistency with other acceptable moral rules. For example, it may be proposed and discussed whether the above rule is to be replaced with something like: "For every x and for every y, x has a duty to y that x does not lie to y, unless this is done to prevent some great disaster." In examining such modifications, the participants in the discussion will typically ask each other to perform some further shoehorn maneuvers.

Notice now that between two people who both regard all and only white human beings as members of the moral community, a discussion of this sort goes on in much the same way as it does between two people who regard all and only human beings as members of the moral community or between two people who regard all and only rational beings as members or between two people who regard all and only members of their own tribe as members. They will all use words like *everyone* (i.e., a variable bound by a universal quantifier) at various points in their discussions, and the fact that they have different sets of individuals in mind when they say *everyone* will usually not create any difference in how their discussions proceed. The results of such a discussion usually hinge on how participants in the discussion react to shoehorn maneuvers that they perform and it is reasonable to expect that someone who regards only members of his tribe as members of the moral community will dislike the idea of "someone" (i.e., some member of his tribe) lying to him in the same way and to the same degree as a person who regards all rational beings as moral agents will dislike the idea of "someone" (some rational being) lying to him.

Of course, there may be some minor differences in the way these discussions proceed: for instance, when examples are introduced in a discussion, those who regard all rational beings as members of the moral community may choose an example that would never be used by people who regard only members of their own tribe as members of the moral community. Moreover, those who would think that it is impossible[3] for blacks to be members of the moral community would never mention blackness as a property of some moral agents or patients in their discussions. But then, blackness is not likely to be mentioned in a discussion about lying even by those who do regard black humans as members of the moral community. And given that people can use only a relatively small number of examples in each moral discussion that they have, we can conclude very little from their examples: namely, we can conclude that they regard the individuals that appear as agents or patients in their examples as members of the moral community, but we cannot conclude anything about the individuals that do not appear in their examples. It follows that we can often listen to a moral discussion about, say, the permissibility of lying (or injuring or stealing or whatever) and understand it perfectly without having any idea whether the participants in the discussion regard only members of their own tribe or all rational beings as members of the moral community.

Moreover, a *participant* in a moral discussion need not know who is regarded as a member of the moral community by the other participant. In a moral discussion one may appreciate and respond to various arguments about how everyone has a duty (to everyone) to behave without knowing who is intended as *everyone* by his interlocutor. It follows that two people who differ in their views about membership in the moral community can still have a perfectly successful moral discussion about whether a certain moral rule is to be accepted or rejected. The only condition is that none of them insists on using an example that the other would reject because it takes as agents or patients individuals that are, according to the view of the latter, outside the moral community, and that none of them introduces into the discussion (as possibly belonging to the members of the moral community) properties that, according to the view of the other, it is impossible for the members of the community to have. In the course of such a discussion the participants might or might not be aware that their views regarding the membership in the moral community differ: neither the disagreement nor the awareness of the disagreement need preclude them from reaching a conclusion about how moral agents (whoever they are) have a duty to moral patients (whoever they are) to behave.

Not only can two people who differ in their views regarding membership in the moral community have a discussion about and agree to assent to a particular moral rule; they can also agree in assenting to the same complete system of moral rules. People can disagree as to who counts as *everyone* in moral contexts, while being in perfect agreement about all rules about what everyone's duties to everyone are.

It is a virtue of my analysis of the notion of morality that it is capable of accommodating the controversial character of questions about membership in the moral community and the fact that we can engage in moral discussions in spite of disagreements that we may have regarding membership in the moral community. This has been accomplished by analyzing morality in terms of argument-places for moral agents and for moral patients without attempting to build into the analysis any specification as to who moral agents and moral patients are. Any analysis that insists that morality *by definition* is concerned with behavior of and/or toward human beings or sentient beings or rational beings or individuals of any other definite type, necessarily ignores disagreements about questions concerning membership in the moral community as well as the fact that we can successfully engage in moral discourse in spite of such disagreements.[4]

The features of questions about membership in the moral community that I have presented in this section, namely their importance, the controversial character of most available answers to them, and their relative independence from questions about content of moral rules, places certain constraints not only on the analysis of the notion of morality but also on any further remarks that we may want to make about these questions as well as on any attempt to answer them. For example, we should be suspicious of answers to these questions that are not capable of being accompanied by some convincing explanation as to why people have ever been tempted to disagree about them.

The relative independence of questions about the content of moral rules (where content is expressed by means of variables) and questions about membership in the moral community (questions about what the domains for these variables are) also has an important consequence for Hare's account of moral reasoning. Probably the most significant aspect of his account is that it refutes moral relativism (in at least one sense of the word *relativism*). He has argued that a full understanding of what moral discourse is commits us to a particular way of resolving moral disputes and that, in each case of a moral problem, acceptance of this method commits everyone to endorsing the same solution as the correct one. His view implies that any moral disagreements that still exist among us must be a result of either our insufficient knowledge of the relevant facts or our insufficient appreciation of what moral discourse is or some other sort of logical error.

Hare's argument has been criticized in various ways, but I want to set most of such criticisms aside and assume, for the sake of argument, that the argument is acceptable (with such modifications as may be required by my discussion in the earlier chapters). What exactly does Hare's argument prove?

It proves only that fully rational and fully informed participants in any moral discussion (that will typically involve arguments based on the shoehorn maneuver) are bound to reach agreement about the *content* of moral rules. In other words, it proves that in a discussion centered around something like "For every x and for every y, x has a duty to y that x behaves in such and such a way toward y," fully rational and fully informed participants are bound to agree about what the "such and such a way" is. However, nothing in Hare's argument shows that such participants in moral discourse must agree about the domains that x and y range over. Appealing to the results of the shoehorn maneuver may be a very powerful technique of argumentation, but it cannot help us in resolving disputes about membership in the moral community. Saying, as we do when we appeal to the shoehorn maneuver, "your claim commits you to the rule that everyone has a duty to everyone to behave in such and such way, and this commits you to . . . ," cannot resolve the question of who counts as everyone for the purposes of such arguments. Hare's argument should therefore be regarded as an argument against relativism concerning the content of moral rules. Even if we grant that the argument is successful, it does nothing to preclude the possibility of relativism concerning membership in the moral community.[5]

5.2 Membership in the Moral Community and Methods of Moral Argumentation

Although we can successfully engage in moral discourse without having a clear answer to the question about membership in the moral community, we still need an answer to it.[6] In order for our moral conclusions to guide our behavior (which they must be able to do in virtue of the prescriptivity of moral discourse) we must have an interpretation for these conclusions (in the technical sense of *interpretation* that involves specification of domains for variables).

Various ways of specifying the domains of moral agents and moral patients have been proposed, putting various degrees of emphasis on qualities such as being rational, being human, being sentient, being capable of making choices, using language, having a soul, and so on. Such proposals are usually motivated by a wish to include in or exclude from one or both domains a specific group of individuals, such as animals or fetuses.

In order to answer the question as to who the moral agents and patients are, or to criticize any of the answers that have already been offered to it, we must have some idea about the character of the question with which we are dealing.

It could be thought that which types of individuals qualify for moral agents and/or patients is a question of the philosophy of mind or some related branch of philosophy. It seems that this has been the traditional approach to such questions.

The approach seems natural, because investigations of the notions that figure prominently in the most popular criteria of agency and patiency, that is, notions like *rationality, sentiency,* or *consciousness,* belong to that branch of philosophy.[7] And if we want to argue that, say, consciousness is a condition of moral patiency, then it seems desirable and indeed indispensable to have at hand a workable analysis of the notion of consciousness, and such an analysis can be provided by the philosophy of mind.

But such an analysis of the concept of consciousness is pertinent to our question about moral patiency only if we have already decided that consciousness is or may be a condition of patiency. Assuming that the concept of consciousness and the concept of a moral patient are independent, no amount of research in the philosophy of mind can by itself tell us whether we should count consciousness among the conditions of patiency. On the other hand, if one were to deny that the two concepts are independent, one would be committing something analogous to the naturalistic fallacy.

There is only one line of argument within philosophy of mind that can establish a direct connection between the applicability of mental predicates and membership in the moral community without risking such a fallacy. Philosophers such as Hilary Putnam[8] and Amelie Rorty[9] have suggested that applicability of mental predicates could be a matter of decision.[10] One could accept this suggestion and then go on to argue that our decisions about their applicability go together with our decisions to consider or not consider something as a moral agent or patient.[11] On this account there would not be anything wrong with arguing directly from the applicability of a certain mental predicate (say *being conscious*) to moral patiency or agency. This strategy, however, strengthens the link between the boundaries of the moral community and the boundaries of the set of individuals to whom the relevant mental predicates are applicable at the cost of becoming unable to determine the latter in any specific way. As a consequence, even on this view, philosophy of mind cannot by itself determine the boundaries of the moral community in any specific way: it can elucidate how decisions about applicability of mental predicates are made, but it cannot make any such decision for us.

Similar reasoning can dismiss the suggestion that the criteria of moral agency or patiency can be discovered by science, that the question is an empirical one. Science could be of help only in applying a criterion that we have already adopted, through enabling us to construct various tests by means of which we could find out whether fetuses, dolphins, or earthworms have the properties required by our criterion, but no amount of scientific information tells us what the properties are that we should look for.

Such considerations have led many contemporary philosophers to assume that the question as to what domains the variables for moral agents and patients range over is itself a moral question. On the other hand, the analysis of the notion of morality presented in chapter 2 seems to imply that questions about membership in the moral community are not moral questions. If moral claims are to be recognized by their two designated argument-places then it seems to follow that an answer to the question of which sets the variables on these argument-places range over cannot be another moral claim. This is another instance of the general principle that one cannot determine domains for variables of a certain language within that language. Should we then conclude that questions as to who the moral agents and moral patients are are not moral questions? Or should I rather modify the analysis of the notion of morality presented in chapter 2 so as to include these questions?

My inclination is to say that only questions about the content of moral rules are moral questions (where the content is expressed by means of individual variables for agents and patients) and that questions about membership in the moral community are not moral questions. But insofar as this is merely a terminological issue, I do not want to insist on it. My main point in this section and the preceding one is that we should realize that questions about membership in the moral community are different from questions about the content of moral rules (most notably because the latter are and the former are not subject to arguments based on the shoehorn maneuver) and that they are relatively independent. If someone understood the distinction between questions about membership in the moral community and (other) moral questions and still wanted to say that the former are moral questions, albeit of a special sort, I would not want to quarrel with him. Although the analysis of the notion of morality presented in chapter 2 would not be a complete analysis of what he calls "morality" it would still characterize a distinct part of what he calls "morality." (He would need to supplement the analysis presented in chapter 2 so as to arrive at an analysis of his notion of morality.)

Our disagreement would be similar to a disagreement as to whether *existence* is a predicate. The important thing to learn about *existence* is that it behaves in a way that is very different from the way in which (other) predicates behave. It is a terminological question whether we are going to express that insight by saying that it is not a predicate at all, or by saying that it is a predicate that is vastly different from other predicates.

In order to see why I am nevertheless inclined to say that questions of agency and patiency are not moral questions (just as most philosophers prefer to say that *existence* is not a predicate) the reader may consider the following analogy. Laws of physics presumably apply to all and only physical objects. However, laws of physics do not tell us how to distinguish physical objects from nonphysical objects: so far as a physicist is concerned physical objects are whatever his methods and theories apply to. We can ask what the laws of physics are that explain why apples fall down and why hot air balloons do not, but if someone asked what the laws of physics are that explain why pure spirits do not fall down, the only proper answer would be: "Well, pure spirits are not physical objects; physics just does not apply to them." Any discussion as to why pure spirits are not physical objects must be outside physics itself: one cannot ask what is the *law of physics* that excludes pure spirits from the realm of physical objects.

We can engage in investigations about laws of physics without having worked out in advance what physical objects are. On the other hand, we can engage in a philosophical discussion about what physical objects are without knowing too much about the laws of physics. The two types of discussion are therefore relatively independent. Still there is an important connection between the two. Although, in order to discuss what physical objects are, we do not need to know too much about the content of the laws of physics, we do need to know how physicists go about investigating and discussing the laws of physics. Limits to the realm of physical objects are determined by the limits to the applicability of the methods of physics. Limits to the applicability of a certain method are determined by what the method is, but they cannot be discovered simply by one more application of that method.

Morality and physics are analogous in all these respects. Although questions about content of the moral rules and questions about membership in the moral community are distinct in the way that I have presented here, there is an important connection between them. Limits to the realms of moral agents and moral patients are determined by the limits to the applicability of the methods of moral argumentation. This point will be elaborated in chapter 6. Limits to the applicability of the methods are, of course, determined by what the methods are, but a discussion of these limits is not another application of the methods.

My claim that there is a fundamental difference between questions about membership in the moral community and questions about domains over which the variables for agents and patients range is reminiscent of Fotion's claim that there is a fundamental difference between action-rules and range-rules. The difference between Fotion and me is that I give special status only to questions about the most general of his range-rules, while treating the questions concerning all the other range-rules as merely aspects of the ordinary moral questions (in the way that has already been explained in section 3.5).

5.3 An Alternative Way of Discussing Agency and Patiency?

From section 3.5 to this point, I have persisted in treating the criteria for moral agency and moral patiency as having to do with domains for certain variables appearing in moral claims. It is, however, possible to talk about criteria of moral agency and patiency in a different way, a way that incorporates them into the content of moral rules.

That is, instead of saying

> For every x and for every y, x has a duty to y that x behaves in such and such a way toward y

and then saying, in a metalanguage, that the criterion for membership in the set of individuals that x ranges over, that is, in the set of moral agents, is A, and that the criterion for membership in the set of individuals that y ranges over, that is, in the set of moral patients, is P;[12] one can simply say the following:

> For every x and for every y, x has a duty to y that, if x satisfies the criterion A and y satisfies the criterion P, then x behaves in such and such a way toward y.

In the second way of talking x and y can range over wider sets than in the first way.

Why have I chosen the first way of talking rather than the second? This question is particularly appropriate in view of the fact that this choice seems to run against the tendency I displayed in chapter 3, to incorporate within moral claims remarks that are sometimes presented as remarks about moral claims (i.e., in a metalanguage).

Most of the answers that can be given to this question have been implicit in various points that I have already made, but it still seems worthwhile to make them explicit.

(1) In the second way of talking, the domains for variables x and y still must be determined in some way. Moreover, we cannot determine these sets prior to knowing the criteria for agency and patiency, because we must make sure that the sets will include, respectively, all moral agents and all moral patients. But once we make sure that we have included all moral agents and patients in the relevant domains, we have absolutely no reason to include any additional, dangling individuals in them. And if we do not include any additional individuals in them, then the clause "if x satisfies the criterion A and y satisfies the criterion P" becomes dispensable, which brings us back to the first way of talking.

Someone who prefers the second way of talking could respond to this argument of mine by saying that we in fact do not need to know the criteria for agency and patiency in setting the boundaries for sets that x and y range over (in the second way of talking), because we can regard them as ranging over all things, over everything that exists (and this will certainly include all moral agents and patients). However, this maneuver presupposes that the idea of the totality of all objects that is not context-relative makes sense. This presupposition may have Frege's authority behind it, but in spite of that, many contemporary logicians would not be willing to endorse it.[13]

General questions of philosophy of language (or, if you will, metaphysics) that are associated with this presupposition are far too general to be discussed here. My point here is merely that those who reject this presupposition, as many do (i.e., those who believe that for each type of discourse we need to specify the domains for individual variables and that in doing so we cannot profit from some once-and-for-all specification like "everything that exists"), should find it natural to adopt the first way of talking in discussing moral agency and patiency.

(2) We have seen that we can disagree about criteria for membership while agreeing about all (other) moral questions. We can also agree about criteria for membership while disagreeing fundamentally about (other) moral questions. In situations of both these types, the first way of talking enables us to keep the points of agreement and points of disagreement clearly separate. It enables us to say that we agree about the content of moral rules while disagreeing about the interpretation of the variables appearing in them, or that we agree about the interpretation while disagreeing about the content. On the other hand, if we dump the criteria for agency and patiency into the content of moral rules, then it becomes difficult to say what the points of agreement in situations of these two types are. It would not be impossible to say what they are, but it would be very cumbersome, and there are no gains in the second way of talking that would outweigh this cumbersomeness. The clarity of insight into these points of agreement that the first way of talking provides seems to be a reason for adopting it.

(3) The prevailing views regarding membership in the moral community change over time. It does not seem plausible to say that, when that happens, we rewrite, as it were, every rule of our moral code. Our views regarding the moral community can change without much (else) in our moral code changing. In situations of this sort the first way of talking, again, enables us to say much more clearly what has changed (interpretation of the variables for agents and patients), and, in particular, what has not changed (the content of the moral rules).

(4) We should note that there is an important dissimilarity between choosing one of the two ways of talking presented in this section and choosing one of the two ways of discussing questions of specialized branches of ethics, presented in section 3.5. In choosing how to formulate the claims of specialized branches of ethics we must bear in mind that it is often necessary to examine logical relations between these claims and more general moral principles. I have therefore, in section 3.5, argued that we should choose the way of formulating these claims that facilitates this examination.

This reasoning, however, does not apply here. Morality as a whole does not stand to something still more general in a relation that would be analogous to the one that obtains between specialized branches of ethics and general moral principles. That is why what I am advocating here is not analogous to what I have advocated in section 3.5.

None of the considerations that I have adduced in this section amounts to an argument that would show that the second way of talking is mistaken. My point in this section is that the first way of talking is to be preferred, not because the second one has some fatal defect, but rather because the first one enables us to achieve greater clarity. What I want to say in the remainder of this book is not dependent on the choice of the first way of talking over the second: if someone insisted on that, all of it could be reformulated so as to fit the second way of talking, albeit at the cost of considerable elegance.

5.4 Applications

Realizing the independence of and differences between questions about membership in the moral community and questions about the content of moral rules makes us better equipped to deal with certain notoriously problematic formulations that are frequently encountered in moral discussions. The formulations that I am going to consider here are problematic because, in interpreting each of them, we seem to be forced to choose between two undesirable options. One option is to interpret the formulation straightforwardly, in which case we end up with something totally uninformative. The other option is to interpret it as a formulation of a substantive moral claim, in which case we are open to the charge that our interpretation, although we might have correctly guessed the intentions of the person who used the formulation, was arbitrary, and that the formulation itself could as plausibly be interpreted as a formulation of some totally different moral claim. In each of the subsections that follow I summarize why it is that we seem to be faced with these two options and then argue that there is a third option: the formulation can also be interpreted as a remark about membership in the moral community.

5.4.1 Equality

The first group of such formulations are those that involve the words *equal* and *equally*. The standard argument for the triviality of equality is that

> "Equally" means "according to one and the same rule." Whenever we treat according to a rule, we will be treating equally in respect to that rule.
> . . . equality or equal treatment is a derivative criterion inadequate for determining rightness or wrongness. Attempts to elevate it to the status of a sufficient standard involve logical errors that could readily lead to unsatisfactory decisions.[14]

Some political philosophers have chosen to simply ignore such arguments. They proceed as if the arguments had never been produced.[15] Others have taken notice of the arguments and tried to analyze various moral claims involving equality in ways that avoid their impact.

Some moral claims that were traditionally made in terms of equality were surely substantive moral rules. However, once we analyze their contents so as to make their nontriviality clear, we can see that they can be expressed without using the word *equal* or *equally* and, moreover, that expressing them in such a way has considerable advantages.

For example, those who claim that being of the female sex should not in itself be an obstacle to obtaining any job are surely putting forward a substantive moral claim. However, expressing this claim as a demand for sexual equality (as it is often expressed) does not add anything to our understanding of its content nor does it facilitate any discussion that might arise about it. On the contrary, expressing it as a demand for sexual equality can only lead us to confuse this claim with other claims that can also be expressed as demands for sexual equality. Moreover it creates an impression that there is some specially strong unity between this claim and various other claims that can be expressed in terms of equality, an impression that turns out to be mistaken once the contents of these claims are spelled out in some detail.[16]

The philosophical approaches to equality in morals that I summarized so far leave us with the following unpleasant choice: when faced with a claim that *a* and *b* should be treated equally you can either interpret it straightforwardly, in which case you end up with a trivial consequence of the universalizability of moral discourse, or you can embark on a long and complex process of trying to figure out the intentions of the person who made the claim, which may sometimes lead you to something that is nontrivial, but that has very little to do with the notion of equality.

However, when it is said that *a* and *b* should be treated equally, the straightforward interpretation of what is said will be a trivial consequence of the universalizability only under the assumption that both *a* and *b* are indeed moral patients. That assumption need not always be shared by all the participants in the discussion; in some situations some of them may have doubts as to whether, say, *b* is a patient, while agreeing that *a* is. In such situations, saying that *a* and *b* should be treated equally may be a way of pointing out that *b* is, in one's view, a moral patient, and in such situations pointing that out will not be trivial. Notice that someone who uses *equally* for this purpose neither says something trivial nor does he put forward a new substantive moral rule: his point is rather that the moral rules we have agreed to, whatever they may be, apply to *b* as well as to *a*.

Advocating equality between humans and at least some nonhuman animals can, for example, be understood in this way. People who advocate it are offering their answer to the question about membership in the moral community, and they are saying that all members of a certain independently identifiable class are also, in their view, members of the moral community. On the other hand, someone who says that black and white humans ought to be treated equally is probably not trying to point out that both black and white humans are members of the moral community, as it is unlikely that anyone would presently have serious doubts about that; what he has in mind is probably some highly specific moral rule having to do with access to education, hiring practices, or something similar.

Remarks about equality are frequently used in a way that creates an illusion that they constitute an important part of justification for some specific moral claim, but if the above considerations are correct they can never play such a role. When remarks about equality are used as imprecise formulations of substantive moral claims, then they are not independent of these claims and so cannot be used to justify them. When they are used to make wholly trivial points, they obviously cannot serve as justifications for anything. And finally, when remarks about equality are used for saying something about membership in the moral community they are again not justifications for one moral rule rather than another, but they could be justifications for applying these rules to specific individuals.

5.4.2 Equal Consideration

A special group of attempts to make the word *equal* operative in moral discourse are principles of "equal consideration." This group needs to be dealt with separately.[17]

As I am interested only in the general characteristics of these principles (and in particular in the role of *equal* in them) I shall not discuss what it is that we should consider equally—interests, needs, potential happiness, life plans, preferences, or something else; I shall be talking simply about "the principle of equal consideration of X."

Let us first ask ourselves why anyone would think that principles of equal consideration are significant moral principles. The answer is, I think, as follows.

Suppose we have a moral rule saying that we should give Y to everyone in proportion to his X. Someone is about to apply this rule to two individuals: a and b. In order to do so he measures their X and finds out that a has 8 units of X while b has 5. It would seem that the rule now requires that he gives more Y to a than to b. However he decides to discount a's X by 50%; after the discounting a is left with 4 units, while b still has 5. Therefore he gives more Y to b than to a. Now it seems that the principle of equal consideration of X is called for precisely to prevent anyone from reasoning and acting in this way.

But this is mistaken. The principle of equal consideration of X is not necessary for the purpose because the initial moral rule is sufficient to do the job. The rule required that Y be distributed in proportion to X and this was not done in the example. In the example, Y was given in proportion to CX where C is some coefficient that varies from individual to individual, and this is not what the rule required. What was wrong in the example was simply that the initial rule was violated; we do not need to invoke any further rules to account for our feeling that something went wrong. The principle of equal consideration of X is therefore redundant.

Moreover, suppose that, contrary to the above argument, the principle of equal consideration is not redundant, and that we need it in order to exclude the reasoning that we encountered in the example. This will still not make the moral system foolproof. Someone could still reason as follows:

> I have just measured a's and b's X, and now I am going to apply the principle of equal consideration of X. I shall now pause and consider the results of my measurements equally. Here I am, fully appreciating that a's X equals 8, while b's X equals 5. Having thus satisfied the principle of equal consideration, I am now going to apply the discounting

procedure to the results of my equal consideration of their *X*. I shall namely reduce the result of equal consideration of *a*'s *X* by 50%, and I shall therefore give to *a* less *Y* than to *b*.

Now if we think that the principle of equal consideration of *X* was necessary to prevent the reasoning that was displayed in the first example, then we should also think that a further principle is necessary to exclude the reasoning exemplified here, namely the principle of equal consideration of the results of equal consideration of *X*. But as the reader already guesses, the story cannot end here. We can now produce a third example, where someone will get around that principle. This could lead to a promulgation of a third principle of equal consideration, and so on, *ad infinitum*. In other words: we either do not need the principle of equal consideration of *X* or we need an infinite hierarchy of principles of equal consideration.

The above criticisms apply to principles of equal consideration insofar as we construe them as saying that we should consider equally the *X* of every moral patient. However sometimes we encounter principles that tell us that we should consider equally *X* of every member of some independently identifiable class (e.g., of every human being, every rational being, or every sentient being). Someone who puts forward a principle of equal consideration in that form is telling us something important: he is telling us that all members of that class are, according to him, moral patients.

So the way to make sense of principles of equal consideration is to treat them as remarks about membership in the moral community. Once we realize that, it follows that the only arguments worth having about such principles are the arguments about exactly how the relevant class should be specified (i.e., who the moral patients are).

5.4.3 Respect for Persons

The argument that I have used in the preceding subsection against principles of equal consideration can also be applied to moral principles, such as the one put forward by Dworkin,[18] that are formulated in terms of "equal concern" and "equal

respect." The distinction between questions about membership in the moral community and (other) moral questions
can, however, be of help in dealing with the principle of
"respect for persons" even independently of the above made
comments about the notion of equality that apply to it when it
is presented as a principle of *equal* respect for persons.

Respecting someone as a person obviously cannot mean
holding him in esteem. The sense of "respecting" that we have
in "respecting someone as a person" must therefore be different from what we have in "respecting someone for his
diligence" or "respecting someone for his artistic achieve-
ments." In order to find out what the relevant sense is, we
should consider some other examples that involve respecting
someone as a member of a certain class.

Suppose a visitor to a meeting of the Board of Governors
starts interrupting speakers, yelling at them, asking questions
that have nothing to do with what is on the agenda, and so on.
It would be natural to accuse him of not respecting members
of the board. If he says that he indeed does not hold them in
esteem, our reply would probably be "Nevertheless, you ought
to respect them as members of the board." In this sense,
respecting someone means recognizing him as a member of a
certain class (occupant of a certain role) and according to him
whatever is appropriate to accord to members of that class.
The class in question need not be associated with any sort of a
higher rank: an instructor who grades students' papers slop-
pily and with considerable delays, never shows up for office
hours, and so forth, can be accused, in the same sense, of not
respecting his students. This is because he is not giving them
the treatment that one is supposed to give the occupants of
the role of a student (regardless of their merits and of whether
one holds them in esteem). In other words, he can be accused
of treating his students as if they were not his students.

An important feature of the notion of respect for individuals as members of a certain class is that it incorporates
reference to a set of rules that tell us how members of that
class are to be treated. However, use of the phrase "respect for
————" in this sense does not in itself convey the content of
these rules, it merely refers us to them. In the first example,

we understood immediately the point of the accusation that members of the board were not respected as members of the board, because we were already familiar with the relevant set of rules: we already knew that participants in formal meetings are supposed to follow the agenda, to speak only when they have been granted the right to speak, and so on. In the second example we understood the accusation because we already knew that there were rules requiring instructors to hold office hours, grade papers promptly and carefully, and so forth.

Now imagine that you are visiting a country with a totally different civilization. You know that a special role is played in their society by people called *schmersons*. You also know how schmersons are selected and what their functions are. One day you meet one of the schmersons and spend a few minutes with him in what seems to you to be a perfectly normal conversation. After that you are accused, "How could you behave so disrespectfully to a schmerson? I understand that you might not hold him very much in esteem, but still you ought to respect him *as* a schmerson." You ask innocently what you did wrong, and you get an angry reply: "It's obvious: you failed to show respect for a schmerson." In that case your understanding of what is going on would be imperfect: you would understand that there are some rules specifying how one is supposed to behave to schmersons and that you have just broken one of them, but you would not know what these rules are, and what exactly the content of the rule that you have broken is. If you wanted to understand the situation fully you would have to learn the rules. No amount of conceptual analysis of "respecting someone as a schmerson" would tell you what the rules are.[19] The content of the rules is not packed into that notion.

Now what is it to respect individuals as members of the class of persons (rather than the class of students or the class of schmersons)? According to the above pattern of analysis it is to recognize that they are persons and to accord to them whatever is appropriate to accord to persons. In other words, it is to apply to them the rules that specify what the proper ways of treating persons are. What sort of rules could these be? Outside a special context, the most plausible candidate for the relevant set of rules seems to be the set of moral rules. If this reasoning is correct, then respecting someone as a person is nothing but applying moral rules to him. But as we have seen in the example of schmersons, the notion of respecting someone as a member of a certain class always points to a set of rules without telling us the content of these rules. Therefore, we should say that respecting someone as a person means applying moral rules to him, whatever these rules turn out to be.

This is an important insight. It entails that we cannot build a moral system by analyzing what it "really" means to respect persons. We cannot take the principle of respect for persons as our basic moral principle and then derive specific moral rules from it. It follows that much of the contemporary literature involving "respect for persons" is misguided, as it attempts to do precisely that. Such attempts are bound to involve arbitrariness[20] and to be open to attacks in which an opponent may claim, equally well, that the principle of respect for persons in fact entails exactly the opposite.[21]

Someone who wants to learn or discuss a particular set of moral rules is in no way helped by being told that he should respect persons as persons (just as in the example of the foreign country, we were not helped by being told that we should respect schmersons as schmersons). A particular set of moral rules must be learned or justified independently of uses of the phrase "respect for persons." It is only after we have familiarized ourselves with a particular set of moral rules that we are able to say about its violations that they constitute not respecting persons as persons.

Now, does all this entail that exhorting someone to respect *a* as a person is always pointless? As the reader has perhaps already guessed, the answer to that question will follow the pattern established in the preceding subsections. It all depends on who *a* is.

If our interlocutor has no doubts about *a*'s membership in the moral community, then it is indeed pointless: our interlocutor then already agrees that moral rules (whatever they are) are to be applied to *a*. He might be unaware of what the relevant rules are, but if this is the case he will not be helped by being told that he should respect *a* as a person; and if he is already aware of what the relevant rules are then he does not need any additional exhortations.

However, there could be situations in which our interlocutor is uncertain as to whether *a* is a member of the moral community. In such a situation, telling him that he should respect *a* as a person (i.e., that moral rules, whatever their content is, are to be applied to *a*) has a point: it can be a way of telling him that we hold the view that *a* is a member of the moral community and suggesting that he adopt the same view.

5.4.4 Everybody Should Count for One

The type of reasoning used in this section comes close to what Mill could have had in mind when he was answering Herbert Spencer's objection to utilitarians in a footnote to the fifth chapter of *Utilitarianism.*

Spencer, just like today's proponents of principles of equal consideration, concern, and respect, has argued that the principle of utilitarianism is not sufficient to generate a system of morality and that utilitarians are themselves committed to another, more basic, moral principle, namely the principle that everybody has an *equal* right to happiness.[22] Mill acknowledged Spencer's point insofar as it resembled Bentham's dictum that everybody should "count for one, nobody for more than one," but at the same time strongly disagreed with Spencer's giving to it the status of an additional moral principle.

When we subject this dictum to the arguments that we have previously used we can see that it is either trivial (if *everybody* is understood as "every member of the moral community")[23] or a specification of the membership in the moral community (if *everybody* is understood as referring to every member of some independently specified class). It is neither more nor less basic than the principle of utilitarianism because it does not belong to the same hierarchy of principles.

Mill did not elaborate on the status of this dictum and was satisfied with describing it as an "explanatory commentary" on the principle of utility. While this is in many ways an imperfect characterization of its status, it does express an important insight that such a dictum differs radically from substantive moral principles and that we can agree with it without agreeing with its being a moral principle in the same way in which the principle of utilitarianism is.

5.4.5 Value

Some philosophers have been tempted by the idea that we all have intrinsic value (or inherent value, or worth) and that the notion of such value plays an important role in ethical arguments.[24] They claim

(1) Every individual that has value ought to be treated in ways that respect its value.

However, what counts as treatment that respects someone's value is far from obvious. We need arguments if we are ever to figure out how to go about respecting individuals' value. Therefore (1) needs to be construed as

(2) Every individual that has value ought to be treated in ways that respect its value, whatever these ways turn out to be upon further moral investigation.

Assuming that the *ought* in (2) is a moral *ought*, the claim may strike many people as trivial, but its proponents believe that it is not. They believe that (2) is a substantive moral claim insofar as it excludes utilitarianism. Whatever the treatment that respects one's value turns out to be, it cannot, they believe, turn out to be treatment in accordance with the utilitarian moral code.

When the claims that the utilitarians sometimes make are presented as claims that valuable individuals ought to be harmed in order that the best consequences be produced, then these claims may appear to be disrespectful of their value. This way of presenting utilitarian claims is, however, tendentious, as it creates a false impression that the good consequences that utilitarians are concerned about are somehow disembodied and separate from the valuable individuals. As a matter of fact, these consequences are always embodied in certain individuals, and typically the individuals in which they are embodied are ones whom the proponents of these views would regard as valuable. When the problematic claims of utilitarianism are presented as claims that we sometimes ought to harm valuable individuals in order to help other valuable individuals, then it is no longer obvious that these claims are disrespectful of value.

Whether utilitarianism is disrespectful of value of individuals and whether it is a correct moral theory is something that we can establish only by pursuing further moral investigation. A refutation of utilitarianism is not packed in (2). This leads me to believe that (2) amounts to no more than

(3) Every individual that has value ought to be treated in accordance with the requirements of morality, whatever these requirements turn out to be upon further moral investigation.

But (3) is indistinguishable[25] from

(4) Every individual that has value is a member of the set of moral patients.

When (4) is supplemented by a criterion of the relevant kind of value, say,

(5) Every individual that has the property P has value.

then they entail

(6) Every individual that has the property P is a member of the set of moral patients.

Now (6) finally tells us something useful. We can, at least in principle, find out whether a certain individual has the property P (presumably by some sort of empirical investigation) and if it does, this, together with (6), will tell us that the ways in which we treat it are subject to moral considerations. On the other hand, it is not clear how (4) and (5) can be useful, except insofar as they, taken together, entail (6). It therefore seems that the only reason that an ethicist could have for claiming (4) and (5) would stem from the belief that they are more obvious than (6), or that it is easier to defend them and then deduce (6) than to defend (6) directly, or perhaps that the only way to defend (6) is via (4) and (5).

Is such a belief justified? If we want to arrive at (6) is it really necessary, or at least helpful, to bring the notion of value into the argument? In order to be able to answer that question we need to know what sort of value this value is, which amounts to understanding the type of discourse in which ascriptions of this value are defended and criticized.

A defender of (4) and (5) can respond to this question in several different ways. One way would be to say that what is meant by *value* is the value of some specific type other than the moral one. This would, however, make (4) problematic. It is not clear why the individuals that have a certain nonmoral value should be regarded as moral patients. It may be that they should, but some further arguments seem necessary to convince one of that. I do not see any reason to believe that it will be easier to show that the individuals having this nonmoral value (whatever it is) should be regarded as moral patients than it would be to show that the individuals having the property *P* should be so regarded.

Alternatively, a defender of (4) and (5) could say that by *value* he means neither aesthetic nor moral nor any other specific type of value, but simply *value* or, if you want, *value in general*. He would then, however, have to face the problem of elucidating the idea of value in general. We have some idea as to what *moral value* means because our ordinary language has moral discourse as one of its segments; we have some idea as to what the aesthetic value is because it also has aesthetic discourse as its segment; and so on. But our linguistic intuitions do not give us any clue as to what could be meant by *value* when it is not made clear that it is either a moral value or an aesthetic value or . . . . There is no such thing as "discourse of values in general."

It is worthwhile to reconstruct here the path that leads philosophers to the mistaken idea that *value in general* makes sense. They begin by noticing that in everyday communication there is moral discourse, aesthetic discourse, and so forth. In exploring such types of discourse they notice obvious similarities among them, similarities that can be expressed by saying that they are all types of evaluative discourse. This realization makes it possible for philosophers to produce (in addition to separate accounts of the functioning of each of these types of discourse) general accounts about the functioning of various types of evaluative discourse, accounts that explore the similarities and differences among them. So far, so good. But indulging in such exploration of evaluative discourse for a while seems to lead people to think that, if there are general philosophical theories about evaluative discourse, then there must be such a thing as general evaluative discourse—that is, that there must be a type of discourse that is evaluative discourse *simpliciter*.

But this last step is fallacious. We can see that it is fallacious if we compare the path sketched above with the following possible path.

Among the games that people play I notice games such as bridge, poker, canasta, and so on. I notice that there are obvious similarities among them, and I can express that by saying that they are all games with cards. I can even write a book about card playing in which I discuss the similarities and differences among various games with cards. But from the existence of general books about card playing, it does not follow that there is such a thing as general card playing, that there is a game with cards that would be card playing *simpliciter*.

Finally, one may try to interpret the *value* in (4) and (5) as moral value. But, without some further explanation, it is entirely unclear what it means to ascribe moral value to an individual (rather than to behavior of a moral agent toward a moral patient). Such an ascription could be interpreted as an ascription of some virtue to the individual in question, but it does not seem that this is what is meant.[26]

The only way of interpreting (4) so that it is both meaningful and easily acceptable is to treat it as the stipulative definition of *value*. "Individuals that have value" is then simply a fancy label for members of the set of moral patients. On this interpretation (5) and (6) stand or fall together: whatever supports (5) would also support (6) directly; and (4) turns out to be merely a device for introducing an unnecessary terminological embellishment into the discussion.

6

Myself and Others

6.1 Contingent Limitations on the Use of the Shoehorn Maneuver

In chapter 5 I discussed the status of questions about membership in the moral community but did not attempt to offer any answers to them. This chapter is an attempt to answer these questions.

As I suggested in section 5.2, in order to understand where the boundaries of the moral community are, we must look at the limitations on the use of the technique of argumentation that is characteristic of moral discourse. Consequently, we must now examine the limitations on the use of the arguments based on the shoehorn maneuver.

We seem to face the limitations to the applicability of arguments based on the shoehorn maneuver when, after presenting someone with such an argument, instead of receiving any specific answer, we hear something like: "This is impossible, I simply cannot imagine myself as having these properties."

The limitations, however, are of two different kinds. In investigating the use of the shoehorn maneuver it is important to distinguish practical limitations to its application, that is, those that can in principle be overcome by the use of a suitable "shoehorn," from the limitations that cannot be overcome, even in principle. Only this latter kind of limitation, which is discussed in section 6.2, can be expected to generate consequences for our investigation of the moral community. In this section, I discuss some of the merely practical limitations on the use of the shoehorn maneuver in order to delimit them from the limitations that really interest us.

Now, if arguments based on the shoehorn maneuver are to work, then it must be possible for our partner in moral discussion to do what we are asking him to do, namely it must be possible for him to put himself in the shoes of the relevant moral agent and/or patient. This is not always easy and may sometimes demand considerable effort on the part of our interlocutor. In such cases, if we want the discussion to proceed as smoothly as possible, we may indeed need to supply him with a shoehorn.

Take, for example, a case in which our interlocutor is 5'7" and myopic. Suppose that in some discussion we have asked him to put himself in Jones's shoes. Jones is 7'5" and is intently watching something going on behind a 6' wall.[1] In this situation, our interlocutor may have some difficulty putting himself in Jones's shoes. He can easily imagine that he has Jones's height and vision and that he is watching what is going on behind the wall. But if he is fully to put himself in Jones's shoes then it seems that he should also be able to imagine that he is watching ———, where "———" is filled by some description of what Jones is watching that is more informative than "what Jones is watching" or "what is going on behind the wall." However he cannot imagine that he is watching ——— because he does not possess sufficient information about what is going on behind the wall and, being 5'7" and myopic, he is unable to acquire it.

Our interlocutor's difficulty will have a simple remedy if we know what is going on behind the wall. We can then pass this information on to him. Instead of telling him "Imagine that you have Jones's height and vision and that you are watching what is going on behind the wall," we can give him the more precise instruction "Imagine that you have Jones's height and vision and that you are watching ——— going on behind the wall." Indeed it seems that our interlocutor is entitled to such a shoehorn. If we care about the outcome of the discussion then it seems only rational to provide the interlocutor with all the information that we consider relevant (unless it is obvious that he already possesses it).

There may be other situations in which we do not possess the information that our interlocutor is missing but we also do not think that such information is really relevant for the argument that we are trying to make. If we were trying to show, for example, that it is morally wrong to attack Jones from the back while he is looking over the wall, then we probably would not suspect that the precise content of what is going on behind the wall will be relevant for the argument. In that case, it will be sufficient to ask our interlocutor to simply imagine that he is watching whatever it is that is going on behind the wall (in precisely these words).[2] Whatever difficulties our interlocutor might have imagining the aspects of the situation that neither we nor he suspect to be relevant they will not affect the argument that we are trying to make.

Finally, there may be situations in which our interlocutor is unable to put himself in the shoes of another because he lacks the relevant information and we are unable to supply him with that information (because we lack it ourselves) even though we think that the particular aspect of the "shoes" that we are ignorant of might turn out to be relevant for the outcome of the argument. It is only in this type of situation that we have a real difficulty. Notice, however, that this type of difficulty does not seem to be caused by the fact that our moral discussions are based on the shoehorn maneuver. In any discussion (whatever the realm of discourse and whatever the argumentative technique employed) we will have difficulties if both parties to the discussion lack some information that they consider relevant.

Moreover it is always possible, at least in principle, to overcome this difficulty by simply acquiring the relevant information. If our attempt to use a shoehorn maneuver in some moral discussion reveals that we (as well as our interlocutor) lack some relevant information, this suggests that we are not yet ready for this stage of the discussion. The proper strategy is then to put the proposed maneuver "on hold" and acquire the information necessary for its successful performance. If our interlocutor complains that he cannot put himself in Jones's shoes because he does not know what is going on behind the wall and if we think that this difficulty is relevant for the argument that we are trying to make, then it seems that we should suspend our discussion until we acquire the necessary information.

In many situations we shall be able to resolve the problem by simply asking Jones what it is that he is watching, but if that is impossible, periscopes, ladders, binoculars, spies, television cameras, and helicopters can all help us to overcome our limitations and obtain the information that we are currently missing. Once the relevant information is obtained it will be possible for the shoehorn maneuver to be performed and for the discussion to continue.

In our attempt to find out what is going on behind the wall we may, of course, encounter all sorts of practical difficulties. Sometimes these difficulties will be so serious that it will be practically impossible to overcome them. If a lifetime of research turns out to be necessary to find out what is going on behind the wall, then we shall probably be forced to give up the whole argument (unless it is very, very important). But so far we have not encountered any situation in which it would be in principle impossible to complete the shoehorn maneuver.

Of course, given that the information necessary for performance of the shoehorn maneuver typically includes information about what other people see, feel, think, desire, and so on, someone who adopted radical skepticism about other minds and who therefore thought that it is in principle impossible for him to acquire any information about what goes on in other people's minds would have a serious difficulty completing any shoehorn maneuver. I shall, however, proceed under the assumption that my readers are under no temptation to embrace radical skepticism about other minds.

But, although radical skepticism can be left aside, there are some philosophically respectable arguments that are skeptical about our ability to ever find out and imagine certain specific aspects of what is going on in other minds.

If we tell a color-blind person "imagine that you see this object as green and that one as red" he will not be able to do it, and it seems to be in principle impossible to provide him with the information that would enable him to do the imagining required. Now, average people who are not normally considered to be color-blind are in exactly the same position when compared with members of some groups whose power of color discrimination is above the average. Similarly there are people of exceptional musical ability who can perceive that a certain tone is, say, C-sharp without using any measuring instruments and without having to compare it with tones of the known pitch. They simply hear it as C-sharp. Not having perfect pitch, I am unable to imagine what it is like to hear sounds the way they do. Some animals possess sonar-like organs and are able to orient themselves in space and perceive objects around them with the help of such organs. We are unable to imagine what it would be like to perceive objects around us in that way. If it were necessary to imagine these things in order to complete a shoehorn maneuver required by some moral argument (which, in real-life moral discussions, it never is), we would be facing a very serious difficulty. The difficulty that one can have imagining such things seems, at first, to be much deeper than any difficulty of the "what is going on behind the wall" type.

But, no matter how deep the difficulties that we encounter in such cases may seem, they are still remediable in principle. We all know that training and/or medical intervention can enable people to have sensory experiences that they did not have before. The cases of such expansion of human sensory capacities give us reason to believe that subjecting ourselves to some form of training or medical intervention could enable us to overcome the limitations that we see in the above examples: we may acquire the capacity of seeing the difference between two shades of blue that now seem indistinguishable or hearing C-sharp as C-sharp or even perceiving objects by the way they reflect sound (or ultrasound) that we emit, and if we come to have such experiences at least sometimes, then we will not have any difficulty imagining that we have them at other times. Such an increase in the range of our experiences may require a level of technological development that we do not presently possess, and in some cases it may be obtainable only by processes that are so long and/or costly and/or risky that we would consider them to be practically impossible. But such an improvement in our ability to have certain types of experiences and a consequential improvement of our ability to imagine such experiences seems to be possible in principle. This leads me to conclude that all these difficulties that result from our ignorance of what it is like to have certain experiences can be assimilated to the difficulties of the first ("what is going on behind the wall") type: in all of them we are prevented from completing the shoehorn maneuver because of some sort of ignorance, and in all of them the relevant sort of ignorance can in principle (if not in practice) be overcome. The examples that we have been considering on the last few pages have therefore failed to reveal any limitations on the use of arguments based on the shoehorn maneuver that would be a direct consequence of the features of the maneuver itself.

6.2   Essential Properties

However, such limitations do exist, and we will now start considering them in the hope that this will be of some help in our investigation of the limits of the moral community. The role of the discussion of all these other, contingent limitations on the application of the shoehorn maneuver was principally to ensure that they are not confused with the logical limitations that we are going to consider now. (The two are easily confused because phrases of the form "I cannot imagine . . ." are frequently used to express both types of limitations.)

In order to remove any doubt about the existence of such limitations we may begin by considering a very clear-cut example. Suppose that in the course of some argument I tell you "Imagine that you possess the property of being identical with the number 17." You might, at first, attempt to comply by imagining that you are some sort of a creature that has the shape of digits *1* and *7* or that you have seventeen pieces of something or that you are the seventeenth member of some group. But if I make it clear that I did not mean anything like that and that I want you to imagine that you are literally identical with the number 17, a mathematical "object," you would be puzzled and would probably reply that it is impossible for you to do that.

The impossibility that we encounter here does not seem to be a practical one. The problem is not a consequence of your not possessing sufficient information about the property of being identical with the number 17 or about anything else. No process of learning, no matter how long and complex, will ever enable you to imagine that you are identical with the number 17. Your inability to imagine that you possess that property seems to be of the same type as your inability to imagine a round square. Just as there is something contradictory about a thing being both round and square at the same time, so there seems to be (at least from your perspective) something contradictory about an individual being yourself and possessing the property of being identical with the number 17 at the same time.

(It could be argued that one's being identical with the number 17 can be excluded by purely "grammatical" considerations, that is, that the property of being identical with the number 17 is of such a *type* that attributing it to oneself is a violation of logical syntax, in which case we do not need to postulate the contradiction between being oneself and being identical with the number 17. Those who feel inclined to endorse this move may take some other property as an example, such as the property of being a sandy beach.)

On the basis of this example we may conclude that there are cases in which it is impossible in principle to carry through a shoehorn maneuver and therefore impossible in principle to successfully use an argument that would be based on such a maneuver. These are the cases in which the participant in the discussion who is asked to put himself in the shoes of some other individual finds a contradiction between being himself and having the properties possessed by that other individual.[3]

The example of being identical with the number 17 was an extreme one: it seems that everyone who attempts to imagine that he is identical with number 17 is bound to see a contradiction in the idea that something is himself and the number 17 at the same time. On the other extreme are the examples in which everyone would find it equally clear that there is no such contradiction, such as "being a red-haired individual" or "being exactly 5'7" tall." When asked "Imagine that you are a red-haired individual," it is highly unlikely that anyone would reply "I can't do that because there is a contradiction between being myself and being red-haired (instead of having the color of hair that I actually have)."

Somewhere between these two extremes we shall find examples that will not generate such uniform responses. If I tell someone "Imagine that you are a human being who has lived all his life in some isolated tribe that has had very little contact with the rest of the world," I would not be at all surprised if I got the reply that he cannot do that and if he went on to say that it is impossible for any individual to be himself unless it is a human being that belongs to either Western civilization or some other civilization that is sufficiently similar to it. On the other hand I would also expect to encounter many people who would not see any logical obstacle to imagining that they themselves have been living in such a tribe. (They would almost certainly encounter many nonlogical obstacles resulting from their insufficient familiarity with the life in such a tribe, but these practical difficulties are not under consideration here.)

Similarly, if I made an experiment of asking various people to imagine that they possess the property of being a dog, I would expect that with some people I would get a reply such as, "It is logically impossible for something to be a dog and myself at the same time, therefore I can't do that," while the others would not see anything logically problematic with imagining that they are dogs (although they might still be prevented from imagining that by some nonlogical obstacles).

Various other examples where people would differ in the same way can be given, and the ratio of those who think that what they are asked to imagine involves a contradiction to those who think that there is no such contradiction will differ from one example to the other. It is more likely, for instance, that someone will see a contradiction between being himself and being a dog than between being himself and being a human being living in an isolated tribe.

What emerges from these examples can be formulated by saying that each one of us treats certain properties as his *essential* properties.[4] These are the properties that are logically necessary for one's being oneself. Everyone treats his not being a number as an essential property of himself, and no one treats his having the color of hair that he has as an essential property of himself. But we differ in which properties each of us considers essential, as is shown in the examples that involve being a dog (rather than a human) or being a member of the isolated tribe (rather than of Western civilization). You may treat your being a human (and not a dog) as an essential property of yourself, while I may treat neither that property nor any analogous property as an essential property of myself.

I am not implying here that anyone among us would be able to produce a complete list of his essential properties.[5] It is rather that when I consider any given property, I can say whether it is one of my essential properties or not. I am also not implying that when asked whether a certain property is one of his essential properties everyone will always be able to give the answer right away. In some cases, analysis, discussion, additional thought-experiments, and some pondering may be called for before one is able to answer such a question. It is through such investigations that one gains insights into what one's essential properties are.

Such investigations may also lead a person to conclude that a property that at first seemed to be an essential property of his is in fact not so (e.g., because treating it as essential is incompatible with something else that he wants to hold) or that he is committed to regarding as an essential property of himself something that, at first, did not seem to be one. But no matter how carefully each of us conducts an investigation into the essential properties of himself, the various outcomes of the investigations are still likely to differ from one individual to another.

Some brief remarks in Hare's recent writings show that he has considered the line of argument that I am pursuing here and decided to reject it:

> It is sometimes said that stoves, mountains, and trees are outside the scope of morality (we cannot have duties to them) because we cannot put ourselves in their positions. I think that this is badly expressed. We can put ourselves in their positions, but, since when we do this we have no

sentience and therefore no concerns, it simply does not matter to us what happens to us if we turn into such things.[6]

In other words, Hare seems to think there are no limits to the applicability of arguments based on the shoehorn maneuver and that the moral community thus has no boundaries. It is just that in some cases the performance of a shoehorn maneuver involves imagining a complete lack of any experience, an experiential blank.

What makes Hare's strategy appear plausible is that he concentrates on examples such as "stoves, mountains, and trees." As long as one deals only with such examples, it might appear that it does not matter very much whether one adopts his approach or the one taken here.

Things, however, begin to look different when one takes into account the example of, say, dogs. It would be difficult to deny that dogs are sentient and that they have experiences of some kind. Therefore a person who can imagine himself being a dog will be imagining something when he puts himself in the shoes of a dog: the shoehorn maneuver will definitely not result in an experiential blank. This fact, however, in no way prevents another person (who also acknowledges that dogs have experiences of some kind) from saying that *he* cannot imagine being a dog, that it is logically impossible for something to be himself and be a dog at the same time. What the latter person says is not defective in any obvious way, and it therefore needs to be accommodated as such within one's theory. The approach advocated here does precisely that. Hare's rejection of the idea that there are logical limits to the application of the shoehorn maneuver, on the other hand, renders his theory incapable of accommodating the position of the latter person. (Hare himself might not be such a person, but that in no way dispenses with the requirement that his theory accommodate the position of such a person.)

Numerous other examples that confirm this point can be produced. A married couple is a being that, unlike "stoves, mountains, and trees," clearly exhibits sentiency, but I cannot imagine that I *am* a married couple, and I suspect that few people could. An individual consisting of someone's left thumb, the area of his cortex that registers sensations from the left thumb and the connecting nerves (and nothing else) is a sentient being, but again, I cannot imagine being that individual, and I doubt that many people can.

6.3   Conclusions about the Moral Community

Let us now see what consequences regarding the moral community are emerging from these considerations about the method of moral argumentation.

First we should note that in making an argument that involves an agent-oriented maneuver we always display at stage 2 (i.e., in moving from "Everyone has a duty to ———" to "You have a duty to ———") that we are regarding our interlocutor as a moral agent. In understanding stage 2 our interlocutor displays that he regards himself as a moral agent.

Similarly, in making a patient-oriented maneuver we must regard our interlocutor as belonging to the set of individuals that the variable for patients ranges over, that is, we must regard him as a moral patient.

Now every moral discussion is a two-way street (otherwise it would not deserve to be called a "discussion"). That is, whenever I produce a moral argument, I must be prepared for the possibility that my interlocutor will choose to reply with a counterargument that will involve either a patient-oriented or an agent-oriented shoehorn maneuver. In order to be prepared for such a possibility I must regard myself as a moral agent and a moral patient.

Moreover, moral arguments are typically not isolated one-shot transactions but elements of a larger whole of moral discourse. If I direct a particular moral argument at someone, I must be ready not only to receive a reply from him, but also, if the need arises, to direct further moral arguments to him. These further arguments may involve both agent-oriented and patient-oriented maneuvers (regardless of whether the initial argument involved an agent-oriented or a patient-oriented maneuver). This entails that, when I direct a moral argument to someone, I must regard him both as a moral agent and a moral patient.

We can summarize these results in the following important conclusion:

> Each participant in moral discourse necessarily regards himself and his partners in this discourse as both moral agents and moral patients.

Now, who else is a member of a moral community? For example, is the number 17 a moral agent? Given that the number 17 is not a participant in moral discourse it is not a moral agent by virtue of the above conclusion; but could it be a moral agent by virtue of something else?

Suppose that the number 17 is a moral agent. That would mean that the participants in moral discourse make moral claims in which they take the variables for moral agents to range over some set that includes the number 17. If the participants in moral discourse really intend these claims as moral claims, then they must be prepared to subject them to standard methods of moral argumentation. As the standard methods of moral argumentation involve the shoehorn maneuver, this entails that a participant in moral discourse would have to be prepared, at least in principle, to imagine that he possesses the properties that are possessed by the number 17, such as the property of being identical with number 17. But no participant in moral discourse regards as imaginable (even in principle) that he himself possesses that property. Therefore, no participant in moral discourse regards the number 17 as a moral agent.

For exactly the same reasons, no participant in moral discourse regards the number 17 as a moral patient.

This can be generalized by saying that a participant in moral discourse cannot regard a certain individual as a moral agent or a moral patient unless he finds the idea that he himself possesses all properties of that other individual noncontradictory (or in the terminology of the preceding section: unless that individual possesses the properties that he regards as his essential properties).

On the other hand, if a participant in moral discourse does find the idea that he himself possesses all properties of a certain individual noncontradictory, then there does not seem to be any obstacle in principle to his carrying out the shoehorn maneuver in which he puts himself in the shoes of that other individual. And if he finds this typical technique of moral argumentation to be applicable to such an individual, then it seems that we can say that he regards that other individual as a moral agent and a moral patient.

All this enables us to formulate the following two conclusions:

> For a given participant in moral discourse, the set of moral agents is the set of individuals such that, for each of them, he regards possessing all of the individual's properties as logically compatible with being himself.

> For a given participant in moral discourse, the set of moral patients is the set of individuals such that, for each of them, he regards possessing all of the individual's properties as logically compatible with being himself.

As the conditions for being a moral agent are exactly the same as the conditions for being a moral patient, these two conclusions have an important and obvious consequence:

> The set of moral agents for a particular participant in moral discourse and the set of moral patients for this same participant are one and the same set.

We have noticed in the preceding section that people differ as to which properties they treat as their essential properties and that a certain individual may therefore have the properties that are logically compatible with my being myself but that are logically incompatible with your being yourself. The above therefore entails that:

> Membership in the moral community is always relative to a particular participant in moral discourse.

In other words, a certain individual may be a member of the moral community *for me*, but not a member of the moral community *for you*.

I should perhaps emphasize at this point that I do not regard the question as to what my essential properties are (or what is logically compatible with being myself) as in any sense preceding the question as to who the members of the moral community are for me. A person may sometimes have very strong intuitions that certain individuals are members of the moral community and may then shape his answer to the question as to what his essential properties are, so that it fits these intuitions, just as a person may sometimes have very strong intuitions that a certain property is an essential property of his and then shape his answer to the question about the boundaries of moral community so that it fits these intuitions. All this is compatible with my thesis. The thesis is simply that the two questions and the answers to them always go together.

Further consequences of the conclusions formulated here will be unpacked in chapter 7.

6.4   Personal Identity across Possible Worlds

The argument so far, and in particular the sketchy account of "being myself" that I offered in section 6.2, is likely to give rise to the following comment:

> When I put myself in the shoes of someone else I imagine myself as having properties that I do not actually have. That is, I consider a possible world in which I have these properties. In doing so I must rely on some account of transworld identification that enables me to say that the particular individual in that other world is myself. The remarks that you made in section 6.2 seem to be a part of some theory that, according to you, each of us uses in identifying himself across possible worlds. How are these remarks supposed to fit the larger context of a general theory of transworld identification?

In this section I attempt to answer this comment, while leaving its basic assumptions unchallenged. In section 6.5 I consider an approach to the problem that rejects some of these assumptions.

Let us first look at the matter in the context of what is presently the most popular theory of identity across possible worlds, namely the one formulated in Kripke's *Naming and Necessity*.[7] This theory claims that possible worlds are given by stipulations that we make concerning them and that such stipulations include stipulations to the effect that a certain individual in some possible world is identical (in the strict sense of *identical*) with some individual that we know from this, actual, world. Kripke's statement of this view is accompanied by his well-known mockery of those who think that transworld identification must be the result of inspecting the properties that objects have in different possible worlds, "as if we were looking at them through a telescope."[8]

However, according to Kripke, our stipulations of identity across possible worlds are constrained by the requirement that an object in some possible world that we stipulate to be identical to a certain object from the actual world must possess the essential properties of that object. The stipulation that in some possible world, Nixon is an inanimate object is Kripke's example of a stipulation that would be defective because it would violate this requirement.[9] Possession of certain properties is therefore necessary but never sufficient for transworld identification; what is sufficient is possession of these necessary, essential properties plus a stipulation.

These features of Kripke's theory are compatible with the intuitions about *being myself* that were expressed in section 6.2. What I have said there is merely that there are some properties that are necessary for being myself. Kripke's criticisms of those who think that transworld identification is a matter of necessary *and sufficient* properties do not affect me, as I have never claimed that there are properties such that possession of these properties is sufficient for being myself. It is compatible with the account of section 6.2 that the transworld identification of myself is a matter of possession of these properties plus stipulation. In fact, the characterization of the shoehorn maneuver on which my account is based probably commits me to assigning this role to stipulation.

But Kripke does not merely tell us that individuals have some properties that are essential, he also tells us where to look and where not to look for these essential properties. For him, the essential properties need not be the same as the ones we consider important[10] nor the properties that we use to fix the reference. He avoids developing a full-fledged positive theory about essences, but he does insist that the essence of a thing involves its origins and substantial makeup.[11] It is because of this aspect of Kripke's theory that my account of what is essential to myself will have to depart from it. What follows is an examination of the strategies that can be used to justify this departure.

First, I could argue that Kripke's views about the essentiality of an individual's origins are simply wrong, which would entail that a departure from them should be welcomed. However, I am not going to develop this strategy here, as such general criticisms of Kripke's theory have already been produced and some of them are rather well-known.[12]

It is much more interesting to grant, for the sake of argument, that Kripke's theory is basically correct and then try to show that the term *myself* (as used by a given individual) may be regarded in such a way that the theory does not apply to it (at least not directly). In this way the account of section 6.2 (and everything else in this book that hinges on it) could be made acceptable even to those who would not want to abandon Kripke's theory under any circumstances.

We should note here that there is no reason to expect that questions about transworld identification of the reference of *myself* (as used by a given individual) will be answerable by a straightforward application of any general theory of transworld identification. Words like *I* and *myself* occupy a special role in our language. It may therefore turn out that the first-person questions about personal identity across possible worlds are questions of a special kind and that in order to deal with them we need to construct a special account that will not follow directly from some general theory of transworld identification that we otherwise consider plausible.

Identification over time within a single possible world is an important precedent that might support the suggestion that we may need to construct a special account in order to deal with first-person questions about personal identity across possible worlds. We already know that first-person questions about personal identity over time create special problems and that we need a special philosophical theory to deal with them, a theory that does not follow directly from some general account of how we identify and re-identify individuals over time. That is why there is a special field of philosophical investigation known as "the problem of personal identity." Some results in this field[13] have even shown that what really interests us in situations in which we use the language of personal identity is a relation that is strictly speaking not a relation of identity at all because it does not have the logical properties of identity, such as transitivity and symmetry. In trying to resolve the problem of personal identity across possible worlds, it may be useful to bear in mind these results of investigation of the problem of personal identity over time.

All examples that Kripke gives of identity of persons across possible worlds are given in the third person. In these examples he insists that it is an essential property of, say, Queen Elizabeth that she originates from a particular sperm and egg. Now, we may find it acceptable and even useful to use the sperm-and-egg criterion when we are discussing identity of persons across possible worlds in the third person (just as in the third person considerations of personal identity over time we often find the bodily criterion acceptable and even useful) and still (on the basis of the above precedent of personal identity over time) reject it as a criterion when we are discussing the question in the first person.

The motivation for divorcing the first-person criteria of personal identity across possible worlds from the Kripkean (sperm-and-egg) essences is rather strong. I can entertain a supposition that my age and genetic information according to which my body has developed are different from what they actually are, and this involves the supposition that I originate from a different sperm and egg. For example, I can consider the possibility that I possess many of the properties that are actually possessed by Nixon, while granting to Kripke that it is impossible for Mane Hajdin to possess all these properties. In fact, I frequently do entertain such suppositions and so probably do most of my readers. When in some conversation I invoke the possibility of my possessing properties that are incompatible with my originating from the sperm and egg from which I actually originated, my interlocutors usually appear to understand what I am saying: they do not react to it in the way in which they usually react to absurdities.[14] When my interlocutors invoke analogous possibilities, it appears to me that what they are saying is intelligible and that I understand it. The "appearances" of understanding that most of us have in such conversations seem to be too systematic to be mere appearances. They are certainly systematic enough that we are entitled to an explanation as to why we so systematically appear to understand each other from anyone who wants to insist that we really do not.[15] Kripke, however, boldly ignores the task of providing such an explanation.[16]

Moreover, the first person statements that individuals make about what properties it is and what properties it is not possible for them to have (i.e., the statements that led us to introduce, in section 6.2, the properties that are essential to being oneself) seem to be immune to corrections that would follow directly from results of scientific investigations (it is not even clear which science would be relevant here). No amount of biological knowledge can, for example, compel one to say that it is possible (or that it is not possible) for something to be himself and be a dog at the same time. Kripkean essences associated with the names such as *Queen Elizabeth, Nixon,* or *Mane Hajdin* are, on the other hand, discoverable by scientific investigation.

In the context of investigating membership in the moral community, additional motivation for keeping the properties that something must have in order to be myself distinct from the Kripkean essence of Mane Hajdin stems from the fact that, taking originating-from-a-certain-sperm-and-egg to play the role that is assigned to essential properties of myself in sections 6.2 and 6.3 would have the highly implausible consequence[17] of restricting my moral community to persons of my age and genetic makeup.[18]

On the other hand, it certainly seems plausible to say that in this world, at least at this moment, I am identical with Mane Hajdin. According to Kripke, *Mane Hajdin* is a rigid designator and statements of identity that have rigid designators on both sides of the identity sign are always necessary. If *I*, as used by a given person, behaved as a rigid designator (as Kripke believes it does),[19] then the statement that I am identical with Mane Hajdin would be necessary and one would not be able to avoid the consequence that the essential properties that are associated with the term *Mane Hajdin* (in particular Mane Hajdin's having originated from a certain sperm and egg) are equally closely associated with the term *I* as used by me. Therefore, if I want to avoid that consequence, as I do, I must show that *I* and *myself* (as used by a given person) need not behave as rigid designators. This can be shown either by establishing that there is a sense of *I* and *myself* such that they are descriptions in disguise or by constructing some account of the meaning of these words that would show how they are radically different from both rigid designators and descriptions. I am going to consider the first of these two lines of argument now and the second in section 6.5.

Let us introduce the semi-technical term *myself*$_p$ to designate my present temporal stage,[20] and the term *myself*$_c$ for the continuant[21] of which myself$_p$ is a temporal stage. In the ordinary language, words *I* and *myself* can be used both for talking about myself$_p$ and for talking about myself$_c$:[22] use of tense and context usually make it clear which of the two is intended. The two terms thus, in spite of the appearance of artificiality, represent two senses that the ordinary word *myself* actually has.

Philosophical debate about personal identity over time presupposes that there is a way in which the notion of myself$_p$ is more basic than the notion of myself$_c$. The whole problem of personal identity over time can, therefore, be regarded as a problem of how we should analyze myself$_c$ in terms of myself$_p$. What we are after when we are investigating the problem of personal identity[23] over time is some relation, call it (as Parfit and Lewis do) *R*, which is such that we can say that myself$_c$ is a collection of all and only those things that stand in *R* to myself$_p$. Different theories of personal identity over time differ in what they tell us about what precisely *R* is. Some theories may put special emphasis on the relation that obtains between a mental state that takes another mental state as its content and that other mental state; that is, some on direct connections by memory and/or intentions, some on continuous chains of such connections, some on the sameness of character, some on embodiment of the relevant mental states in the living organisms that are related in a certain way, and so on. What all these views have in common is that they treat the idea of $myself_c$ as something that I, as it were, construct, taking $myself_p$ as the starting point (and then adding to $myself_p$ whatever is related to it by R). It may even be said that this secondary status of $myself_c$ is something that is implicit in regarding the problem of personal identity over time as a problem.

Now, if the notion of $myself_p$ is, as the discussion of personal identity over time assumes, more basic than the notion of $myself_c$, then it seems to follow that, when we are trying to establish some relation between $myself_c$-in-this-world and $myself_c$-in-W (where W is some other possible world) we should not apply our preferred theory of transworld identification directly.[24] Whatever theory of transworld identification we accept, we should apply it to the more basic notion of $myself_p$ first and so establish the relation between $myself_p$-in-this-world and $myself_p$-in-W. If $myself_c$ is in general a collection of all and only those things that stand in R to $myself_p$ then $myself_c$-in-W will be a collection of all and only those things in W that stand in R to $myself_p$-in-W.[25]

Moreover, if we look back on what was said about the shoehorn maneuver in the preceding chapters, in light of the distinction between $myself_p$ and $myself_c$, we shall immediately see that many arguments based on the shoehorn maneuver have to be interpreted in terms of $myself_p$ rather than $myself_c$. For example, when I am told, in some moral discussion, "Imagine that you, yourself, are in pain" or "Imagine that you, yourself, desire X," I am not supposed to imagine merely that the history of my life includes, at some point or other, being in pain or a desire for X. Imagining that certainly would not achieve the results that my interlocutor intends. On the other hand, it also does not seem that he wants me to imagine that I have been and that I shall continue being in pain throughout my life or that a desire for X has persisted and will persist throughout my life. What my interlocutor wants me to imagine in these cases is that $myself_p$ includes feeling pain or a desire for X.

It is up to Kripkeans to decide whether they want to say that $myself_p$ is a rigid designator. Even if they do, and if they consequently choose to regard the relation between $myself_p$-in-this-world and $myself_p$-in-W as, literally, a relation of identity, it is a consequence of the above argument that $myself_c$ will still not be a rigid designator. And whatever the essential properties of $myself_p$ are, they will not have anything to do with any sperm and egg, because $myself_p$ is in general not inserted in history by a meeting of a sperm and an egg. Moreover, if the transworld identification is to be established between $myself_p$-in-this-world and $myself_p$-in-W first, and not between $myself_c$-in-this-world and $myself_c$-in-W right away, then $myself_c$-in-this-world and $myself_c$-in-W need not originate from the same sperm and egg.[26]

So far, my argument within this section has been addressed mainly to those who regard Kripke's theory of transworld identification as, in general, plausible. What about the opposite camp? How does the shoehorn maneuver fare within the context of Lewis's counterpart theory?

At first sight, Lewis's theory may seem inhospitable to the very idea of the shoehorn maneuver, because, according to the theory, I can say that an individual is $myself_p$-in-W only if it is a counterpart of $myself_p$-in-this-world, and I can say that only if $myself_p$-in-W, in the relevant respects, resembles $myself_p$-in-this-world more closely than do other things in W. The shoehorn maneuver, on the other hand, often involves considering $myself_p$-in-W as very different from $myself_p$-in-this-world, while at the same time imagining that other individuals in W resemble $myself_p$-in-this-world much more closely.

The phrase "in the relevant respects, resembles" in the preceding paragraph means something like: resembles in the respects that govern the counterpart relation that is appropriate to the context. Different contexts require different counterpart relations, that is, counterpart relations governed by different relations of resemblance. It is therefore important to realize that the point made in the preceding paragraph does not depend on the details of our view as to what the counterpart relation appropriate to our context is and thus does not depend on what precisely the "relevant respects" are. Whatever they are, shoehorn maneuvers will often involve imagining that some individual in W is, in those respects, more similar to $myself_p$-in-this-world than is $myself_p$-in-W to $myself_p$-in-this-world.[27]

Consider the following, rather typical, use of the shoehorn maneuver. If I have made the claim that it would be morally permissible for me to treat Mary in a certain way, I may be asked to consider the world, say W, in which I have the properties that Mary actually has and in which someone who has the properties that I actually have is treating me in the proposed way. Given that this other person (the agent in W) has precisely the properties that I have in the actual world, no one can be a better candidate for my counterpart in W. The person with the properties that Mary has (the patient in W) is bound to be a worse candidate. It is impossible to tailor the counterpart relation so that, in this example, the patient in W turns out to be my counterpart, and the agent in W turns out not to be my counterpart.

One can ensure that the patient in W is my counterpart by selecting a suitably undemanding counterpart relation (say, the one that makes any rational being a counterpart of mine),[28] but under such a counterpart relation, the agent in W is bound to be my counterpart too (and so are probably many other individuals in W). Again this strategy does not give us what we need in order to fit such shoehorn maneuvers into the framework of the counterpart theory: we need a transworld relation that is, in the example we are using, going to pair me in the actual world with the patient in W and not with the agent in W.

In spite of this seeming inhospitability of the counterpart theory to the shoehorn maneuver, and in spite of the fact that the early version of the theory was definitely unable to accommodate it,[29] the current version of the theory accommodates it without difficulty. That is because there is, in its current version, more to the counterpart theory than counterpart relations. It now allows for settling the questions of transworld identification of $myself_p$ by stipulation from among $myself_p$'s counterparts in the relevant world (when there are more than one).[30] One can thus say that what, in performing a shoehorn maneuver, enables me to say that a certain individual is myself$_p$-in-W is that it is a counterpart of myself$_p$-in-this-world in virtue of some relatively undemanding counterpart relation; and that, from among many individuals in W who are my counterparts in virtue of that relation, I have stipulated that it, and no other individual, is myself$_p$-in-W.

What I said in section 6.2 about the essential properties of myself can be accommodated within Lewis's theory as being about that (relatively undemanding) counterpart relation that sets the boundaries to the pool of individuals from which such stipulations are made.

6.5 Transfer of Consciousness within a Single World

At the beginning of section 6.4 it was assumed that whenever I imagine that I have properties that I do not actually have, this amounts to my considering some possible world, distinct from the actual one, in which I have these properties.[31] However, not all philosophers would agree with that assumption. It can be argued that there is an important difference between thought-experiments that involve my imagining that I have some combination of properties that neither I nor anyone else actually has and thought-experiments (which are particularly prominent in moral discourse) that involve my imagining that I have some combination of properties that I do not actually have but that someone else does actually have. While it must be acknowledged that the former kind involves consideration of another possible world, it can be claimed that (contrary to the assumption made at the beginning of section 6.4) the latter kind should not be analyzed in terms of possible worlds at all.

Such a view is entailed by the current version of Lewis's theory.[32] The version of the view that is more directly related to our present purposes is, however, the one that has been formulated by Zeno Vendler.[33]

A summary of the main argument in favor of such a view is as follows. Speaking informally, we can say that a possible world is given by the set of all propositions that are true in that world. Propositions, whatever exactly they are, are things that cannot contain ineliminable indexicals. For example, that there exists an individual possessing such and such properties is a proposition that may be true in some possible worlds and false in others. Possible worlds are individuated in such a way that a world in which this proposition is true and a world in which it is false must be distinct worlds. But, if I say not only that there is an individual with such and such properties but, in addition, that I am, myself, the individual with these properties, I shall not succeed in expressing a new proposition. Insofar as this utterance does express some proposition, the indexical in it must be eliminable, and if we eliminate the indexical, we are back to the proposition that there is an individual with these properties; if I insist that the indexical is ineliminable, then what I insist on is not a proposition at all.[34] Consequently, when I am engaged in a thought-experiment that involves my having the properties that I do not actually have but that someone else does actually have, what I am engaged in need not be regarded as my considering another possible world. This is because all relevant propositions have the same truth value in the possible world I am considering as in the actual one: what seems to be different *(my* having these properties) is not a proposition that would be true in that world and false in the actual one, because it is not a proposition at all. We should therefore say that what I consider in such a situation is a different *point of view*, a different perspective, on the actual world.

This argument seems rather unproblematic. It may indeed be a good idea to adopt the way of talking and thinking about possible worlds that is recommended in this argument, rather than the way that was used in section 6.4. It may also be a good idea to regard the shoehorn maneuver in the light of this argument, that is, as something that does not always involve consideration of a different possible world but that may simply consist in a shift of perspective within the actual world.

It may now seem that the acceptance of this argument and the rejection of the way of thinking presented in section 6.4

supports some conclusions regarding moral discourse: if the limitations on the use of the shoehorn maneuver (that I discuss in sections 6.2 and 6.3) are associated with problems of transworld identification, and if we can get rid of transworld identification in the shoehorn maneuver (as the argument just presented enables us to do, at least sometimes), then it becomes easier to accept the view that all such limitations are only apparent.[35]

On the other hand, I think that the argument about different perspectives within a single world will not carry this burden. In the remainder of this section, I argue that the claims of section 6.2 (and their consequences in section 6.3) are independent of our acceptance or rejection of this argument by showing how such claims can be accommodated within the framework generated by the argument as easily as they can be accommodated within the framework of section 6.4. In other words, I regard the shift from section 6.4 to section 6.5 merely as a shift to a different, probably better, way of imbedding my analysis of the shoehorn maneuver in the wider context of theories about modalities and not as a contribution to the substance of that analysis.

Vendler puts considerable emphasis on the analogy between my imagining that the combination of properties that someone else actually has is a combination of properties that I myself have and my imagining that some past or future moment of the history of the actual world is present.[36] These analogies are supposed to make it easier for us to accept that there are no limits to my putting myself in the shoes of others: I can imagine anyone's properties as my own, just as I can imagine any moment of the history of this world as present.

However, there is an important disanalogy between the two. When I acknowledge that I can imagine anyone's properties as my own, that does not mean that I can imagine the properties of any individual within the actual world as my own. The Empire State Building, the fingernail on my right index finger, and the sheet of paper on which this sentence is written, are all individuals of this world, but most of their properties I cannot imagine as mine, as there would be something contradictory about that. Only some privileged individuals (e.g., normal human beings) are such that I can imagine all of the properties of any of them as mine. On the other hand, no moments in the continuous history of the actual world are privileged in that way.

The point that I have just made is very obvious, and Vendler certainly would not want to deny it. He in fact seems to acknowledge it when he says that one can put oneself in the position of "any deserving individual."[37] Furthermore, the acknowledgment of this point is also implied by his use of the expression "anchors to subjectivity" for such individuals.[38] However, he never explains what makes an individual "deserving," or why some individuals are and some are not "anchors to subjectivity." He is too busy emphasizing that "transference of consciousness" (his term for the shoehorn maneuver) is possible between me and *any* deserving individual. What I want to emphasize is that it is possible between me and any *deserving* individual (and only between me and any deserving individual). Some of Vendler's remarks make it obvious that he thinks that cats, for example, are deserving individuals,[39] while computers are not,[40] but it is left unclear why he thinks that his readers will take this particular selection of deserving individuals as unproblematic. It certainly seems conceivable that someone would want to accept Vendler's general theory while picking out some other individuals as deserving. Vendler's theory, therefore, needs to be supplemented by some elaboration of the notion of deserving.

In other words, we need some account of what the points of view or perspectives or (in terms of Vendler's useful metaphor) anchors to subjectivity are among which transference of consciousness is possible. In my imagination I can, as it were, move from the anchor to subjectivity that constitutes me to another one by imagining its properties as mine. I can, in imagination, anchor myself to this same world by that other anchor to subjectivity, but we should not forget that there can be no anchoring (even anchoring-in-imagination) without an anchor, that is, that we can imagine being anchored to the world only by some anchor to subjectivity, and that a world comes equipped with only so many anchors. How the anchors to subjectivity are scattered around a particular world must be based on something in the description of that world[41] (although it is not a part of the description of the world that a particular anchor is mine).

It seems, therefore, that it must be acknowledged that there are properties that something must have in order to be an anchor to subjectivity, that is, in order to be one of the points among which transference of consciousness is possible. If Vendler acknowledges that there are such properties he will already be making a decisive step toward acknowledging the intuitions that guided section 6.2.[42] That there are properties that something must have in order to be an anchor to subjectivity is compatible with Vendler's claim that what is anchored by the anchors (the "transcendental self") has no essence.

I hope that I have just shown that the talk about properties that are "essential to my being myself" (if interpreted as talk about the properties that something must have in order to be an anchor to subjectivity) is not inappropriate in the context of Vendler's theory (in spite of some appearances to the contrary). What I still must do, in order to show that the account presented in sections 6.2 and 6.3 can fit the framework of Vendler's theory, is to show that the relativist aspects of my account can be accommodated within the framework. To that end let us introduce the term *accessibility* for a binary relation that can hold between anchors to subjectivity.[43] We can say that the anchor to subjectivity *b* is accessible from anchor to subjectivity *a* if and only if there are no insurmountable obstacles to transference of consciousness from *a* to *b* (to *a*'s imaginatively putting himself in the position of *b*). Vendler thinks that every anchor to subjectivity is accessible from any anchor. But once we start thinking in terms of accessibility, we see that there is no good reason to accept Vendler's belief in unrestricted accessibility. It is indeed far from obvious that the accessibility relation must be either symmetrical or transitive. We should notice again that Vendler's repeated insistence that what is anchored by the anchors, namely, "the transcendental self," has no essence and that there is therefore nothing about it to limit accessibility does not amount to an argument for unrestricted accessibility among anchors to subjectivity, because it does not entail that there is nothing about anchors themselves to limit accessibility.[44]

We can now introduce another term into this framework. We shall say that a certain property is an *essential* property of a particular anchor to subjectivity if and only if it is shared by all the anchors that are accessible from it. If Vendler's belief in unrestricted accessibility were warranted, then we would be entitled to say that all anchors to subjectivity share the same essence. But, if there are no reasons to believe in unrestricted accessibility, then we must suppose that different anchors to subjectivity will, in general, have different essences.

Now, if the essential properties of the particular anchor to subjectivity that constitutes *me* are understood in this way, then they turn out to play the same role as what I have called the "essential properties of myself" in section 6.2. This enables us to accommodate everything that was said in sections 6.2 and 6.3 within a framework that incorporates all the important insights of Vendler's theory (most notably the insights that transference need not be analyzed in terms of possible worlds and that it involves a transcendental self that has no essence). There does not seem to be anything in arguments that support these insights to exclude the account that I have sketched.

7

Consequences

7.1 Relativism

In this chapter I discuss what consequences the general account of the boundaries of the moral community presented in section 6.3 has for disputes that regularly arise about these boundaries.

It may, first, be interesting to note how the account of membership in the moral community that was offered there relates to various traditional criteria for membership in this community, such as being rational, being sentient, having a soul, being human, and so on.

The account offered does not directly conflict with any of these criteria. It merely places the question as to whether, say, rationality is relevant to membership in the moral community in a different context from the one in which it has traditionally been asked. A person who accepts the account of membership in the moral community given in section 6.3 still must resolve for himself whether rationality (or sentience, or humanity, etc.) is an essential property of *him* or not. The answer to this question will determine whether rationality is relevant to membership in the moral community *for* this particular participant in moral discourse. That everyone must answer such questions for himself does not mean that there is no room for argument and discussion in dealing with them. For example, I may be initially inclined to say that rationality is not an essential property of myself, and you may then, in a discussion, point out to me that certain other beliefs that I hold commit me to treating rationality as an essential property of myself. But although it is possible to produce such arguments, they are, in a sense, *ad hominem* and there are no conclusive arguments through which we could achieve complete uniformity among the ways in which each of us sets the boundaries to his moral community.

The view that I am advocating can be described as relativism about questions concerning membership in the moral community.[1] However, in describing this view as relativism, we should bear in mind the results of section 5.1 where it is argued that questions about membership in the moral community are independent of questions as to which moral rules we are going to adopt. The relativism that I am advocating here is therefore perfectly compatible with nonrelativism about questions of the latter type.

7.2   How to Argue with Radical Racists

There are many people who may be reluctant to accept the view about membership in the moral community that is presented here precisely because of its relativism. In this section I try to convince them that the consequences of accepting this relativism are not as drastic as they seem.

Consider the example of *radical racism*. Someone is a radical racist if he regards human beings of certain races (or all races other than his own) as not being members of the moral community. For him, whatever moral rules he has agreed to simply do not apply to members of other races (variables for agents and patients in these rules do not range over them). Colloquially put, members of other races "don't count" for him.

I label this view *radical racism* in order to distinguish it from *ordinary racism*. An ordinary racist does accept the members of other races as members of the moral community; however, he fashions his moral rules in such a way that it is morally permissible or even required that everyone who happens to be a member of his own race treats anyone who happens to be a member of some other race in ways that put members of these other races in a position that is in some respects substantially inferior to the position of members of his own race. Unlike a radical racist, an ordinary racist tries to justify his views by moral arguments, and is prepared, at least in principle, to put himself in the shoes of members of the other races. Only the case of radical racists is relevant for my discussion here, but in the course of this discussion it will be important that we do not confuse radical racists with ordinary racists.

It may be worthwhile to note that radical racism is rare these days.[2] Most of the views that we call racist are of the ordinary kind. It is extremely unlikely that a white North American would be a radical racist with respect to black North Americans.

But, although unlikely, it is possible that a white North American would say that for him blacks "don't count," that they are for him outside the scope of morality. If someone did say such a thing, in which way could we criticize him?

If we are guided by my account of membership in the moral community we could certainly ask him whether he can imagine himself to be a member of the black race, but if he is really a radical racist he will insist that he cannot imagine such a thing and that belonging to the white race is an essential property of himself. We may then try to construct arguments that would show him that treating his membership in the white race as one of the essential properties of himself is inconsistent with something else that he holds. It may be possible to talk a radical racist out of his position by such arguments. But we can certainly imagine a case of a perfectly consistent radical racist, whose radical racism would survive all such arguments.

The relativism about questions concerning membership in the moral community that I have advocated here seems to suggest that there is nothing that we can do about such a consistent radical racist. This implication is something that most people will find repugnant, which is why it is important to show that there are ways of criticizing radical racism (and other similar views) that are compatible with my argument.

Among the conclusions that we have reached in section 6.3 there is one that we can exploit for this purpose, and this is the conclusion that, for each user of moral language, the set of moral patients necessarily coincides with the set of moral agents. This thesis implies that although we cannot rationally compel someone to admit that a certain individual is either a moral agent or a moral patient by starting from scratch, we can convince someone that a certain individual is a moral patient once we hear him talking about this individual as a moral agent.

Now, people are much more tempted to be radical racists when they are looking at questions of moral patiency than when it comes to agency. It seems very easy to claim that someone is not a moral patient and that we therefore do not owe him anything. The thesis that moral patiency is tied with moral agency has the consequence that this easiness is only apparent.

Suppose that someone purports to be a radical racist and is perfectly consistent in his radical racism as long as the question is whether members of the relevant race are moral patients. The trick that may be useful to play on him consists in describing to him very vividly various situations in which members of that race performed acts that would normally be considered wrong when performed by moral agents. Chances are that such stories will, at some point, prompt him to say something like "How could they do such a [morally] bad thing." As soon as he utters this, he has lost the game as we will be quick to point out to him that his remark treats members of that race as moral agents, which entails that he can, after all, make sense of his being a member of that race, which entails that when we come back to the question of moral patiency he will no longer be able to claim that he cannot make sense of his being a member of that race, which entails that he is, after all, committed to treating them as moral patients.

One instance of such spontaneous moral reaction on the part of someone who purports to be a radical racist can therefore be sufficient to destroy his position.

This technique of persuading the radical racists leads us to another, more fundamental way of dealing with them. It consists in abandoning the moral context and shifting to prudential discourse—more precisely to prudential consideration of our participation in moral discourse.

Although it is logically possible to stay out of moral discourse completely, each person will usually have good prudential reasons to enter into it, as it enables him to enlist the cooperation of others in maximizing his own well-being (think in particular of the situations of "Prisoner's Dilemma"). The benefits that a person can expect to receive from that cooperation typically outweigh the sacrifices that he can expect morality will require him to make.[3] Each one of us can therefore expect to become better off by entering into moral discourse.[4]

We can now make a prudential argument for taking certain individuals, say human beings of a certain race, as partners in moral discourse, which is similar to this familiar prudential argument for not staying out of moral discourse in general. It is logically possible for you to decide that you shall never enter a moral discussion with any member of a certain race. However, if you make such a decision, you have a considerable price to pay, as there will be fewer means available to you to ensure that the behavior of these individuals contributes to, or at least does not interfere with, your well-being. Your relation with these individuals will become reminiscent of the Hobbesian state of nature, as you, to a large extent, must rely on sheer force as a means of influencing their behavior. This way of dealing with others is costly and not very efficient. Moreover, it has limited application, as more complex forms of behavior are beyond the reach of physical coercion. On the other hand, if you choose to enter into moral argumentation with the human beings of that race it is rather likely that you will be able to influence them to behave in ways that contribute to your well-being with less effort (moral discussion is generally easier than exercise of physical force), and more efficiently, and that you will be able to get them to cooperate with you in fairly complex endeavors (into which people usually cannot be coerced by physical force). Admittedly, once you take them as partners in moral discourse you must accept that the moral rules you assent to will require you to make some sacrifice for their benefit. But it is still to be expected that the total package of consequences of taking these human beings as your partners in moral discourse will be better for you than the total package of consequences of not taking them as partners in moral discourse. Therefore, just as you have prudential reasons for entering moral discourse rather than staying completely out of it, you can also have prudential reasons for entering moral discourse *with specific individuals,* rather than refusing to do so.

Acceptance of this argument, on the basis of the first conclusion of section 6.3, commits you to treating these individuals as both moral agents and moral patients. This is how radical racism can be refuted on prudential grounds.

7.3   Stable and Unstable Membership in the Moral Community

Users of moral language generally agree in treating all individuals to which the prudential argument of the preceding section happens to apply as members of the moral community. The set of individuals to which the argument applies includes most human beings, regardless of their race. If some user of moral language gets tempted by radical racism or some other view that would result in excluding such individuals from his moral community, we can always remind him of the prudential reasons that he has for keeping them in.

Of the individuals to which the prudential argument applies I shall say that their membership in the moral community is *stable.* By characterizing their membership as stable I mean that it can be grounded by the prudential argument, that the argument makes them relatively secure against losing their membership, and that it makes them securely established as members of the moral community for practically all[5] participants in moral discourse.

The crucial premise in the prudential argument was that the individuals under consideration can be better influenced by moral arguments than by sheer force. While such a premise is true of most humans, it would not be true of, for example, (nonhuman) animals. When facing a hungry lion, the most prudent strategy is definitely not to address moral arguments to it. This fact does not preclude such animals from being members of the moral community for at least some participants in moral discourse, but even when they are counted as members, their membership is much more precarious. There is nothing as compelling as the prudential argument of section 7.2 to ground the membership of animals in the moral community. We can express this by saying that individuals to whom the prudential argument does not apply must be regarded as *unstable* members of the moral community (if they are to be regarded as members of that community at all).

It needs to be emphasized that unstable membership in the moral community is not a lesser *degree* of membership: as has been shown in section 3.7, membership in the moral community does not admit of degrees. From the viewpoint of someone who accepts certain unstable members as members, they are on a par with other members. The difference is a difference in the stability of membership and not in what the membership involves.[6]

In determining whether an individual qualifies for stable membership in the moral community we must ask the following questions:

1. Is the individual in question already a participant in moral discourse? If it is not, is it possible for us to teach and/or motivate it to become one? How much effort would we have to put into that?
2. Does the individual in question regard *us* as members of the moral community (or, in case it is still not a participant in moral discourse, would it regard us as members if it became a participant)? If not, can we persuade it to regard us as members (e.g., by convincing it that it would be prudent for it to regard us as members)? How much effort would it require to persuade it?[7]
3. Is the individual in question in the position to benefit or harm us? How much can it benefit or harm us? How do the net benefits resulting from its cooperation with us compare with what morality is likely to require us to do for it (if we decide to count it as a member of the moral community)?
4. How easily can the individual in question be influenced by other means (e.g., by physical force)?

When we have answers to these questions we will be able to decide whether the individual in question can be better influenced by moral arguments than by alternative methods, to behave in ways that contribute to our well-being, which is the criterion for stable membership in the moral community. In most cases answers to questions listed under (1) will be decisive.

The distinction between stable and unstable members enables us to acknowledge the importance of insights behind two influential views regarding membership in the moral community, while granting that the opponents of these views are not totally misguided.

The first is the view (or rather a family of distinct but similar views) that the ability to use language is a criterion (or perhaps even the criterion) for membership in the moral community. In the view that I am defending, the ability to use language is indeed relevant for membership in the moral community because it is a necessary condition for being a stable member (being able to use language is certainly a necessary condition for being able to use it so as to engage in moral discourse). But it is merely a necessary condition. Moreover, its being necessary for stable membership does not preclude participants in moral discourse from counting creatures who cannot use language as unstable members. (At least some participants in moral discourse do not regard their ability to use language as an essential property of themselves.)

The other, closely related view is contractarianism—the view that regards morality as a sort of "contract"[8] that we enter into because, for each of us, it is prudent to do so. It seems to follow from the contractarian view of morality that members of the moral community are all and only those beings that are such that we can profit from entering into this "contract" with them, and a necessary condition for our being able to profit from a contract is that the other party is able to understand and follow the contract.[9]

One important thing to note about contractarianism in general is that, although there may be good grounds for saying that it is prudent to engage in moral discourse and contractarians may be right in emphasizing that, there are no good grounds for building the thesis that it is prudent to engage in moral discourse into an analysis of the notion of morality. We can imagine that there are no prudential reasons in favor of engaging in moral discourse and that moral discourse still goes on. It may be unlikely that it would go on, but the supposition that it would seems perfectly intelligible, and this suggests that it is not part of the notion of morality that it is prudent to engage in moral discourse.[10]

What I have to say about the application of contractarianism to the question of membership in the moral community is parallel to the comment that I have just made about contractarianism in general. Contractarians are right in emphasizing that there is a group of individuals (that includes most humans, but excludes nonhuman animals) that are such that we have prudential reasons to take them as partners in moral discourse, that is, to "contract" with them, and thus to regard them as members of the moral community. But participants in moral discourse can still include in the moral community individuals that they are not compelled to include by prudential reasons. In fact, many participants in moral discourse do include in the moral community some individuals that they are not prudentially required to include, for example, nonhuman animals. The views of such participants in moral discourse may be problematic, but it does not seem that they are rendered unintelligible by what morality is.

The terminology introduced in this section enables us to express the important insights contained in the contractarian view of the moral community by saying that there are individuals whose membership in the moral community is stable, as well as to say that it is a weakness of such a view that it does not seem to allow for unstable membership in the moral community.[11]

7.4 Applications

Most of the discussions of the questions of membership in the moral community in contemporary philosophical literature appear in the context of attempts to solve some highly specific problem such as the problem of abortion. The discussion of membership in the moral community in this book is, on the other hand, motivated primarily by theoretical concerns and not by a wish to provide a ready-to-use solution to any such problem. However, our understanding of the position defended in this book will be enhanced if we look briefly at what it implies (and what it does not imply) about various specific issues.

7.4.1 Animals

We have already looked at the case of nonhuman animals and concluded that they could be, at best, unstable members of the moral community. Of course if it turned out that, say, dolphins in fact have moral discourse or that they are capable of learning it, then the argument of section 7.2 could conceivably apply to them as well, and they would then be stable members; in saying that they are at best unstable, I assume that dolphins do not have the capabilities required to participate in moral discourse.

Now, whether nonhuman animals are going to be unstable members of the moral community or not members at all, will, according to my account, be relative to particular participants in moral discourse: some will be able to make sense of the supposition that they, themselves, possess properties of various nonhuman animals, some will not. We can also expect that animals of different species will fare differently: there will be more people who will be able to make sense of the supposition that they possess properties of apes or dogs than people who will be able to make sense of the supposition that they possess properties of earthworms or lobsters.[12] Even within the same species different animals may fare differently.[13]

Some people may be initially inclined to say that there is no contradiction between being themselves and possessing properties of certain animals because they do not realize that something else that they hold commits them to there being a contradiction there, while others may say that there is a contradiction while being committed by their other views to there being no contradiction there. In such cases there will be room for discussion and argument: a suitable argument may convince such people that their views need to be adjusted. The best strategy in discussions about moral standing of animals seems to be to concentrate on such cases without hoping to convince everyone that animals belong or do not belong to the moral community.

It is also a consequence of my view that those who count nonhuman animals as members of the moral community must count them as both moral patients and moral agents. This may seem to be grossly counterintuitive. While we are used to the idea that nonhuman animals may be regarded as moral patients by some people, regarding them as agents seems ludicrous. But is it?

Saying that nonhuman animals can be regarded as moral agents, and that many people are committed to regarding them as such, does not entail the highly implausible consequence that those who regard nonhuman animals as agents will very often be in the position to say that an animal has violated some moral claim (nor does it entail that they will ever be in the position to say it). Saying that many people are committed to regarding animals as moral agents entails only that they do not regard the possibility of animals doing something morally wrong as excluded on grounds that would precede production of any moral arguments. It entails that they are open to moral arguments through which it can be established whether the animal in question did something morally wrong or not.

Suppose that both you and I regard dogs as members of the moral community, that is, that you are able to make sense of the supposition that you possess the properties of a dog and that I am able to make sense of the supposition that I possess the properties of a dog. Suppose, moreover, that I have said "Fido did something morally wrong in biting the postman." You would probably want to disagree with that. The important thing to notice is that you can articulate your disagreement by means of an argument. You can ask me to universalize my claim and you can then point out to me that this commits me to saying that I, myself, would be doing something wrong if I were to bite the postman (or anyone sufficiently like the postman) while possessing the properties that Fido actually possessed in that situation. You can then ask me to imagine that I possess these properties. You can point out to me that this involves my imagining that I have been conditioned to bite all intruders, that I am unable to distinguish the postman from possibly vicious intruders, and that I therefore, when the postman appears, have an irresistible urge to bite him. After thinking about all these aspects of the situation, I would probably withdraw the claim that I have made. Most, if not all claims, that could be made to the effect that behavior of an animal was morally wrong would probably have the same fate.

The important thing to notice is that what was described in the preceding paragraph was a moral argument par excellence. Saying that animals are regarded as moral agents by some people means only that these people are in principle prepared to go through such arguments, but it does not entail anything as to what the conclusions of such arguments will be.

What I have said so far may be sufficient to convince my reader that saying that animals are regarded as moral agents by some people does not generate any obviously absurd consequences. But the reader may still wonder what is the point of saying that animals are regarded as moral agents by some people (and moreover that all those who regard them as moral patients are committed to regarding them as moral agents as well) if even these people are never going to agree to any claim that would say that an animal has done something morally wrong (has violated a moral duty).[14] Saying that animals are regarded as moral agents by these people is certainly highly unnatural, so if we are to accept this way of talking it must bring some theoretical gain that would outweigh its unnaturalness.

The gain that such a way of talking brings is that it enables us to distinguish participants in moral discourse who are in principle prepared to go through moral arguments that take animals as moral agents, as in the example of biting the postman (no matter how rarely they actually go through such arguments), from participants in moral discourse who would never go through such arguments because what they regard as essential properties of themselves logically excludes their having the properties of the relevant animals. And this distinction, although admittedly of limited practical importance, is of theoretical interest. It is, namely, important to realize that, although practically no one would ever endorse the claim that Fido did something morally wrong in biting the postman, people refuse to endorse it for different reasons: some refuse to endorse it because they think that a moral argument against it can be produced and some because they think that Fido is not a member of the set of moral agents (and that no moral argument is therefore appropriate).

7.4.2   Inanimate Nature

Some people with mystical inclinations might claim that they can imagine that they possess properties of plants, mountains, and rivers, that there is nothing contradictory about a thing being one of themselves and a plant at the same time. If they are sincere, then plants, mountains, and rivers are members of the moral community for them. Their membership is, of course, unstable. But a great majority of the participants in moral discourse would find their possession of the properties of plants, mountains, or rivers incompatible with being themselves.

Consequently, whenever we are faced with something that appears to be a moral claim that takes objects of inanimate nature as members of the moral community, we must interpret it as (*a*) directed toward only a small number of mystics; or (*b*) not a moral claim at all, but a claim that belongs to some other type of discourse;[15] or (*c*) an abbreviated expression of some very complex moral claim that does not take inanimate objects as members of the moral community, but something else (e.g., a claim that we have a duty to preserve a certain area of wilderness may be an abbreviated expression of a duty to produce certain benefits for future generations of humans where these benefits are supposed to follow by some complex chain of causal connections from preservation of that area of wilderness). Interpretation (*c*) will be appropriate in most cases, but when the person who made the claim that we are trying to interpret insists that (*c*) is not what was intended, (*b*) or (*a*) may be appropriate.[16]

7.4.3   Fetuses

It seems fairly uncontroversial that we cannot in any serious sense communicate with fetuses, much less have moral discussions with them, which seems to exclude their having stable membership in the moral community. So far as unstable membership is concerned, what some people regard as their essential properties seems to be incompatible with the properties of fetuses, while what some other people regard as their essential properties seems to allow their possessing properties of fetuses.

We should, however, bear in mind that the observation that people differ in this respect (and that there are probably no compelling arguments by which one group could convert the other) does not dispose of the problem of abortion. In making this claim I not only have in mind the well-known argument of Judith Jarvis Thomson[17] to the effect that abortion may be permissible, in at least some cases, even if fetuses are moral patients, but also the arguments that defend a relatively conservative position on abortion without according membership in the moral community to fetuses. This includes not only the standard arguments that appeal to brutalization and similar side effects,[18] but also Hare's argument, which hinges on the assumption that some future humans will be glad that the fetuses from which they developed were not aborted.[19]

Whatever one might think about Hare's argument, it is important to notice that it treats these future humans as moral patients that are relevant for the duty not to have or perform abortions and that the argument does not need to treat fetuses as anything more than a link in the causal chain through which we affect these future humans. This aspect of Hare's argument needs to be emphasized, because the argument has been criticized as if it regarded fetuses as moral patients.[20]

7.4.4 Infants

What was said above about fetuses also applies to infants. Given that we cannot take them as partners in moral discourse, they do not enjoy stable membership. The difference between infants and fetuses, however, is that more people can imagine themselves as infants than as fetuses. More participants in the moral discourse therefore grant unstable membership to infants than to fetuses. But it is possible to consistently hold that one's essential properties exclude one's having properties of an infant.

There is one popular argument that people may be tempted to use against those who would claim that they cannot make sense of the supposition that they have the properties of infants, and it may be worthwhile to see why it does not work. This is the argument that it must be logically possible for me to possess properties of an infant because I actually possessed these properties once. The first reply to that argument may be that its premise is simply false. If I adopt a theory of personal identity over time that gives particular prominence to direct memory connections and if I do not remember my infanthood, then I can say that there is an important sense of *I* such that I have never possessed the properties of an infant.

But suppose we have adopted some theory of personal identity over time in which it is true that I possessed the properties of an infant once. Recall that, in the terminology of section 6.4, that means that I, myself$_c$, had these properties, which in turn means that myself$_p$ is related by relation R to something that had such properties. Recall also that the shoehorn maneuver typically requires me to imagine that myself$_p$ possesses the relevant properties. But the fact that myself$_p$ is related by R to something in the past that possessed certain properties does not entail, without further argument, that it is possible for myself$_p$ to possess these properties. This is the second reply to the popular argument.

Readers who are upset by the suggestion that there may be no conclusive argument against those who would not count infants as moral patients should bear in mind that one's not counting infants as moral patients need not have any drastic manifestations in one's behavior, because one's dealing with infants may be constrained by duties that one has to others. For almost every infant, there is someone around who is sufficiently emotionally attached to it that he would suffer if the infant were maltreated, and one probably has a duty to these people not to make them suffer in that way. One could also reason in a manner analogous to Hare's argument about abortion and claim that one's dealing with infants is constrained by one's duties to future adults into which these infants are going to develop. Finally, the familiar argument (also used in discussions of abortion and cruelty toward animals) that certain forms of treatment of individuals that are not moral patients, but sufficiently resemble moral patients, are morally wrong because they may brutalize those who engage in them and make them more likely to maltreat moral patients is particularly persuasive when applied to the case of infants.

7.4.5 Members of Future Generations

It is unlikely that anyone would see any logical obstacle to imagining that he, himself, lives at some future time. Therefore, for practically all participants in moral discourse, there do not seem to be any obstacles to counting members of future generations as members of the moral community.[21] In spite of that fact, many people may intuitively feel that future members of the moral community are somehow still not in quite the same group as the present members of the moral community. We can see that this intuition is justified if we reflect on the fact that, although members of future generations may be almost universally regarded as members of the moral community, their membership is still unstable.

The prudential argument of section 7.2 does not apply to members of future generations for at least two reasons. First, it is impossible for us to take future humans as our partners in any form of discourse. We can at most have one-way communication with them (we can leave them messages) but this is insufficient for engaging in *discourse.*

Second, even if it were by some miracle possible to discuss moral issues with members of future generations, it seems that we would not have good prudential reasons to do so, because (causation working as it does) the ways in which their acting in accordance with moral rules contributes to our well-being are bound to be rather limited.[22]

7.4.6 Computers

Very few people today would say that possessing the properties of a computer is compatible with being themselves. Present-day computers do not seem to be serious candidates for members of the moral community. However, if we assume that there are, in principle, no limits to computers' reaching any degree of sophistication and complexity, then it seems conceivable that some people will be able to imagine themselves with the properties of highly sophisticated future computers and will count them as members of the moral community. There certainly does not seem to be a strong reason why I would have to regard it as an essential property of mine that my body is made of relatively soft materials. In fact, many readers of science fiction that uses highly sophisticated computers as characters react to depictions of behavior of and toward these computers in the ways in which we normally react to artistic depiction of behavior of and toward members of the moral community.

The interesting question, however, is whether computers could be stable members of the moral community. If we are free to assume that computers can reach any degree of sophistication, then we could presumably also teach them to engage in moral discourse (which involves teaching them to act on the results of that discourse). However, we would have the prudential reason of section 7.2 for actually engaging in moral discourse with them only if that were the most efficient way to influence them to behave in ways that contribute to our well-being. It is rather unlikely that this condition will be satisfied. In answering the question listed under (4) in section 7.3 we shall see that, when we want a computer to do something for us, we can straightforwardly program it to do that, and this will usually be a more efficient way of achieving our goal than convincing it by moral arguments to do the same thing, even if the latter option were available. The only scenario in which we would have prudential reasons for directing moral arguments to computers is one in which it is possible to influence them by means of such arguments, and in which it somehow became difficult to influence them by straightforward reprogramming. This could happen if computers were equipped with devices by means of which they could defend themselves against being reprogrammed. In this, admittedly very unlikely, situation, we would have grounds for regarding computers as stable members of the moral community.

7.4.7 Organizations and Groups

The fact that a certain group or organization has as its members only members of the moral community, that is, individuals whose properties I can imagine as mine, does not entail that I should be able to imagine the properties of that group or organization as mine. In fact, people are generally unable to imagine properties of groups or organizations as their own. These properties include, for example "having 7,123 regular members and 1,738 associate members" or "being hierarchically structured." My having any of these properties seems clearly impossible. Anything that could have 7,123 regular members and 1,738 associate members or be hierarchically structured would not be me.

This fact entails that people are generally committed to not regarding any group or organization as a member of the moral community, regardless of its size and how formal or informal it is. (Including families, corporations, nations, and states.)[23] Therefore, all moral claims that appear to express duties of or to groups or organizations must be interpreted as abbreviations for complex systems of moral claims that would express duties of or toward members of these groups or organizations (and possibly other individuals that are not their members, but are in some other way related to them).

I am of course aware that some philosophers would insist that such interpretations of claims that appear to express duties of or to groups are not satisfactory, that they do not capture the whole meaning of these claims. Such arguments would have to be met on a case-by-case basis. One would have to see precisely which element of the meaning of these claims is alleged to be missing and to show how it can be accommodated; there is no general reply to all possible arguments of this sort. Entering into case-by-case investigation of these arguments would however lead me too far away from the main concerns of this book.[24]

7.4.8 Criminals

This subsection does not deal with all people who have committed criminal offenses at some point in their lives (a majority of them are unanimously regarded as members of the moral community), but rather with those few criminals whom we would tend to characterize as "monstrous."[25] *Monstrous* is, of course, an extremely vague characterization, but its vagueness does not affect the point that I want to make here.

When we ask someone to imagine that he is about to commit such and such monstrous crime, we should not be surprised if, at least sometimes, we receive the reply "No, I can't imagine that. Anyone who would be inclined to do such a thing would not be me." People who respond in such a way do not regard monstrous criminals as members of the moral community. If we continue discussing questions related to monstrous criminals with these people, we will often note that their reactions are perfectly in line with not regarding monstrous criminals as members of the moral community. That is, when monstrous crimes are described to them, they tend to feel the same sort of horror that they feel when they hear about earthquakes, floods, and dangerous diseases (rather than an inclination to criticize these crimes morally). And when the question of how we should deal with monstrous criminals is raised, they tend to approach it in the same manner in which they approach questions as to how we should protect ourselves against earthquakes, floods, or dangerous diseases (i.e., in the way that is totally unlike the way in which they would approach, e.g., the question of what punishment is appropriate for tax evasion).

If what is implicit in this approach were to be philosophically articulated in a theory of punishment, the result would be something that is radically different from what we find in standard theories of punishment. Unlike the standard theories, which all assume that punishment is in need of moral justification and attempt to provide such justification, this theory would dispense with the need for moral justification of punishment of monstrous criminals. If monstrous criminals are not members of the moral community, then whatever we do to them simply cannot be morally wrong (except perhaps because of its side effects) and is therefore not in need of moral justification.

It seems that, several centuries ago, this way of thinking about criminals was widely accepted. At some periods it was even manifested in the legal institution of outlawry. Although it is not so widely spread any more, I would like to suggest that it still informs much of popular thinking about crimes, criminals, and punishment.

I do not want to claim that this approach would survive philosophical scrutiny (nor that it would not). This topic would need to be investigated separately. What I do want to claim is that the philosophical investigation of punishment needs to take this approach seriously.[26] Philosophers who want to come to terms with "common moral consciousness" over the issue of punishment should, in particular, recognize the presence of this approach in popular attitudes toward punishment.

We should note that it seems that we will not always be able to overcome someone's refusal to regard monstrous criminals as members of the moral community by appealing to the prudential argument of section 7.2, as there seem to be some criminals to whom it does not apply. It seems that at least some criminals display inability (or perhaps extremely stubborn unwillingness) to engage in moral discourse.

Thus, it has been alleged by Yochelson and Samenow that failure to put oneself in another's position is typical of what they call "criminal personality."[27] It is controversial whether such remarks are justified and how large the segment of criminal population to which they might apply is. But if such remarks are justified, then it follows that the criminals to whom they apply are precluded from having stable membership in the moral community.

7.4.9   The Insane and the Mentally Retarded

What can be said about membership of the insane in the moral community[28] (both those who display tendencies toward criminal behavior and those who do not) and the severely mentally retarded is largely analogous to what has already been said about the membership of monstrous criminals and infants. "Someone insane or severely retarded would not be me" is for many (but not all) people a perfectly natural response to the request "Imagine that you, yourself, are insane or mentally retarded." These people are committed to not regarding the insane and mentally retarded as members of the moral community. Moreover, the argument of section 7.2 does not apply to the seriously insane and severely mentally retarded, which precludes them from having stable membership in the moral community.

A popular argument that is sometimes used against those who claim that being insane or mentally retarded is logically incompatible with being themselves is "But you can *become* insane or retarded,[29] therefore being insane or retarded must be compatible with being yourself." This argument is analogous to the argument about infants that we have considered in section 7.4.4.

The reply is also analogous. First, it is not clear that I can become insane or retarded. On some accounts of personal identity over time, I cannot become insane, because "my" becoming insane breaks the relation that is, on these accounts, necessary for personal identity. Second, even if I grant that myself$_p$ might be related by relation R to something in the future that is insane or retarded, that does not entail, without further argument, that it is possible for myself$_p$ to be insane or retarded.

Now suppose that someone is perfectly consistent in not regarding the mentally retarded as members of the moral community and that he therefore advocates a policy of wide-ranging slaughter of the mentally retarded. (Everything that I say below about the mentally retarded, *mutatis mutandis*, applies to the insane.) He admits that the benefits of this policy are relatively slight: there will be some savings to those who would otherwise be required to bear the cost of keeping the retarded alive. But he regards these benefits as sufficient to justify the policy, because, given that he does not treat the retarded as moral patients, he does not think that there is any loss to weigh these benefits against. Is there any way to morally criticize his proposal?

In reply we can certainly appeal to some of the already familiar side effects of such policies: people who are emotionally attached to the mentally retarded may suffer if the retarded are slaughtered, and the whole process may brutalize those who carry it out and make them more likely to treat humans who are not retarded in the similar manner.

There is one additional side effect that we can appeal to in this case (and perhaps also in the case of monstrous criminals).

Namely, those who implement the policy of slaughtering the retarded would presumably slaughter those humans whom they *believe* to be retarded. The person who proposed the slaughtering policy may regard being retarded as incompatible with being himself and may consequently be unable to imagine that he is retarded, but he will certainly be able to imagine that he is a human being of normal intelligence who is falsely believed to be retarded. If he puts himself in the shoes of such humans and imagines that he is being slaughtered as a result of the proposed policy he may be led to abandon the proposal. He should also put himself in the shoes of the humans of normal intelligence who will not actually be slaughtered but who will fear that they might be slaughtered because someone might come to believe, falsely, that they are retarded, and this will probably also push him in the direction of abandoning the proposal.

The person who proposed the slaughtering might, however, respond to this argument by revising his proposal and building into it that the retarded will be slaughtered only after their retardation has been established by complex tests that will minimize the chance of mistake. But then we can ask him to imagine that he is a human of normal intelligence who is forced to submit to these tests in order to prove that he is not retarded. Considering such a scenario may also lead him to abandon his proposal, because these humans will probably be very annoyed and humiliated by being forced to submit to these tests. The result can be reinforced by asking him to put himself in the shoes of all those who will not actually be forced to submit themselves to these tests, but who will be very annoyed by the idea that they live in a society in which they may be forced to submit to them.

Much of what I have said in this book implies that many of us cannot sincerely and consistently claim to regard all human beings (in the biological sense) as members of the moral community. Yet, there is a reason why various political slogans that imply that all human beings are members of the moral community are so rhetorically powerful. The foundation of their appeal lies in the fact that we all strongly resent having to prove that we qualify for membership in the moral community. We all find it reassuring to know that something very simple, such as presenting our human bodies, will be sufficient to secure for us the treatment that is accorded to members of the moral community.

Everyone has moral reasons for maintaining conditions in which those human beings whom he regards as members of the moral community will continue to feel this reassurance. As a means to that end, everyone may have moral reasons to treat human beings that he does not regard as members of the moral community as if they were members of the moral community.

Appeals to side effects, such as the one that has just been made, are often sufficient to convince those who do not regard certain individuals as members of the moral community to treat them in ways that those who do regard them as members will find morally acceptable. That possibility, together with the possibility (discussed in sections 7.1 and 7.2) of rational argumentation about the membership itself, entails that the consequences of relativism about membership in the moral community are not as disturbing as they may have seemed to be at first.

Notes

Introduction

[1] R. M. Hare, *Freedom and Reason* (Oxford: Clarendon Press, 1963).

[2] R. M. Hare, *Moral Thinking: Its Levels, Method, and Point* (Oxford: Clarendon Press, 1981).

[3] R. M. Hare, *The Language of Morals* (Oxford: Clarendon Press, 1952).

[4] Hare, *Moral Thinking*, 208.

[5] See, for example, Louis P. Pojman, "Is Contemporary Moral Theory Founded on a Misunderstanding?" *Journal of Social Philosophy* 22, no. 2 (Fall 1991): 51.

[6] Alfred Jules Ayer, "Critique of Ethics and Theology," chap. 6 in *Language, Truth and Logic* (London: Victor Gollancz, 1936).

[7] R. M. Hare, "Comments," in Douglas Seanor and N. Fotion, eds., *Hare and Critics: Essays on* Moral Thinking (Oxford: Clarendon Press, 1988), 202.

[8] Hare is certainly aware of this problem as can be seen from section 8.4 of *Freedom and Reason* where he himself raises a closely related question. In offering my answer to the problem I explain why I think that the remarks he makes in this section are not sufficient to close the issue. Moreover, as the importance of the consequences of universalizability has been boosted in Hare's more recent writings, the problem is of more interest now than it was at the time when *Freedom and Reason* was written.

[9] Robert L. Arrington has argued in chapter 6 of *Rationalism, Realism, and Relativism: Perspectives in Contemporary Moral Epistemology* (Ithaca, N.Y.: Cornell University Press, 1989) that we become acquainted with the concept of morality when we are given certain paradigmatic moral principles, such as "One ought to tell the truth" and "One ought to keep one's promises." To oversimplify a bit, his analysis of the concept of morality says that morality is whatever includes and is built around such principles. He believes that no further analysis of the concept is necessary (or

likely to be successful) and would therefore regard much of the enterprise of this book as misguided (see esp. pp. 285–86 of his book). What Arrington overlooks, however, is that sentences such as "One ought to tell the truth" or "One ought to keep one's promises" can be used to express nonmoral rules (e.g., rules of law or of prudence). Full understanding of the concept of morality therefore must involve more than familiarity with such examples.

[10] See Hare, *Moral Thinking,* 11–12.

Chapter 1

[1] Hare, *Freedom and Reason* (Oxford: Clarendon Press, 1963), 165; *Moral Thinking: Its Levels, Method, and Point* (Oxford: Clarendon Press, 1981), 100; and review of *Contemporary Moral Philosophy,* by G. J. Warnock, *Mind* 77 (1968): 437. In his article "Prudence and Past Preferences: Reply to Wlodzimierz Rabinowicz," *Theoria* 55 (1989): 155, Hare says that "it is not clear that prudential judgements are universalizable in the same way as moral judgements (though there may be *a* way in which they are universalizable)."

[2] See Hare, *Freedom and Reason,* 36.

[3] Hare, *Moral Thinking,* 56.

[4] Susan Wolf, "Moral Saints," *The Journal of Philosophy* 79 (1982): 419–39. Wolf's argument was criticized by Robert Merrihew Adams in his article "Saints," *The Journal of Philosophy* 81 (1984): 392–401. Adams misses the point of Wolf's article by placing excessive importance on Wolf's use of the word *saint* which is not at all essential to her argument. To be on the safe side, I shall avoid that word in presenting her argument.

[5] Wolf, "Moral Saints," 435.

[6] Ibid., 432.

[7] Michael Slote, in chapter 4 of *Goods and Virtues* (Oxford: Clarendon Press, 1983), defends a view that is basically the same as Wolf's, namely the view that there is such a thing as admirable immorality. Unlike Wolf, he does provide at least one example of behavior that may be viewed as admirable and grossly immoral by citing Winston Churchill's ordering of the firebombing of civilian

targets in certain German cities at the time when that was not indispensable to Allied victory.

However, the impact of Slote's argument is spoiled by his going to unnecessary length (especially in section 5) to defend his own view on what is and what is not admirable. Many readers may find these views somewhat idiosyncratic and Slote's arguments for them unconvincing, and this may distract them from appreciating the important consequences about the nature of moral discourse that follow from the mere intelligibility of such views.

[8] Needless to say, one may strongly feel that the life of a given person is admirable, without being able to formulate precisely enough the qualities that make it admirable. This, however, is a contingent matter which is compatible with saying that universalizability is a feature of this type of discourse.

[9] Cf. Wolf, "Moral Saints," 436.

[10] It is an important defect in Frankena's recent criticism of Hare that he seems unaware of the fact that Hare has said this ("Hare on Moral Weakness and the Definition of Morality," *Ethics* 98 [1988]: 781–82).

[11] A different and much older way of achieving the same result is by constructing prudential arguments that take as their factual premises some claims about divine punishments and rewards. However, contemporary game-theoretic arguments have the obvious advantage of being less dependent upon such controversial assumptions.

[12] While most contemporary authors who discuss the relation between prudence and morality argue about something like (*a*) without even mentioning anything like (*b*), Hare seems to be aware of the importance of arguing for (*b*). However, even he is not careful enough in keeping the two lines of argument distinct. He begins the argument of the first half of chapter 11 in *Moral Thinking* as something that is intended to convince an amoralist who simply refuses to use moral words. One is thus led to expect that the argument will be an argument for (*b*). However, in the course of presenting the argument Hare slips into talking about the extent to which prudential principles *coincide* with moral principles (*Moral Thinking*, 193), which sounds much more like (*a*). Moreover, his argument concentrates on the relation

between prudence and what he calls, "intuitive-level moral think-ing," which leaves it unclear as to what he thinks about the relation between prudence and moral discourse at its critical level. The distinction between (*a*) and (*b*) will be important for the argument of chapter 7.

[13] Louis Pojman's remark that "what I bind myself *to*, I can unbind myself *from*" ("Is Contemporary Moral Theory Founded on a Misunderstanding?" *Journal of Social Philosophy* 22, no. 2 [Fall 1991]: 51) therefore applies to (*a*), but not to (*b*).

[14] A detailed discussion of situations of precisely this sort can be found in part 1 of Derek Parfit's *Reasons and Persons* (Oxford: Oxford University Press, 1984). Parfit, however, neither uses the term *discourse* nor makes the distinction between a type of dis-course and a view or a theory within discourse of a certain type. Consequently, the matter that I would discuss in terms of one type of discourse delegating its authority to another type of discourse, he discusses in terms of one *theory* telling us to believe another *the-ory*. In spite of this, much of what Parfit says in part 1 of *Reasons and Persons* can be easily reformulated to fit my framework and should be read by anyone who is tempted to think that there must be something wrong with a type of discourse (theory) that gives us a one-way ticket to another type of discourse (theory).

[15] In his recent article "On There Being Some Limits to Morality," *Social Philosophy & Policy* 9, no. 2 (1992): 63–80, John Kekes advances a thesis that is in many respects similar to the one I am advancing in this section. However, even he eventually succumbs to the temptation to smuggle in the idea that certain kinds of con-siderations are absolutely overriding. In his case, considerations about what he calls "the protection of the self" are absolutely over-riding. Given that selves differ, Kekes believes that these con-siderations would delegate their authority to other kinds of pre-scriptive discourse in ways that differ from person to person. Implicit in his argument, however, is that, for any given person, considerations about "the protection of the self" provide an order-ing of different kinds of prescriptive discourse that would somehow not be just one among many alternative orderings. My argument here shows that this cannot be so: the discourse that deals with "the protection of the self" (whatever precisely that is) is bound to be on a par with any other kind of prescriptive discourse.

[16] Hans Kelsen, *General Theory of Law and State*, trans. Anders Wedberg (New York: Russell & Russell, 1961), 374.

[17] Within a particular type of discourse a person can perhaps reach a conclusion that, if he had been in a position to create or not create other types of prescriptive discourse, he should have decided not to create them. But such conclusions are of limited practical importance because none of us shall ever be (nor has anyone ever been) in such a position; nor shall any of us ever be in the position to extinguish a type of prescriptive discourse at will. Moreover, such conclusions are completely irrelevant if our aim is to understand the world of prescriptive discourse as it is, and not as it should have been (in some sense of *should*).

At most, a person can decide that he will not engage in certain types of prescriptive discourse. If many people make such decisions with respect to the same type of discourse, then it may perhaps be extinguished at some point in the distant future. Again, this possibility is not of much relevance if our aim is to understand the world of prescriptive discourse as it is now.

[18] It can be said that this dread finds its philosophical expression in Kant's idea that the existence of God, which guarantees what he calls "the exact harmony of happiness with morality" (and so eliminates the possibility of conflict between moral and prudential considerations), simply must be accepted as a "postulate of pure practical reason" (*Kant's Critique of Practical Reason and Other Works on the Theory of Ethics*, trans. Thomas Kingsmill Abbott, 6th ed. [London: Longmans, 1909], 221).

[19] W. K. Frankena, "The Concept of Morality," in G. Wallace and A. D. M. Walker, eds., *The Definition of Morality* (London: Methuen, 1970), 153–54 (article first published in 1967). Cf. J. L. Mackie, *Ethics: Inventing Right and Wrong* (Harmondsworth, England: Penguin Books, 1977), 106–7.

[20] Frankena, "The Concept of Morality," 170–73.

[21] T. L. S. Sprigge, "Definition of a Moral Judgement," in *The Definition of Morality*, 119–45 (article first published in 1964).

[22] Jan Narveson, *The Libertarian Idea* (Philadelphia: Temple University Press, 1988).

[23] Ibid., 125.

[24] H. J. McCloskey, "The Complexity of the Concepts of Punishment," *Philosophy* 37 (1962): 310.

[25] The argument that follows is presented as an argument about moral discourse but applies to other types of prescriptive discourse as well. No type of prescriptive discourse can be successfully distinguished from the others in terms of sanctions that back up its prescriptions. The argument can be regarded as a generalization of some aspects of Kelsen's analysis of legal discourse.

[26] Narveson seems to acknowledge this when he says that "for an act to be obligatory or wrong is for it to be the case that its performance or nonperformance *should* be universally reinforced, positively or negatively" (*The Libertarian Idea*, 223, italics mine; cf. 125, 264), but he avoids spelling out the consequences of that acknowledgment.

[27] Cf. Kelsen's criticism of the "concept of jurisprudence as prophecy" in *General Theory of Law and State*, 165–69.

[28] Cf. Kelsen's argument involving a similar infinite regress in *General Theory of Law and State*, 59–60.

[29] Note that my point here is not that there cannot be a nonmoral prescription telling us to apply sanctions of the sort *S* whenever moral prescriptions are violated, but that it is implausible to try to build reference to such prescriptions into one's analysis of the notion of morality.

Narveson's response ("Comment on Hajdin on Sanctions and Morals," *Dialogue* 32 [1993]: 761–65) to the argument of this section (originally published as "Sanctions and the Notion of Morality," *Dialogue* 32 [1993]: 757–60) is therefore not sufficient to refute it. Central to his response is the argument that prescriptions about the application of sanctions are ultimately nonmoral and that there is nothing implausible about their being nonmoral. A further argument would, however, be needed to convince one that it is not implausible to say that there is a *conceptual* connection between such nonmoral prescriptions and morality.

[30] While this line of reasoning about moral discourse is implausible, an analogous line of reasoning about legal discourse leads to a

result that is much more plausible, namely to Kelsen's analysis of law as essentially a system of prescriptions about application of sanctions, rather than prescriptions backed up by sanctions (the latter are, for him, merely a way of presenting the former).

Chapter 2

[1] Needless to say, imagining myself as having properties that I do not actually have always involves imagining myself as not having some of the properties that I actually have.

[2] The term was coined by Alfred F. MacKay in "Extended Sympathy and Interpersonal Utility Comparisons," *The Journal of Philosophy* 83 (1986): 305–22. MacKay is critical of the philosophers whose accounts of morality give prominent place to the shoehorn maneuver and probably intended the term to be somewhat ironic. Although I do not share his views about this technique of argumentation, I have found that the term that he has coined is a very convenient tool for referring to it. (Compare the history of the term *impressionism*, which was intended as derisive by the critic who invented it.) Alternative terms could be *transference of consciousness* or *empathetic identification*.

[3] C. I. Lewis, *An Analysis of Knowledge and Valuation* (La Salle, Ill.: Open Court, 1946), 545; cf. *The Ground and Nature of the Right* (New York: Columbia University Press, 1955), 91.

[4] Thomas Nagel, *The Possibility of Altruism* (Oxford: Clarendon Press, 1970), especially chapter 9, section 2; cf. *The View from Nowhere* (New York: Oxford University Press, 1986), especially chapter 7, section 3.

[5] Zeno Vendler, "Changing Places?" in Douglas Seanor and N. Fotion, eds., *Hare and Critics: Essays on* Moral Thinking (Oxford: Clarendon Press, 1988), 171–83. See also "A Note to the Paralogisms," in Gilbert Ryle, ed., *Contemporary Aspects of Philosophy* (Stocksfield, England: Oriel Press, 1976), 111–21; *The Matter of Minds* (Oxford: Clarendon Press, 1984).

[6] John C. Harsanyi, *Essays on Ethics, Social Behavior, and Scientific Explanation* (Dordrecht, Netherlands: D. Reidel Publishing Company, 1976).

[7] Mary Bittner Wiseman, "Empathetic Identification," *American Philosophical Quarterly* 15 (1978): 107–13.

[8] G. J. Warnock's article "Morality and Language: A Reply to R. M. Hare," in Donald B. Cochrane, Cornel M. Hamm, and Anastasios C. Kazepides, eds., *The Domain of Moral Education* (New York: Paulist Press, 1979), 107–14, while in many respects unfair to Hare (Warnock himself describes it as "excessively polemical" in the introduction to his collection *Morality and Language* [Oxford: Basil Blackwell, 1983], 7, where it is reprinted) contains (page 113) an argument against him which is similar to the one that I am presenting in this subsection. Hare's reply ("A Rejoinder," in *The Domain of Moral Education*, 118) to Warnock's argument seems to consist in pointing out that one does not fully understand a universal prescription unless one has imagined a situation in which one is treated in accordance with that prescription. In my way of presenting the matter, this amounts to saying that stage 1 and stage 2 naturally lead one to stage 3 because one does not fully understand the contents of the universal prescription that one assents to at stage 1 without performing the shoehorn maneuver required by stage 3. The possibility of going through stages 1, 2, and 3, and still, at stage 4, dismissing the whole exercise as morally irrelevant is therefore important because it shows that this counterargument of Hare's is not sufficient to save his view about the connection between universalizability and the importance of the shoehorn maneuver in moral discourse.

In earlier polemic with Warnock over what was substantially the same question, Hare used the strategy of claiming that assenting to a prescription necessarily involves a sort of desire that it be acted on (in his review of Warnock's *Contemporary Moral Philosophy*, *Mind* 77 [1968], 439). My discussion of assenting to a prudential prescription in the remainder of this subsection is implicitly a response to that strategy. Cf. J. A. Brunton's distinction between "practical" and "theoretical" sincerity in "Restricted Moralities," *Philosophy* 41 (1966): 118.

[9] Ingmar Persson, "Hare on Universal Prescriptivism and Utilitarianism," *Analysis* 43 (1983): 43–49; Fred Feldman, "Hare's Proof," *Philosophical Studies* 45 (1984): 269–83; G. F. Schueler, "Some Reasoning about Preferences," *Ethics* 95 (1984): 78–80; R. M. Hare, "Some Reasoning about Preferences: A Response to Essays by Persson, Feldman, and Schueler," *Ethics* 95 (1984): 81–85; MacKay, "Extended Sympathy and Interpersonal Utility

Comparisons"; R. B. Brandt, "Act-Utilitarianism and Metaethics," in *Hare and Critics*, 27–41; Allan Gibbard, "Hare's Analysis of 'Ought' and its Implications," in *Hare and Critics*, 57–72; R. M. Hare, "Comments," in *Hare and Critics*, 215–22 and 229–34.

[10] In section 8.4 of his *Freedom and Reason* (Oxford: Clarendon Press, 1963).

[11] The crucial first paragraph in section 8.4 of *Freedom and Reason* is, in fact, less than perfectly clear on what the relevant connection between morality and people's interests is supposed to be. At the beginning of the paragraph we are told that (*a*) "aesthetic questions have no bearing on other people's interests," (*b*) "or, we might add, other people's interests on aesthetic questions," and given that this is said in the context of distinguishing aesthetic and moral questions, we may assume that the opposite is supposed to hold of moral questions. What is said at the end of the same paragraph, however, seems to contradict (*a*) (the existence of ugly things often violates people's interests), and so it seems that (*b*), which at the beginning of the paragraph was introduced in a casual way, almost as an afterthought, in fact has to do all the work. Moreover, Hare does not quite tell us what the status of (*b*) is. If the relevant paragraph were read in isolation from the rest of the book, the most natural reading would be that (*b*) is a conceptual truth, which would entail that it is, after all, not sufficient to characterize moral discourse as prescriptive, universalizable, and overriding. On the other hand, if (*b*) is not a conceptual truth, then one would want to know more about what kind of truth it is supposed to be before deciding whether to accept it. Cf. *Moral Thinking: Its Levels, Method, and Point* (Oxford: Clarendon Press, 1981), 54.

[12] We can call the whole of stage 1 universalizing in the wider sense of the word.

[13] When we say that universalizability is a feature of moral discourse we mean that one cannot regard a claim as moral without recognizing requests for such reconstructions as legitimate. We do not mean that one cannot regard a claim as moral if one is unable to *actually* produce such a reconstruction.

In other words, if one assents to a moral claim, one must *believe* that it is deriv*able* from some universal claim (that one would also be willing to accept), but the moral (rather than nonmoral) status of the claim is not jeopardized by one's inability to produce the derivation. If challenging our interlocutors to universalize their claims is to be (a part of) a technique of moral argumentation, then the claims in question must have the status of moral claims, independently of whether those who put them forward are able to successfully respond to the challenge.

If someone believes that the claim he has put forward is so derivable but it turns out that he is unable to produce the relevant derivation (and this may turn out only after a long discussion), then we can say that he has not succeeded in justifying the claim, but it would be obviously wrong to say that the claim has never been a moral claim at all. We cannot say that intending a claim as moral entails the ability to produce the derivation, precisely because it would lead to this obviously wrong consequence.

In Hare's writings this difference, between believing that a claim that one assents to could be universalized (which is a necessary condition for regarding it as a moral claim), and being able to universalize it (which is a part of the ability to justify it), has not been made sufficiently clear. If he had spelled out this difference, he would have made it clearer how metaethical issues (about what makes something into a piece of moral discourse) are intimately connected with and yet distinct from normative-ethical issues.

[14] For example, we all know that in ordinary language, as Donnellan has shown, the very same expressions can be used referentially (in which case they are akin to individual constants) and attributively (in which case they are not): Keith S. Donnellan, "Reference and Definite Descriptions," *The Philosophical Review* 75 (1966): 281–304.

[15] The reader might wonder why I talk about these arguments as being performed on certain argument-places rather than on certain terms (namely the terms that fill these places). After all, moral claims that we usually discuss are normally not open claims but rather claims in which the argument-places are occupied by something. My intention is not simply to generate a pun on the word *argument*. When stage 1 and stage 2 are considered separately, they could indeed be described as being performed on certain terms. But each of the two stages consists precisely in eliminating the term on which it is performed and replacing it with another term. Consequently, the term on which stage 2 is performed cannot be the same as the term on which stage 1 was

performed. What the two stages have in common are only the argument-places on which the replacements are performed, which is why, when we are describing such an argument as a whole, we must talk about its being performed on argument-places rather than on terms.

[16] The use of the word *addressed* in this sense has been strongly criticized by H. L. A. Hart in *The Concept of Law* (Oxford: Clarendon Press, 1961), 21–22. I believe that Hart is right in pointing out the important differences between this use of the word and its other uses, but I also believe that his criticism is too strong. In other words, I do not think that there is anything wrong with using the word in this way (as Austin and many of those who were influenced by him did) as long as we are aware of the differences that Hart has pointed out.

[17] The purpose of the word *intended* here is to distinguish the argument-places for prudential agents from argument-places that contain terms that turn out to refer to these same individuals, although the person who formulated the claim did not, in structuring it, have the intention that the terms that appear there refer to the individuals of whom it can be said that they follow or violate the claim. For example, a person who puts forward the claim that it was imprudent of Peter to bet that the next person with whom Paula will have an affair will be a psychologist, obviously did not intend the phrase "the next person with whom Paula will have an affair" to refer to someone of whom it can be said that he followed or violated the claim. Rather, he intended Peter as the prudential agent. But it may turn out that Paula will have an affair with Peter. Similarly, when prudential agents are represented by an individual variable, it may turn out that this variable ranges over the same individuals as some other variable that appears in the claim.

[18] The aim of the qualification "or its negation" is to make this definition of moral agents applicable to claims that say that something is morally permissible. These claims cannot be, strictly speaking, followed, and they certainly cannot be violated, but their negations can be. A similar qualification should be a part of the fully precise definition of a prudential agent.

[19] The explanation given in note 17, above, *mutatis mutandis,* applies here as well.

[20] Notice that it is irrelevant here that it may be impossible to imagine oneself as a weapon. We understand that the argument is inappropriate before we even try to put ourselves in the shoes of the weapon, simply in virtue of understanding the structure of the claim and the intentions of the person who structured it. In a discussion about the claim "Paula has a duty to Peter not to insult him in front of John," putting oneself in the shoes of John is similarly without much relevance (except indirectly).

[21] Except by Nagel: see chapter 7, section 3 of *The View from Nowhere*.

[22] See note 18, above.

[23] See note 17, above.

[24] The term *moral patient* is coined by analogy with the term *moral agent*. The use of the term *moral patient* does not have such a long and respectable history as that of the term *moral agent*, but several philosophers have already used it in the sense that is roughly the same as the sense in which I am using it. Examples are: N. Fotion, *Moral Situations* (Kent, Ohio: The Kent State University Press, 1968); G. J. Warnock, *The Object of Morality* (London: Methuen, 1971), 151; Thomas McPherson, "The Moral Patient," *Philosophy* 59 (1984): 171–83; and Jan Narveson, "The How and Why of Universalizability," in Nelson T. Potter and Mark Timmons, eds., *Morality and Universality* (Dordrecht, Netherlands: D. Reidel Publishing Company, 1985), 3–44. Narveson, in note 10 to "The How and Why of Universalizability" says that he takes the word *patient* from David Gauthier's article "Reason and Maximization," *Canadian Journal of Philosophy* 4 (1975): 424. This may leave his readers with the mistaken impression that no one has used the word in this way before 1975, while it was in fact used in this way by N. Fotion as early as 1968. The way in which all these philosophers use the term *moral patient* should not be confused with the related but importantly different way in which it is used by Tom Regan and those who take Regan's work as their starting point.

[25] The reader should notice that what I have built into the notion of morality here is merely that in moral discourse we employ arguments based on agent-oriented and patient-oriented shoehorn maneuvers.

That we employ such arguments does not entail anything about what we do when we are faced with two such arguments that pull in opposite directions (neither of which contains any error). Hare believes that in such a situation we simply add up the results of these arguments. But as Michael Gorr points out ("Reason, Impartiality and Utilitarianism," in *Morality and Universality*, 132) it is possible to argue that, in such a situation, the shoehorn maneuver that involves the lowest preference-satisfaction is always decisive (in a manner reminiscent of Rawls). Nothing in the nature of the arguments based on the shoehorn maneuver (as I have presented it) compels us to adopt either the first or the second, or any third way of dealing with these situations. Cf. J. W. Roxbee Cox, "From Universal Prescriptivism to Utilitarianism," *The Philosophical Quarterly* 36 (1986): 1–15; Ingmar Persson, "Universalizability and the Summing of Desires," *Theoria* 55 (1989): 159–70.

What the proper way of dealing with these situations is, is certainly an extremely important question and a full account of the methods of moral argumentation would have to provide an answer to it; but the answer (whatever it is) need not be incorporated into the analysis of the notion of morality and I am therefore not going to discuss the question here.

Saying that we employ the arguments based on agent-oriented and patient-oriented shoehorn maneuvers in moral discourse is sufficient to distinguish this discourse from other types of prescriptive discourse. Any disagreements that we might have about the proper procedures for balancing the outcomes of such arguments against each other should therefore not preclude us from agreeing with the analysis of the notion of morality that I have offered here.

Much of what recent critics (see note 9 above) of Hare's account of the shoehorn maneuver have said therefore does not affect my analysis because their criticisms are principally aimed at the aspects of his account that involve adding up the results of shoehorn maneuvers (he thinks that it is an easy thing to do, while they think that it is impossible).

[26] Although Hare often (e.g., in *Moral Thinking*, 41, 59) presents universalizing as a process that results in a claim that contains no individual constants and in which the individual variables are bound by universal quantifiers, he sometimes (e.g., in "Universalisability," in *Essays on the Moral Concepts* [London: Macmillan, 1972], 13–28) writes as if it were sufficient for a claim to contain no individual constants in order to be acceptable as a result of universalization. The argument about *Excalibur* is not affected by

this ambiguity as it can be adapted to both these ways of understanding universalizability. However, the ambiguity becomes relevant if we try an alternative argument against Hare that differs from the one given in the main body of the text in not using a proper name (such as *Excalibur*), but an existential quantifier.

Consider the claim: "Anyone who has the property *F* ought to give *something* to everyone who has the property *G*." Normally, this claim would be rendered as not containing any individual constants but as containing a variable bound by an existential quantifier. What would Hare say about such a claim?

If he decided to stick to the former, stricter way of understanding universalizability, it seems that he would have to say that this claim still needs to be universalized in some way, which strikes one as unnatural.

He could avoid this charge if he opted for the latter way of understanding universalizability (as nothing but elimination of individual constants). But if the notion of universalizability is to be understood in this way, then it becomes too weak for other important purposes. At stage 1 of arguments that involve the shoehorn maneuver we need the former, stronger way of understanding universalizability because at that stage we need to get a variable bound by a *universal* quantifier at the relevant argument-place (otherwise we would never be able to proceed to stage 2).

The obvious way out of this dilemma is to adopt the stronger way of understanding universalizability but to restrict the requirement of universalizability in moral discourse to argument-places for moral agents and argument-places for moral patients.

[27] To be precise, I have to say that my view results in a simpler final analysis of the notion of morality only on the background of other departures from Hare's analysis that I have advocated. Hare's view on this matter did provide for a simpler analysis of the notion of morality when taken together with all other elements of his analysis of that notion, but I hope that I have shown that some of these elements are untenable.

[28] Hare, *Moral Thinking*, 115.

Chapter 3

[1] It is possible to hold both these views, but in that case the considerations of section 3.2 apply.

[2] See part 3 of Hare's *The Language of Morals* (Oxford: Clarendon Press, 1952) for a discussion of the logical relationships among most of these words. In chapter 4 I discuss the question as to whether the noun *right* belongs in the same family of interdefinable words.

[3] ξ and χ are placeholders for either individual variables or individual constants. Of course, when these places are filled by variables, the claim must be completed by suitable quantifiers.

[4] I use the words *obeyed* and *violated* here in such a way that a claim is obeyed by a certain agent if and only if it is not violated by him. This way of talking is somewhat unusual. In normal parlance we would not say that during the last five minutes I kept obeying the moral rule that prohibits murder, unless I had been subjected to a temptation to murder someone during that time. Likewise, we would not say that I obeyed a moral rule that requires one to save those who are drowning in one's vicinity simply by virtue of the fact that no one was drowning in my vicinity. In the way of talking that I am advocating, all these things could be said. In fact it could be said that during the last five minutes I obeyed nondenumerably many moral rules.

Such consequences of this way of talking may sound paradoxical, but they are not any more paradoxical than the well-known paradox of material implication (in fact it is a version of the same paradox). As we have all learned, acquiescing to the notion of material implication in spite of its being somewhat unnatural has important theoretical rewards; and acquiescing to the use of the word *obey* that I am advocating here has similar rewards.

I, of course, just like anyone else, intuitively feel the difference between obeying a rule in an interesting way and obeying it in an uninteresting way. I merely think that there is no reason for restricting the use of the word to interesting cases of obedience.

I do not think that in advocating this way of using the word *obey* I am introducing a new sense of the word. That is, I believe that this way of using it is well within the limits set by its ordinary meaning. That we usually do not use the word in this way need not be accounted for by the features of its meaning because it can be accounted for simply by the fact that it would be, for most everyday purposes, uninteresting.

It is a feature of this use of the word *obey* that, in the majority of instances in which we can say that someone obeyed a moral rule, praise is not even prima facie appropriate. We praise people only in those relatively rare situations when the circumstances bring them close to violating a moral rule and they still do not violate it. On the other hand, for every violation of a moral rule, blame might be prima facie appropriate. This is analogous to our not praising a scientific claim that contains material implication whenever we see something that confirms it, but only when it survives some crucial experiment. On the other hand, a single falsification makes it appropriate to reject or modify a scientific claim.

[5] Some deontic logicians prefer to avoid conditionals within the scope of the operator of obligation and to render what we would normally call conditional duties in other ways because they believe that ordinary conditionals within the scope of the operator of obligation lead to paradoxes (versions of the so-called Ross's Paradox that was originally formulated in terms of disjunctions). However, von Wright, who himself held such a belief for a long time, has more recently argued, in part 2 of "Norms, Truth, and Logic" in *Practical Reason* (Oxford: Basil Blackwell, 1983), that such maneuvers become unnecessary once the nature of the alleged paradoxes is properly understood.

[6] Some people do not like to make moral claims that are too complex. They prefer to express their moral views by making claims whose contents are simple and then saying about each of them that it has such and such exemptions or holds only under such and such conditions or applies only in such and such situations. In other words, instead of expressing all the subtleties and complexities of their moral outlooks within the contents of their moral claims, they prefer to express some of them in the form of metalinguistic remarks about the claims they make.

While such a practice could conceivably be convenient for some purposes, it is definitely not conducive to the most fruitful philosophical discussions. It is not clear how one should go about investigating logical relations between a moral claim that holds only under certain conditions and a moral claim that holds only under some other conditions. Only if these claims are reformulated by incorporating the relevant conditions into their contents, so that we deal with the claims that have conditional contents but hold unconditionally, does the investigation of their logical relations become a manageable task.

[7] It may be worthwhile to note that this is not something that would be peculiar to moral claims: there are other types of speech acts for which an analysis in terms of illocutionary force and propositional content is useful but incomplete in a similar way. See my "Is There More to Speech Acts Than Illocutionary Force and Propositional Content?" *Noûs* 25 (1991): 353–57.

[8] We may link both of them with claims in which agents and/or patients are represented by variables bound by existential quantifiers, but such claims usually play a less important role in moral arguments.

[9] Even those who, like Christopher Stone (*Should Trees Have Standing?: Toward Legal Rights for Natural Objects* [Los Altos, Calif.: William Kaufmann, 1974]), think that the domains of moral agents, and especially of moral patients, are much wider than most people think, have to put some boundaries on them. No one has argued, for example, that mathematical objects can belong to the set of moral patients.

[10] See note 4, above.

[11] I am assuming here that before we try to investigate logical relations between any two claims we shall put some effort into formulating them as precisely as we can (and precise formulations often turn out to be rather complex). I would find it redundant to even mention this assumption were it not for the fact that it is a strategy characteristic of some moral philosophers to pick up a pair of generally accepted moral claims in their everyday, simplified, easy-to-remember formulations that will often be mutually inconsistent, and then marvel over the alleged fact that logic does not apply to moral discourse, or applies only in some peculiar way (so that two inconsistent claims can both be acceptable), without making any attempt to check whether there are (possibly complex, but still) acceptable reformulations of these claims that would make them consistent. It is, by the way, interesting that the philosophers who repeatedly play this trick on moral claims rarely attempt it on scientific claims, although the latter are as susceptible to it as the former. With the exception of Hegelians, philosophers do not marvel over the fact that everyday, simplified, easy-to-remember formulations of the laws of science often generate inconsistencies.

The difference between reasonably precise formulations of
moral claims and their everyday, simplified, easy-to-remember formulations is important in interpreting some pronouncements of
moral philosophers that might appear to be in opposition to the
argument that I am making in this section. Thus, for example,
Alan Goldman has suggested in *The Moral Foundations of Professional Ethics* (Totowa, N.J.: Rowman and Littlefield, 1980) that
some professional roles may turn out to be "strongly differentiated," which in his terminology means that they have their own
moral principles that may override the principles of ordinary
morality. If this is interpreted as meaning that the principles of
some branches of professional ethics may override everyday, simplified, easy-to-remember formulations of ordinary moral
principles, then it is perfectly compatible with what I am saying in
this section. This interpretation of Goldman's view is compatible
with the assumption that acceptability of the rules of any professional ethics ultimately depends on their being consistent with
general moral principles in their precise formulations. Indeed,
some such assumption seems to be implicit in Goldman's own
investigations.

Benjamin Freedman has attempted to defend a view similar to
Goldman's in "A Meta-Ethics for Professional Morality," *Ethics* 89
(1978): 1–19. Concerning Freedman's article, I have nothing to
add to Mike W. Martin's fully convincing criticism in "Rights and
the Meta-Ethics of Professional Morality," *Ethics* 91 (1981): 619–25.
See also Freedman's response "What Really Makes Professional
Morality Different: Response to Martin," *Ethics* 91 (1981): 626–30,
and Martin's final reply "Professional and Ordinary Morality: A
Reply to Freedman," *Ethics* 91 (1981): 631–33.

[12] Treating the discourse of medical ethics as a special type of discourse might appear to be morally innocuous if one restricts
one's attention to some specific contents of medical ethics (the
contents that one happens to find morally acceptable). But notice
that if one treats medical ethics as discourse separate from moral
discourse, that is, as discourse that has its own technique of argumentation, different from moral argumentation, then these
contents will be open to revision without any further reference to
morality, and (depending on what the relevant techniques of
medical-ethics argumentation are supposed to be) the results of
following these revised contents could be morally disastrous.
Therefore, if there were a special discourse of medical ethics,

then (in the absence of some further argument) it would be morally advisable not to enter into it and to discourage everyone from entering into it. Similarly, in the absence of some further argument, it is unclear that it would be prudent to engage in this discourse (unless one were bribed to do so).

[13] N. Fotion, "Range-Rules in Moral Contexts," *Mind* 72 (1963): 556–61; "'All Humans Ought to Be Eliminated,'" *Ethics* 87 (1976): 87–95.

[14] What is given as an example of a range-rule here is an agent-range-rule. In order to deal with the example fully we would need one more range-rule, dealing with the patients.

[15] Michael Tooley, *Abortion and Infanticide* (Oxford: Clarendon Press, 1983), 96–99.

[16] Tooley's discussion is formulated in terms of having rights, rather than being a moral patient: I have reformulated it in order to avoid opening here the issues related to rights that will be discussed in chapter 4. Tooley's own understanding of what it is to have rights allows this reformulation.

[17] The term *moral community* has already been used by contemporary philosophers in similar ways, for example, by Mary Anne Warren in "On the Moral and Legal Status of Abortion," *The Monist* 57 (1973): 43–61. However, the term is sometimes used in an entirely different sense, namely to denote a group of people that share the same moral principles. My use of the term has nothing to do with this second sense.

[18] All this has already been pointed out by Andrew Oldenquist in "Rules and Consequences," *Mind* 75 (1966): 180–92; cf. Hare *The Language of Morals*, section 4.1, and *Freedom and Reason* (Oxford: Clarendon Press, 1963), 124. Unfortunately, many philosophers still need to be reminded of this point.

[19] Derek Parfit, *Reasons and Persons* (Oxford: Oxford University Press, 1984), 443.

[20] See the example of "The Harmless Torturers" in Parfit, *Reasons and Persons*, 80.

[21] Parfit himself, in fact, believes something stronger than this but acknowledges (*Reasons and Persons*, 82) that his stronger view is controversial and that something like what I have formulated here is sufficient for most ends and purposes.

[22] This is the reply to the view that the relevant ascriptions of virtues are not at all analyzable in terms of ascriptions of duties. My opponent might, however, defend a weaker view that these ascriptions of virtues are partially analyzable in terms of ascriptions of duties, that is, that they are to be analyzed in terms of ascriptions of duties and something else. In that case, the reply would apply to that "extra" element in the meaning of virtue-ascriptions: it would then not be clear why one should regard that extra element as belonging to moral discourse. How exactly that would affect the status of virtue-ascriptions would of course depend on what the extra element is supposed to be.

[23] Anyone who is tempted to invoke ancient Greek ethics in discussions of the problems of contemporary ethical theory should consider the following warning from Jonathan Barnes:

> Aristotle's notion of ethics is not quite the same as our present notion of moral philosophy: if we ascribe to Aristotle the aims and interests of Kant or Mill or their modern successors, we shall be in danger of misunderstanding him.
> (It is important not to be misled here by translated terminology. Aristotle refers to his book as *ta ēthika*: the title transliterates to 'The Ethics' but translates rather as 'Matters to do with Character.' Again, English translations abound with such phrases as 'moral virtue': but 'moral virtue' renders either *ēthikē aretē* [properly: 'excellence of character'] or else the plain *aretē* ['excellence' . . .].)
> . . . Indeed, despite the political and social ambience of the *Ethics*, Aristotle shows a remarkable indifference to the effects of the good man's actions on his fellows . . .
> This theory . . . is, I think, well removed from anything that we might be tempted to think of as a system of morality.

(Jonathan Barnes, Introduction to *The Ethics of Aristotle* [Harmondsworth, England: Penguin Books, 1976], 27, 31.)

[24] The same type of argument I am using in this section against those who regard some virtue-ascriptions as not analyzable in

terms of duty-ascriptions can be used against those who would argue that certain sorts of ecological concerns (that are sometimes termed "moral") cannot be expressed so as to fit my analysis of morality. That is, the argument against them would be that most of such concerns ultimately have something to do with how ecological policies affect moral patients, and that it is not clear why any outstanding concerns (that cannot be so analyzed) should be regarded as moral. In fact it seems that at least one of the proponents of such views would be happy to accept this argument as he himself suggests that (in order to understand such concerns fully) "we may need to become less moralistic" (John Rodman, "The Liberation of Nature?" *Inquiry* 20 [1977]: 103).

[25] See, for example, Harry S. Silverstein, "Universality and Treating Persons as Persons," *The Journal of Philosophy* 71 (1974): 57–71, especially page 64; Robert Nozick, *Philosophical Explanations* (Cambridge, Mass.: Harvard University Press, 1981), 451; cf. Christina Hoff Sommers, "Filial Morality," *The Journal of Philosophy* 83 (1986): 439–56.

Chapter 4

[1] According to an often quoted formulation of this view, "right and duty are different names for the same normative relation, according to the point of view from which it is regarded." (S. I. Benn and R. S. Peters, *Social Principles and the Democratic State* [London: George Allen & Unwin, 1959], 89).

[2] It should be noted that *correlativity* and related terms are not used uniformly in the contemporary philosophical literature about the relation between rights and duties. For example, David Lyons in "The Correlativity of Rights and Duties," *Noûs* 4 (1970): 45–55, uses them in a sense that is much wider than mine.

[3] I shall not attempt to do that because the disagreement between correlativists and such radical anticorrelativists would probably turn out to hinge on very fundamental disagreements about the methods of philosophical analysis and a discussion of these disagreements would lead us too far away from the relatively specific problems of this chapter (see section 3 of the introduction for a brief statement of the methods of analysis on which the investigations in this book are based). An example of such radical

anticorrelativism is Alan R. White, *Rights* (Oxford: Clarendon Press, 1984).

[4] For examples of these objections, see H. L. A. Hart, *Bentham* (London: British Academy, 1962), section 4; David Lyons, "Rights, Claimants, and Beneficiaries," in David Lyons, ed., *Rights* (Belmont, Calif.: Wadsworth, 1979), 58–77; Carl Wellman, *A Theory of Rights: Persons Under Laws, Institutions, and Morals* (Totowa, N.J.: Rowman & Allanheld, 1985), 25.

[5] I use the word *respected* here in a sense that makes it analytic that a right is respected if and only if it is not violated. See note 4 to chapter 3.

[6] This point (we can summarize it as "no violation without a violator") has been elaborated in Heather J. Gert, "Rights and Rights Violators: A New Approach to the Nature of Rights," *The Journal of Philosophy* 87 (1990): 688–94. It has the consequence that every right is a right against someone, in spite of McCloskey's repeated insistence on the opposite. McCloskey claimed, for example, that "the right of the tennis club member to play on the club courts is a right to play, not a right against some vague group of potential or possible obstructors," and that the last person in the universe would still have rights (H. J. McCloskey, "Rights," *The Philosophical Quarterly* 15 [1965]: 118, 119). I have not been able to discern any persuasive arguments for his position, but I believe that it results from his neglect of the distinction between rights and liberty-rights.

[7] This feature of talk about rights is sometimes called the "dynamic aspect of rights" by philosophers who do not find it pernicious. (J. Raz, "On the Nature of Rights," *Mind* 93 [1984]: 200).

[8] In spite of the proliferation of writings about rights in recent years the terminological problem that I discussed in this section has not received sufficient attention, apart from a remark on page 38 of Geoffrey Russell Grice's book *The Grounds of Moral Judgement* (Cambridge: Cambridge University Press, 1967).

   The way of talking about rights that I advocated in this section disposes of the paradox of "a right to do wrong." Saying "It is morally wrong to defend your racist views publicly" and at the same time "You have a moral right to defend your racist views publicly" may *seem* paradoxical; but the seeming paradox disappears when the latter is transformed into "You have a moral right that no one forcibly prevents you from defending your racist views publicly." Cf. Jeremy Waldron, "A Right to Do Wrong," *Ethics* 92 (1981): 21–39.

[9] See, for example, W. D. Ross, *The Right and the Good* (Oxford: Clarendon Press, 1930), 48–50.

[10] Immanuel Kant, *Lectures on Ethics* (Indianapolis: Hackett, 1980), 239–41.

[11] For example, if the duty to abstain from cruelty to animals is not owed to animals but to potential human spectators of such cruelties, then it seems quite reasonable to say that the potential human spectators have some right in the matter.

[12] Hart, *Bentham*, 314.

[13] Lyons, "Rights, Claimants, and Beneficiaries," 68–69.

[14] H. L. A. Hart, "Are There Any Natural Rights?" *The Philosophical Review* 64 (1955): 175–91.

[15] Ibid., footnote 7.

[16] At least this is my reading of his article. The article itself is not entirely explicit on this point. Cf. Frankena's remark on page 213 of his article "Natural and Inalienable Rights," *The Philosophical Review* 64 (1955) in which he says, "I am not sure whether he [Hart] denies that obligations entail rights or not."

[17] For example, if the duty to abstain from cruelty to animals is not owed to animals then it may be that it is owed to potential human spectators of such cruelties.

[18] Hart, "Are There Any Natural Rights?" 183.

[19] Hart's much later article, "Bentham on Legal Rights" (in David Lyons, ed., *Rights*), contains something that might at first glance seem to be an answer to the question that troubles me here, namely the question as to what the ways are in which a right-holder has control over the freedom of another. He says that the "fullest measure of control comprises three distinguishable elements: (i) the right holder may waive or extinguish the duty or leave it in existence; (ii) after breach or threatened breach of a duty he may

leave it 'unenforced' or may 'enforce' it by suing for compensation or, in certain cases, for an injunction or mandatory order to restrain the continued or further breach of duty; and (iii) he may waive or extinguish the obligation to pay compensation to which the breach gives rise" (in Lyons, ed., *Rights*, 141). However, one should not forget that the article in which he says this is an article about *legal* rights. Although these remarks may be fine as parts of an analysis of the concept of a legal right, they are of little use for our understanding of moral rights, which are the subject of his 1955 article. An attempt to include provisions like (ii) or (iii) in an analysis of the concept of a moral right would fail for the same reasons for which Feinberg's analysis (discussed in the next subsection) fails. Concerning provision (i) see subsection 4.4.3.

[20] Hart himself notices this: Hart, "Are There Any Natural Rights?" 177.

[21] Joel Feinberg, "The Nature and Value of Rights," *The Journal of Value Inquiry* 4 (1970): 243–57.

[22] William Nelson, "On the Alleged Importance of Moral Rights," *Ratio* 18 (1976): 145–55.

[23] Point 3 is in fact dubious as Feinberg does not make it clear what rules the institution of claiming in morality could have in addition to the rules for recognizing claimants.

[24] Jan Narveson, "Commentary [on Feinberg's article]," *The Journal of Value Inquiry* 4 (1970): 258.

[25] See note 19, above. Carl Wellman's book, *A Theory of Rights*, also contains suggestions that some of the phrases involving the word *right* that we use in ordinary moral discourse (e.g., "right to social security" discussed on page 181 of the book) should be analyzed in terms of someone's duties (as the "defining core") and a power of waiver (as one of the associated elements). However, this aspect of Wellman's view is not opposed to correlativism, as he claims only that some particular phrases involving the word *right* should be so analyzed and not that it is a feature of the meaning of the word *right* itself.

[26] This type of situation has recently been discussed in detail by Jeremy Waldron. See note 8, above.

Chapter 5

[1] Some readers may be tempted to suggest a very easy way of answering that question. According to this suggestion we should first look at what sorts of properties and relations are ascribed to moral agents and moral patients in the content of our moral rules. In the content of our moral rules we will typically find relations such as lying, stealing, helping, and so on. We should then ask what the individuals are of which it can be meaningfully asked whether they stand in such relations (possess such properties). These individuals are the members of the moral community.

We only need to look at a couple of examples in order to see that this will not do. The relation of injuring would presumably be a paradigm of a relation that is found in the content of a moral rule. This relation is defined for individuals like Peter and Paula, but it is not defined only for them. It makes perfect sense to say that a falling rock has injured someone. However, Paula's injuring Peter would count as a violation of the rule that prohibits everyone from injuring anyone else, but a falling rock's injuring Paula would not. The relation is the same in both cases, but in the first case it takes its terms from the moral community, while in the second, the individual who does the injuring comes from outside the domain of moral agents. Another example is the one that we are already familiar with: Paula's striking Peter as opposed to lightning's striking a tree.

One might now try to rescue the suggestion by arguing that the sense of *strikes* in "Paula strikes Peter" is different from its sense in "Lightning strikes a tree," that we use *strikes* for what are, in fact, two different relations. The word *injuring* and many others might be ambiguous in some similar way. Once we remove these ambiguities we shall be able to apply the suggestion as initially formulated.

However, this reply involves a circularity, as there does not seem to be any way to specify the allegedly different senses of these words independently of specifying the domains of individuals that can enter the corresponding relations.

[2] John Harris, *The Value of Life* (London: Routledge & Kegan Paul, 1985), 10.

[3] Notice that what is relevant here is thinking that it is *impossible* for a certain property to ever belong to a member of the moral community, and not thinking that a certain property never has

belonged and never will belong to a member of a moral community. In moral discussions (and especially in philosophical moral
discussions) we sometimes deal with properties of which we think
never have belonged and probably never will belong, but nevertheless could belong, to members of the moral community.

[4] One example of an analysis of the notion of morality that exhibits
this error is Frankena's analysis, according to which the very
notion of morality requires that moral agents be rational beings
and that moral patients be sentient beings. See his first Carus
Lecture "Must Morality Have an Object?" *Monist* 63 (1980): 3–26.
Another such example is Warnock's analysis: see *The Object of
Morality* (London: Methuen, 1971), 143–52. A similar error is
made by Peter Singer in sections 11.4 and 11.5 of "Reasoning
towards Utilitarianism," in Douglas Seanor and N. Fotion, eds.,
Hare and Critics: Essays on Moral Thinking (Oxford: Clarendon
Press, 1988), where he treats people who differ in their views
about membership in the moral community as having different
notions of universalizability.

[5] Section 3 of "Abortion and the Golden Rule," *Philosophy & Public
Affairs* 4 (1975), in particular, suggests that Hare was not aware of
the problem that I have presented here. Cf. section 11.5 of
Freedom and Reason (Oxford: Clarendon Press, 1963).

[6] Raz at one point ("Principles of Equality," *Mind* 87 [1978]: 326)
seems to be suggesting that there is no independent way of identi-
fying individuals who are moral patients ("moral subjects" as he
calls them), that is, that the question has no answer; but he does
not elaborate the point and makes no attempt to explore the consequences of his suggestion for our moral behavior.

[7] A criterion that may seem to be popular (perhaps even the most
popular) is that of "being human." However, of all those who talk
as if they accept this criterion, very few would, after some questioning and a few thought-experiments, stick to the view that being a
member of the biological species *Homo sapiens* is necessary or sufficient or even relevant for membership in the moral community.
That is, after some questioning it usually turns out that what they
really have in mind as the criterion for membership is some combination of mental properties that are typically, but not necessarily,
instantiated in members of the species *Homo sapiens* and that
could, at least in principle, be instantiated in other types of beings.

This point has been persuasively defended by Michael Tooley in *Abortion and Infanticide* (Oxford: Clarendon Press, 1983).

[8] Hilary Putnam, "Robots: Machines or Artificially Created Life?" *The Journal of Philosophy* 61 (1964): 668–91.

[9] Amelie O. Rorty, "Slaves and Machines," *Analysis* 22 (1962): 118–20.

[10] See also Richard Rorty, *Philosophy and the Mirror of Nature* (Princeton: Princeton University Press, 1979), especially 99, 127, 190–91.

[11] Cf. Ludwig Wittgenstein, *Philosophical Investigations*, trans. G. E. M. Anscombe (Oxford: Basil Blackwell, 1958), IIiv: "My attitude towards him is an attitude towards a soul. I am not of the *opinion* that he has a soul."

[12] *A* and *P* may turn out to be the same criterion.

[13] See Michael Dummett, *Frege: Philosophy of Language* (London: Duckworth, 1973), 567–69.

[14] Richard E. Flathman, "Equality and Generalization, A Formal Analysis," in J. Roland Pennock and John W. Chapman, eds., *Nomos IX: Equality* (New York: Atherton Press, 1967), 49, 51.

[15] See, for example, Kai Nielsen, *Equality and Liberty: A Defense of Radical Egalitarianism* (Totowa, N.J.: Rowman and Allanheld, 1985).

[16] However, the irrational attachment to the words *equal* and *equality* can be so strong that even a philosopher like Bernard Williams, whose own analysis shows that these words are bound to be put to many radically different uses (so that mutually contradictory claims can be defended by appeals to principles involving equality), can still be reluctant to draw the conclusion that it would be best to avoid them in serious discussions. Instead, he is happy to say that "if the idea of equality ranges as widely as I have suggested, this type of conflict is bound to arise with it" ("The Idea of Equality," in Peter Laslett and W. G. Runciman, eds. *Philosophy, Politics and Society*, 2nd series [Oxford: Basil Blackwell, 1962], 129).

[17] Those who put forward such principles sometimes make explicit their hope to avoid the difficulties that beset other principles

involving equality. See, for example, the first paragraph of Stanley I. Benn's article "Egalitarianism and the Equal Consideration of Interests," in *Nomos IX: Equality*, 62.

[18] Ronald Dworkin, *Taking Rights Seriously* (Cambridge, Mass.: Harvard University Press, 1977), 272–78. Dworkin, of course, believes that his principle is a substantive moral principle and actually tries to show that significant claims follow from it—for example, that we should disregard people's external preferences (234–35, 275). But Dworkin's supposed derivation of this claim from the principle of equal concern and respect is arbitrary; his opponent can equally well argue that the principle of equal concern and respect entails that we should be equally concerned with all preferences (personal and external) and there is nothing in the meaning of "equal concern and respect" to decide the issue one way rather than the other. The principle of disregard for external preferences may well be an acceptable principle (see my "External and Now-For-Then Preferences in Hare's Theory," *Dialogue* 29 [1990]: 305–10), but "equal concern and respect" is of no use in establishing it. The impression that the principle of equal concern and respect does entail that only nonexternal preferences are morally relevant may be due to Dworkin's choice to label these preferences "personal." But this choice is itself arbitrary.

[19] Note that we have assumed that you know the functions of schmersons and how they are selected. This knowledge presumably contains all the defining characteristics of the concept of a schmerson. Therefore, it cannot be argued that your trouble is caused by the lack of knowledge of the defining characteristics of that concept.

[20] A typical article on the topic claims, for example, that "treating an individual as a person in the present sense means sensitivity to and sympathy with his needs, interests, problems and difficulties, projects, aspirations, concerns and goals; it means concern, even caring for his welfare, rather than indifference to whether he lives or dies, is happy or miserable, successful or frustrated, failing. It means making him feel that he matters, his life matters." (Haig Khatchadourian, "The Human Right to Be Treated as a Person," *The Journal of Value Inquiry* 19 [1985]: 193). All the things mentioned in this passage are surely important and worthwhile; but can all this really be a part of the meaning of the phrase in question? And if the verb *mean* is not used here in its strict sense, then

we need independent arguments in favor of treating people in the ways that are listed in this passage.

21 It is, for example, common to accuse utilitarians of not respecting a certain individual as a person in situations in which their theory commits them to subjecting that individual to drastic suffering for the sole reason that such suffering will increase the overall utility. But utilitarians, if they wanted to use the language of "respect for persons" could always reply that their opponent is the one who lacks respect for persons because he fails to respect all those other persons whose utility would be increased as a result of the sacrifice. As long as both sides persist in arguing in terms of "respect for persons," the issue is bound to remain unresolved, as there is nothing in the meaning of *respect-for-persons* to decide it either way.

22 This was not intended to imply that everyone should end up with the same amount of happiness.

23 This is trivial because it is analytic that members of the moral community are precisely those who "count for one" for the purposes of moral discourse.

24 Examples range from Kant, via Gregory Vlastos ("Justice and Equality," in A. I. Melden, ed., *Human Rights* [Belmont, Calif.: Wadsworth, 1970], 76–95) to contemporary philosophers such as Tom Regan (*The Case for Animal Rights* [Berkeley: University of California Press, 1983]) and Jean Hampton (*Forgiveness and Mercy* [Cambridge: Cambridge University Press, 1988, co-authored with Jeffrie G. Murphy]).

25 Assuming that (3) is understood as implying that the individuals in question would themselves be wronged if they were not treated in these ways.

26 See, for example, Regan's criticism of "perfectionism," in *The Case for Animal Rights*, 237.

Chapter 6

1 This example is borrowed from Alfred MacKay (who used it in a somewhat different context), "Extended Sympathy and Interpersonal Utility Comparisons," *The Journal of Philosophy* 83 (1986): 318.

[2] Our interlocutor could object that he cannot simply imagine that he is watching "whatever it is that is going on behind the wall" because it is a feature of the process of imagining that it always has to be imagining of something fully specific. This objection has a respectable history: it has been pointed out a long time ago that it is impossible "to have, an idea that shall correspond with the description . . . of the general idea of a triangle—which is neither oblique nor rectangle, equilateral, equicrural nor scalenon, but all and none of these at once" (George Berkeley, *The Principles of Human Knowledge* [Glasgow: Collins, 1962], introduction, section 13).

One could attempt to meet this objection within the field of philosophy of mind by embarking on an investigation of the process of imagining in order to see whether imagining always has to be imagining of something fully specific. However, such investigation would be long and laborious and its results controversial.

Fortunately, we need not meet this objection head-on: we can get around it by using the same strategy that we use to overcome Berkeley's problem with respect to triangles in many cases in which imagining a triangle is not an end in itself but has some further purpose. If I tell someone, in the course of teaching him geometry, "Imagine a triangle," and in reply to that I get the Berkeleyan objection, I would probably say "O.K., maybe you are right, maybe it is impossible to imagine a triangle *simpliciter*, but then please imagine some randomly selected triangle."

Similarly, if my interlocutor insists on imagining some specific scene as going on behind the wall, and I do not think that the content of the scene is relevant for my argument, then I can tell him "O.K., then please imagine the specific scene that you will select by some random procedure from the range of scenes that may be going on behind the wall."

After a shoehorn maneuver is performed in this way there might be some lingering doubt that the particular choice that our interlocutor has made has somehow affected the outcome. That could spoil the effect of the argument. This problem fortunately has a simple remedy. If we have such doubts we can run the experiment several times, each time with a fresh random choice. If we want to know more about how the accuracy of the outcome increases with the number of such repetitions of the shoehorn maneuver, and how to ensure that the selection is really random, we can borrow statistical methods that have already been developed for the purposes of empirical research.

[3] Some authors, such as Zeno Vendler (in chapter 3 of *The Matter of Minds* [Oxford: Clarendon Press, 1984]), insist on the distinction between:

(*a*) I imagine having the property *F*.

(*b*) I imagine *my* having the property *F*.

If one uses a formulation like (*a*) then the sort of contradiction that I am talking about is not obvious. But the appearance created by formulations like (*a*) is without much significance: the contradiction cannot be eliminated by the simple expedient of talking in terms of (*a*). When I imagine having the property *F*, I certainly do not imagine *any* individual's having the property *F*. How does my imagining having the property *F* differ from my imagining any individual's having the property? Well, it differs because it is my imagining *my* having the property *F*.

The difference between (*a*) and (*b*), which is merely a matter of style, should not be confused with the very important difference between both of them on one hand and on the other hand:

(*c*) I imagine Mane Hajdin's having the property *F*.

(I assume here that I am Mane Hajdin.) It seems that formulations of the type (*b*) are sometimes used to express something that would be better expressed by formulations of the type (*c*). See also the following note.

[4] The properties that something must have in order to be *myself* need not be the same properties that something must have in order to be Mane Hajdin, in spite of the fact that *I* as used by me and *Mane Hajdin* as used by anyone happen to have the same reference. The argument presented in this section is only about the former ones and has nothing to do with whatever essential properties might be associated with ordinary proper names like *Mane Hajdin*.

In *Moral Thinking: Its Levels, Method, and Point* (Oxford: Clarendon Press, 1981), 120, Hare insists that the essence that (according to some theories of naming) is associated with an ordinary proper name will not be the essence of *I* as used by the bearer of that name. This claim, with which I agree, does not, however, provide sufficient ground for the much stronger claim that Hare immediately proceeds to make, and with which I disagree, namely that *I* (as used by a specific person) has no essence. That the essence of *Mane Hajdin* is not the same as the essence of myself, does not entail that *myself* has no essence: it may be that it has some other essence. Hare does not consider that possibility, and provides no reason for not considering it, and this seems to be one of the crucial flaws in his argument. (This also applies to what he says in Douglas Seanor and N. Fotion, eds., *Hare and Critics: Essays on* Moral Thinking [Oxford: Clarendon Press, 1988], 281.)

On the next page of *Moral Thinking*, Hare himself characterizes this argument of his as "bald and brief" and tries to remedy this by referring his readers to an article by Zeno Vendler. However, Vendler's theory (both as presented in this article and in some of his more recent writings) suffers from what is basically the same weakness, as I show in section 6.5.

[5] Note also that I have defined my essential properties as those that are necessary for being myself. I am not saying that "being myself" can be reduced to a list of necessary and sufficient properties. See the discussion of Kripke's theory in section 6.4.

[6] Hare, "Comments," in *Hare and Critics*, 283; see also R. M. Hare, "Moral Reasoning about the Environment," *Journal of Applied Philosophy* 4 (1987): 7.

[7] Saul A. Kripke, *Naming and Necessity* (Cambridge, Mass.: Harvard University Press, 1980); first published in Donald Davidson and Gilbert Harman, eds., *Semantics of Natural Language* (Dordrecht, Netherlands: D. Reidel Publishing Company, 1972), 253–355.

[8] Kripke, *Naming and Necessity*, 44, 50. Judging by the fact that it is so often quoted, this mockery seems to have persuaded many people to accept Kripke's theory of transworld identification. This is hardly justified as the following two theses are clearly different:

(*a*) possible worlds are not discovered but stipulated;

(*b*) transworld identification is a matter of stipulation and not of discovery.

The mockery about telescopes contributes only to the defense of (*a*) and not of the more controversial (*b*), which is not entailed by (*a*). It is possible to agree with Kripke in believing that possible worlds are stipulated and not discovered, yet to regard these stipulations as purely qualitative and think that the questions of transworld identification are not to be resolved by further stipulations, but by discovering the consequences of our other stipulations.

[9] Kripke, *Naming and Necessity*, 46.

[10] Ibid., 77.

[11] For a condensed statement of this point see notes 56 and 57 to *Naming and Necessity*. In the main body of the text of *Naming and Necessity* the point is made by means of examples.

[12] See, for example, Michael Dummett, *Frege: Philosophy of Language* (London: Duckworth, 1973) appendix to chapter 5: "Note on an Attempted Refutation of Frege"; John R. Searle, *Intentionality: An Essay in the Philosophy of Mind* (Cambridge: Cambridge University Press, 1983), chapter 9: "Proper Names and Intentionality"; M. S. Price, "On the Non-Necessity of Origin," *Canadian Journal of Philosophy* 12 (1982): 33–45.

[13] The most famous such result is Parfit's theory of personal identity, first formulated in "Personal Identity," *The Philosophical Review* 80 (1971): 3–27. A more recent formulation of Parfit's theory can be found in part 3 of *Reasons and Persons* (Oxford: Oxford University Press, 1984). See also David Lewis, "Survival and Identity," in Amélie Oksenberg Rorty, ed., *The Identities of Persons* (Berkeley: University of California Press, 1976), 17–40; John Perry, "The Importance of Being Identical," in *The Identities of Persons*, 67–90; Derek Parfit, "Lewis, Perry, and What Matters," in *The Identities of Persons*, 91–107.

[14] The only exceptions I have encountered were in conversations with people who have allowed their day-to-day thinking to be influenced by reading Kripke.

[15] One rather uneconomic way of effecting a compromise between Kripke's theory and such anti-Kripkean intuitions is to say that each of us somehow embodies two persons: a "metaphysical" and an "ethical" one, where the former, but not the latter, has its essence determined by the relevant sperm and egg. This has been suggested by Anthony Appiah, "'But Would That Still Be Me?': Notes on Gender, 'Race,' Ethnicity, as Sources of 'Identity,'" *The Journal of Philosophy* 87 (1990): 493–99.

[16] Some Kripkeans may be tempted to argue that the explanation has been provided by Kripke's separation of a prioricity and necessity. That something is conceivable means that we do not know a priori that it is not the case, but, they would argue, because of this separation, that has nothing to do with what is possible. On that interpretation, my sperm-and-egg essence puts limits on what is possible for me to be, but it does not in any way constrain what is conceivable for me to be.

A short response to this is that *if* Kripke's theory really *were* about possibility and necessity in some sense that is unrelated to what is conceivable, then I would be entitled to completely ignore it: what is needed in shoehorn maneuvers is conceivability and not possibility in that other sense (whatever it might be). A longer response is needed, however, because this is not what Kripke's theory is about.

It is indeed part of Kripke's theory that a prioricity on one hand, and necessity and possibility on the other are not related in the straightforward way in which they traditionally have been thought to be related. There are, according to him, situations that are conceivable (i.e., situations that can be "described" without contradiction) and nevertheless impossible. Kripke's theory however does provide for a connection between a prioricity and necessity, only it does so in a more roundabout way. According to Kripke, the following is known a priori:

If I actually originated from the sperm S and egg E, then I necessarily originated from S and E.

The negation of that, namely

I actually originated from S and E, and it is possible that I did not originate from S and E

is, according to Kripke's theory, inconceivable and self-contradictory. It is this kind of connection that enables Kripke himself to appeal to inconceivability in his own discussions of what is necessary (*Naming and Necessity*, 113 [notice the word *imagine* in "what is harder to imagine is her (Queen Elizabeth's) being born of different parents"], 114, 47).

Thus, Kripke's theory allows for my entertaining the supposition that I originated from a sperm and egg different from the sperm and egg from which I actually originated only if I am ignorant (or pretend to be ignorant) about the latter. It does not allow for my entertaining that supposition *together with* my holding the true belief as to what sperm and egg I actually originated from. And yet, I often do (what at least appears to be) precisely that, and I suspect that most people do similar things. When I consider the (apparent) possibility of my possessing the age, genetic makeup, and related features of Nixon, I do not have to forget or repress my knowledge about my actual origin. I can talk about my actual origins and my (seemingly) possible different origins in the same breath, and be (apparently) understood. On Kripke's theory such understanding cannot be genuine, because such talk is self-contradictory. It is a significant weakness of his theory that it offers no account of why the understanding seems genuine and why the supposed contradictions do not seem to be contradictions. The point made in the body of the text thus cannot be dismissed by invoking the Kripkean separation of a prioricity and necessity.

Can the problem that I have raised regarding *I* also be raised regarding ordinary proper names such as *Nixon?* It can. One can complain that it is, according to Kripke, self-contradictory to say "Nixon actually originated from *S* and *E* and it is possible that Nixon did not actually originate from *S* and *E*," while to many people it does not seem self-contradictory. However, here Kripke can produce a reasonably plausible explanation as to why this does not seem self-contradictory. He can say that what the people who do not see the self-contradiction really have in mind is "Nixon originated from *S* and *E* and it is possible that someone who has such and such properties (that are actually possessed by Nixon) did not originate from *S* and *E*," which is, of course, perfectly noncontradictory in any theory. This argument may work in the third person, but it is very difficult to accept it in the first person because an attempt to substitute "someone who has such and such properties" for *I* would simply destroy the first person character of the sentence. The problem that I have raised thus applies to *myself* in a way in which it does not apply to ordinary proper names.

This note was prompted by Randy Carter's comments on my paper "Parfit, Kripke, and Personal Identity Across Possible Worlds," presented at the 1991 Central Division Meeting of the American Philosophical Association.

[17] The same implausible consequence would follow if we based our account of the moral community on some theory that answers the question of transworld identification in terms of "branching off" from a single earlier individual. See, for example, J. L. Mackie, "*De* What *Re* Is *De Re* Modality?" *The Journal of Philosophy* 71 (1974): 551–61.

[18] This has been overlooked by Mary Bittner Wiseman, who seems to think that Kripke's theory entails exactly the opposite, namely that "there is no metaphysical barrier to the empathetic identification of one person with another" ("Empathetic Identification," *American Philosophical Quarterly* 15 [1978], 110). She seems unaware that for any person, most of the other persons around him could not have originated from the same sperm and egg as he did. Cf. Shalom Lappin, "Moral Judgments and Identity across Possible Worlds," *Ratio* 20 (1978): 69–74.

Wiseman, moreover, without providing any argument, interprets (on the same page) Kripke's view that "we cannot imagine . . . that an object, given the object it is, should be of a different kind" as entailing that a person cannot imagine not being a person but as definitely not entailing that a woman cannot imagine being a man (a male person). But this is not such straightforward matter. Until some further argument is provided, the thesis that we cannot imagine an object to belong to a kind different from the kind to which it actually belongs, leaves it up for grabs what counts as *a kind* in the relevant sense. Someone could accept this thesis and at the same time think that *women* rather than *persons* constitute a kind in the relevant sense (in which case he would regard the thesis as entailing that a woman cannot imagine being a man). There is nothing in either *Naming and Necessity* or Wiseman's article that we could appeal to in order to convince him that he is wrong.

[19] Kripke, *Naming and Necessity*, note 12 to the preface.

[20] By "my present temporal stage" I mean my total present mental state, without implying anything as to whether there is some sort of substance (Cartesian Ego) underlying this mental state or whether it is simply a Humean, free-floating, mental state without any underlying substance. The "present" here should not be understood as referring to a single instant, as there are probably no instantaneous mental states, but as referring to some relatively short span of time that is still sufficiently long to accommodate something that can be called a mental state.

[21] Again, "continuant" should not be understood as implying the existence of some continuing substance. Something can be a continuant without being a substance, for example by being a collection of mental states that are interrelated in a certain way.

[22] Cf. David Lewis, "Attitudes *De Dicto* and *De Se*," *The Philosophical Review* 88 (1979): 527, 530–31.

[23] I use the phrase "personal *identity*" in a noncommittal way, that is, I regard this as a phrase that we adopt for the purpose of handling a certain set of issues before we know what the resolution of these issues is. This use of the phrase is compatible with our eventually resolving these issues in terms of relations other than the relation of identity. The same applies to my use of "transworld *identification*."

[24] On this account, transworld identification of myself$_c$ is analogous to transworld identification of John's family (assuming that we are interested in the identification of John's *family*, rather than individuals who happen to belong to that family). If we wanted to connect John's-family-in-this-world with John's-family-in-*W*, we would not apply our preferred account of transworld identification directly. We would first apply the account to John and connect John-in-this-world with John-in-*W*. John's-family-in-*W* would then be a collection of all and only those individuals in *W* who turn out to stand in the appropriate relations to John-in-*W*.

[25] I can, as it were, *access* the lives that I can lead (or could have lead) at different points. When I consider a possible history of my life, it certainly makes some difference whether I imagine myself at the age of 25 (remembering only parts of that life-history prior to that age and merely anticipating all the parts that are supposed to come after that age) or myself at the age of 30 (remembering all things that happened before that age, including what happened at the age of 25). This is so even if we assume that each of these two life histories, when considered as a whole, is indistinguishable from the other. Thinking about personal identity across possible worlds in the way that is suggested here enables us to account for this difference.

[26] The whole of part 4 of Parfit's *Reasons and Persons* is based on the assumption that "sperm-and-egg" can be used as the criterion of personal identity across possible worlds (if not across all possible worlds, then at least across those possible worlds that share some important characteristics of the actual world). He does not provide much of an argument for using this criterion and does not seem to notice that using it does not fit very well with his own theory of personal identity over time (as presented in part 3 of the

same book), which takes myself$_p$ as more basic than myself$_c$. See also subsection 3.6.3, above.

[27] The way of dealing with the truth that I might have been very different from the way I actually am that is presented in David Lewis, *On the Plurality of Worlds* (Oxford: Basil Blackwell, 1986), 254–55, is therefore inapplicable here.

[28] To use the word *counterpart* for such an undemanding relation may be somewhat misleading (in the light of the purpose for which the notion of a counterpart was originally introduced), but it is not incorrect: David Lewis, "Individuation by Acquaintance and by Stipulation," *The Philosophical Review* 92 (1983): 27.

[29] As has been shown by Shalom Lappin, "Moral Judgments and Identity across Possible Worlds."

[30] Lewis, "Individuation by Acquaintance and by Stipulation," 31.

[31] Hare certainly created an appearance of having made this assumption himself. Thus, in "Relevance," (in Alvin I. Goldman and Jaegwon Kim, eds., *Values and Morals* [Dordrecht, Netherlands: D. Reidel Publishing Company, 1978], 83), he says: "Let us simply suppose (*pace* Leibniz) that there are two possible world-histories which are identical in all their universal properties and differ solely in the roles occupied in them by different individuals." However, his recent response to Vendler's criticism (*Hare and Critics*, 285) reveals that he intended such remarks to be interpreted loosely and that he would not really want to endorse the approach presented in section 6.4 (insofar as it is different from the approach that will be discussed in this section).

[32] Lewis, "Individuation by Acquaintance and by Stipulation"; *On the Plurality of Worlds*, section 4.4; "Attitudes *De Dicto* and *De Se*."

[33] Vendler, "Changing Places?" in *Hare and Critics*, 171–83. See also *The Matter of Minds*, and "A Note to the Paralogisms," in Gilbert Ryle, ed., *Contemporary Aspects of Philosophy* (Stocksfield, England: Oriel Press, 1976), 111–21. We should remember that a reference to Vendler's "A Note to the Paralogisms" plays a crucial role in Hare's exposition of his views about the shoehorn maneuver: Hare, *Moral Thinking*, 119.

[34] Cf. John Perry, "The Problem of the Essential Indexical," *Noûs* 13 (1979): 3–21.

[35] Vendler seems to think something like this. In "Changing Places?" after pointing out that Hare has totally overlooked the possibility of this argument, he suggests that its acceptance makes moral thinking easier ("Changing Places?" 182), and in *The Matter of Minds*, 15, after discussing some problems with representing other possible worlds, he says "This difficulty, however, does not apply to the representation of other minds in *this* world."

[36] For example, in section 13.7 of "Changing Places?"

[37] Vendler, *The Matter of Minds*, 17ff, 29.

[38] Ibid., 14.

[39] Ibid., 6.

[40] Vendler, "A Note to the Paralogisms," 117.

[41] "*The world is such* that it contains beings which offer, as it were, anchors to subjectivity" (Vendler, *The Matter of Minds*, 14, italics mine).

[42] These are the intuitions that are swept under the carpet by Vendler's casual use of the notion of "deserving individuals."

[43] The "accessibility" as defined here can be regarded as one among various kinds of accessibility in the sense introduced in Lewis, "Individuation by Acquaintance and by Stipulation," 30–31.

[44] Vendler may be right in insisting that transference of consciousness cannot be understood without the Kantian notion of transcendental self, and it may nevertheless be that transference always involves the empirical self as well, and indeed that it is logically impossible for it not to involve the empirical self. If the transference of consciousness from *a* to *b* did not, in any way, involve *a*'s empirical self, then it would be impossible to characterize it as transference *from a*. In other words, without referring to my empirical self we could not distinguish *my* imagining *b*'s properties as mine from *your* imagining *b*'s properties as yours or

from some unspecified person's imagining *b*'s properties as his (as well as from *b*'s actually, and not in imagination possessing these properties—see James McGilvray, review of *The Matter of Minds, Canadian Philosophical Reviews* 6 [1986]: 253). This would, among other things, have the consequence that it would be impossible to profit from transference in our ethical discussions.

Chapter 7

[1] It is important not to confuse relativism about membership in the moral community with the thesis that criteria for membership in the moral community are vague, as has been done by Jane English, "Abortion and the Concept of a Person," *Canadian Journal of Philosophy* 5 (1975): 235, and David S. Levin, "Abortion, Personhood, and Vagueness," *The Journal of Value Inquiry* 19 (1985): 197–209. The latter thesis is also justified: whatever criterion for membership we adopt, there will probably be a large gray area between the cases that clearly satisfy the criterion and the cases that clearly do not. But the problems that surround membership of, say, fetuses (the class that English and Levin are particularly interested in) in the moral community cannot be accounted for by simply saying that our criteria for membership are vague and that fetuses are somewhere in the gray area. The case of fetuses is not parallel to what we find in the standard examples of things that are in the gray area of a vague criterion, such as roller skates (to take Hart's well-known example) that neither clearly satisfy nor clearly fail to satisfy the criteria for being a vehicle. People who are familiar with the meaning of the word *vehicle* will usually *agree* that roller skates are boundary cases of a vehicle (unless they have some vested interest in disagreeing). The case of fetuses is seriously problematic precisely because there are people who regard fetuses not as boundary cases but rather as clear-cut cases of members of the moral community and also people who regard fetuses as clear-cut cases of nonmembers of the community.

[2] The argument of this section provides, among other things, an explanation of why it is so rare.

[3] Sometimes one might succeed in enlisting the cooperation of others by merely pretending that one engages in moral discourse, but such success is, in general, likely to be limited and short-lived in comparison with what one can achieve by sincerely engaging in moral discourse.

⁴ Considerations of this sort are familiar from, for example, chapter 11 of Hare's *Moral Thinking: Its Levels, Method, and Point* (Oxford: Clarendon Press, 1981). However, in interpreting these considerations it is important to bear in mind the distinction between two ways, discussed in section 1.3 above, in which prudential discourse can delegate its authority to moral discourse, and to interpret such arguments along the lines of the way that is labeled (*b*) in that section (in spite of the ambiguities in the actual formulation of Hare's argument—see note 12 to chapter 1, above).

⁵ That is, all except those who would be unable or unwilling to appreciate the prudential argument of section 7.2.

⁶ In other words, one should not think of the difference between stable and unstable members as analogous to the difference between first-class and economy-class passengers on a plane. Instead, one should think of it as analogous to the difference between passengers with reservations and stand-by passengers on a one-class plane. The difference between the two has to do with *getting* to be on the plane and not with what happens on the plane. Once a stand-by passenger is on the plane, he is on a par with other passengers.

⁷ Questions listed under (2) are not going to be of great practical importance because individuals that otherwise qualify for stable membership will usually also have prudential reasons to regard us as members of the moral community. In practice, no individual is going to be disqualified from stable membership solely on the basis of answers to questions listed under (2).

But we can imagine situations where this would not be so. There can be extraterrestrials who engage in moral discourse among themselves, and who are so powerful that they can significantly harm us, while we are totally unable to influence them in any way. In their case, answers to questions listed under (1), (3), and (4) would all speak in favor of treating them as stable members of the moral community. However, if we also assume that all benefits that they can get from us they can easily get by force, then they would not have any prudential reason for regarding us as members of the moral community (this involves assuming that they are simply not interested in subtle forms of interaction with us, into which we cannot be coerced; that such subtle interaction would not be a benefit to them). In such a case, questions listed

under (2) could play a crucial role in disqualifying them from stable membership in the moral community. (This thought-
experiment is taken from William H. Davis, "Man-Eating Aliens,"
The Journal of Value Inquiry 10 (1976): 178–85.)

This thought-experiment also shows that, although there is, as
a matter of fact, a great deal of agreement as to who stable members are, stable membership in the moral community is also
relative to particular participants in moral discourse. In the experiment, extraterrestrials would presumably be stable members for
each other while humans would be stable members for each
other, but extraterrestrials would not be stable members for
humans nor vice versa. In the remainder of this chapter, however,
I disregard this feature of stable membership.

[8] I put the word *contract* in quotes because of the standard objection
to contractarianism that morality cannot literally be a contract as
morality is what makes contracts binding. This objection can, however, be avoided by a sufficiently careful formulation of the view.

[9] See Jan Narveson, "Animal Rights," *Canadian Journal of Philosophy*
7 (1977): 176–78, and section 3 of his "Animal Rights Revisited,"
in Harlan B. Miller and William H. Williams, eds., *Ethics and
Animals* (Clifton, N.J.: Humana Press, 1983), 45–59.

[10] Not only is it possible that moral discourse would go on even in
the absence of prudential reasons for engaging in it, but there is
not even good reason to dismiss that possibility as a manifestation
of irrationality (unless one simply stipulates that *rational* means
the same as *prudent*). That point is elaborated in my "External
Reasons and the Foundations of Morality: Mother Teresa vs.
Thrasymachus," *The Journal of Value Inquiry* 26 (1992): 433–41.

[11] In *Ethics: Inventing Right and Wrong* (Harmondsworth, England:
Penguin Books, 1977), 194, Mackie makes the following statement, which may appear like a formulation of the same insight
that I am trying to express in this section:

> The claims of these classes [defective humans and non-
> human animals], then, lie outside what I must regard as the
> core of morality. It is only extensions of morality that cover
> them. Moreover, these are gratuitous extensions of morality.

However, when this statement is interpreted in the light of what he
says in the paragraph that immediately follows, it turns out that

"extensions of morality" do not amount to our considering the individuals in question as members of the moral community, but merely to there being some constraints that are placed on our behavior towards them by the duties that we have toward others.

¹² As Michael Fox has put it:

As for animals themselves, it seems altogether too misleading to classify all non human organisms under such a broad heading. Controversies about animals and morals have been most unsatisfactory in this respect, featuring blanket statements about animals' capacities and moral status that utterly fail to differentiate between forms of life as widely separated on the evolutionary scale as oysters and chimpanzees.

(*The Case for Animal Experimentation: An Evolutionary and Ethical Perspective* [Berkeley: University of California Press, 1986], 14).

¹³ For example, it may be that animals of a certain species, when they are raised in natural conditions in which they have to search for food, find ways to overcome obstacles, socially interact with other animals, fight for themselves, and so on, develop, by being exposed to all these experiences, mental life that is fairly complex. It may also be that animals of the same species that are raised on a factory farm, and are thereby deprived of all these experiences, never develop a mental life of comparable complexity. Now it does not seem unreasonable to think that possession of properties of animals in the former group is compatible with being myself and at the same time hold that an individual that would have such a rudimentary mental life as is possessed by animals of the same species that are raised on a factory farm could not be me. (After all, I might not be able to imagine the properties of a human that is raised under similar conditions.)

The possibility of this view constitutes a challenge to an important tenet of vegetarianism. Namely, most vegetarians hold that, if it turns out that universal vegetarianism cannot be achieved, then we should at least provide more natural living conditions for the animals that are to be eaten. But on the view that I have sketched here, this is precisely what we should not do. On this view, if the animals in question are provided with natural living conditions, they will develop a mental life that will make them members of the moral community, and then there will be a serious moral problem about eating them. On the other hand, if we keep them under conditions of a factory farm, then they will not develop a mental life that would make them members of the moral community, and there will consequently be no moral problem about eating them. Providing natural living conditions for these animals and then eating them, far from being the second best option (as vegetarians usually treat it), is, on this view, the only morally problematic one.

[14] It is, by the way, not at all obvious that they are never going to agree to any such claim. At least some dog owners seem to blame their dogs morally from time to time, for example, for disloyalty.

[15] See note 24 to chapter 3.

[16] Incidentally, those who still think that my view that moral agency always goes together with moral patiency is something highly unusual, should take notice of the fact that at least one writer who advocated regarding objects of inanimate nature as patients did not see anything absurd about regarding them as agents as well: Christopher Stone, *Should Trees Have Standing?: Toward Legal Rights for Natural Objects.* (Los Altos, Calif.: William Kaufmann, 1974), 34.

[17] Judith Jarvis Thomson, "A Defense of Abortion," *Philosophy & Public Affairs* 1 (1971): 47–66.

[18] See, for example, Jane English, "Abortion and the Concept of a Person," 241.

[19] R. M. Hare, "Abortion and the Golden Rule," *Philosophy & Public Affairs* 4 (1975): 201–22.

[20] George Sher, "Hare, Abortion, and the Golden Rule," *Philosophy & Public Affairs* 6 (1977): 185–90.

[21] An obstacle may appear if we suppose that future humans may be radically different from present-day humans. But even then the obstacle would not stem from the mere fact that they are future rather than present.

[22] Members of past generations are also usually counted as unstable members of the moral community, but do not qualify for stable membership for reasons that are similar to those that exclude members of future generations. However, questions about membership of past generations in the moral community (unlike questions about membership of future generations) are usually not regarded as particularly pressing questions, for obvious reasons.

[23] The point made here also applies to animal species (even if we assume that individual animals belonging to the species in question are members of the moral community).

[24] By way of illustration, I shall nevertheless look at one example of such an argument. In "Collective Rights and Tyranny," *University of Ottawa Quarterly* 56 (1986): 115–23, Michael McDonald has commented on the case *Wong-Woo, Walia, Fong, and Pater v. Québec Minister of Education and Attorney-General*, in which one of the crucial questions was whether the right to education in the language of a linguistic minority, from section 23 of the Canadian Charter of Rights and Freedoms, is to be interpreted as a right that ultimately belongs to individual members of that minority or to the minority as a whole. Although McDonald's article takes a legal case as its starting point, it does not seem that he intended the argument to be restricted to the legal context, and nothing in the argument precludes its being regarded as an argument about the underlying moral rights as well.

The issue before the court concerned denial of education in English to a relatively small subgroup of the English-language population of Québec. Parents belonging to that subgroup argued that section 23 of the Charter gives to each of them the right to have his children educated in English, while the argument of Québec was that the right declared in section 23 is to be construed as a right of the English-speaking minority taken as a whole, and that denial of English-language education to a small subgroup of that minority does not constitute a violation of that right when it is so construed.

In deciding the case, the court took the position that the whole idea of collective rights is defective and that the right declared in section 23 must therefore be interpreted as the right of individual parents to have their children educated in the language of their linguistic minority.

In commenting on the case, McDonald has argued that the argument of Québec was dismissed too quickly by the Court. He shows (see especially page 121 of the article) that important aspects of what was intended, or of what could have been intended, by section 23 are missed if we interpret it as giving the right to individual parents to have their children educated in the language of their linguistic minority. It seems that he takes this as the basis for his view that the right expressed in section 23 may be a collective right.

What is common to both the position of the Court and McDonald's criticism of that position is the assumption that we

have only two options here: either the right in question is a right
of individual parents to have their children educated in the language of their linguistic minority or it is a collective right of the
minority itself.

But there are other possibilities. An individual member of a linguistic minority usually benefits from the fact that a sufficient
number (a "critical mass") of people around him continues to
speak his language. An important condition for his receiving this
benefit is that education in that language be generally available to
children of his minority. However, his receiving this benefit will
usually not be affected if education in this language is unavailable
to some relatively small subgroup within the minority. Section 23
of the Charter could be interpreted as granting to every member
of a linguistic minority the right that the government increase his
chances of receiving this benefit by making education in the language of the minority generally available to children of that
minority. Interpreting it in that way seems to accommodate all the
important insights presented in McDonald's paper, while avoiding his conclusion that claims expressing collective rights cannot
be interpreted in terms of claims that attribute rights to individual
members of the relevant collectivities.

[25] Some people are inclined to say that all monstrous criminals are
insane. However, not everyone would agree with that, and I therefore discuss monstrous criminals separately from people who are
insane. Those who think that all monstrous criminals are insane may
disregard this subsection and proceed to the next one right away.

[26] A rare example of a contemporary philosopher who does take it
seriously is Christopher W. Morris, "Punishment and Loss of
Moral Standing," *Canadian Journal of Philosophy* 21 (1991): 53–79.
(His argument, however, presupposes an account of membership
in the moral community, or moral standing as he calls it, that is in
many respects different from the account defended in this book.)

[27] Samuel Yochelson and Stanton E. Samenow, *The Criminal
Personality*, vol. 1 (New York: Jason Aronson, 1976), 372–73.

[28] I use the nonmedical term *insane* here (rather than something
like *mentally diseased*) because I do not want to imply that the criteria for belonging to the class that I am talking about are purely
medical.

[29] Cf. Narveson, "Animal Rights," 177.

Bibliography

Adams, Robert Merrihew. "Saints." *The Journal of Philosophy* 81 (1984): 392–401.

Appiah, Anthony. "'But Would That Still Be Me?': Notes on Gender, 'Race,' Ethnicity, as Sources of 'Identity.'" *The Journal of Philosophy* 87 (1990): 493–99.

Arrington, Robert L. *Rationalism, Realism, and Relativism: Perspectives in Contemporary Moral Epistemology.* Ithaca, N.Y.: Cornell University Press, 1989.

Ayer, Alfred Jules. *Language, Truth and Logic.* London: Victor Gollancz, 1936.

Barnes, Jonathan. Introduction to *The Ethics of Aristotle.* Harmondsworth, England: Penguin Books, 1976.

Benn, Stanley I. "Egalitarianism and the Equal Consideration of Interests." In *Nomos IX: Equality,* edited by J. Roland Pennock and John W. Chapman, 61–78. New York: Atherton Press, 1967.

Benn, S. I., and R. S. Peters. *Social Principles and the Democratic State.* London: George Allen & Unwin, 1959.

Berkeley, George. *The Principles of Human Knowledge.* Glasgow: Collins, 1962.

Brandt, R. B. "Act-Utilitarianism and Metaethics." In *Hare and Critics: Essays on* Moral Thinking, edited by Douglas Seanor and N. Fotion, 27–41. Oxford: Clarendon Press, 1988.

Brunton, J. A. "Restricted Moralities." *Philosophy* 41 (1966): 113–26.

Davis, William H. "Man-Eating Aliens." *The Journal of Value Inquiry* 10 (1976): 178–85.

Donnellan, Keith S. "Reference and Definite Descriptions." *The Philosophical Review* 75 (1966): 281–304.

Dummett, Michael. *Frege: Philosophy of Language.* London: Duckworth, 1973.

Dworkin, Ronald. *Taking Rights Seriously.* Cambridge, Mass.: Harvard University Press, 1977.

English, Jane. "Abortion and the Concept of a Person." *Canadian Journal of Philosophy* 5 (1975): 233–43.

Feinberg, Joel. "The Nature and Value of Rights." *The Journal of Value Inquiry* 4 (1970): 243–57.

Feldman, Fred. "Hare's Proof." *Philosophical Studies* 45 (1984): 269–83.

Flathman, Richard E. "Equality and Generalization, A Formal Analysis." In *Nomos IX: Equality*, edited by J. Roland Pennock and John W. Chapman, 38–60. New York: Atherton Press, 1967.

Fotion, N. "'All Humans Ought to Be Eliminated.'" *Ethics* 87 (1976): 87–95.

———. *Moral Situations.* Kent, Ohio: The Kent State University Press, 1968.

———. "Range-Rules in Moral Contexts." *Mind* 72 (1963): 556–61.

Fox, Michael Allen. *The Case for Animal Experimentation: An Evolutionary and Ethical Perspective.* Berkeley: University of California Press, 1986.

Frankena, William K. "The Concept of Morality." In *The Definition of Morality*, edited by G. Wallace and A. D. M. Walker, 146–73. London: Methuen, 1970.

———. "Hare on Moral Weakness and the Definition of Morality." *Ethics* 98 (1988): 779–92.

———. "Must Morality Have an Object?" *The Monist* 63 (1980): 3–26.

———. "Natural and Inalienable Rights." *The Philosophical Review* 64 (1955): 212–32.

Freedman, Benjamin. "A Meta-Ethics for Professional Morality." *Ethics* 89 (1978): 1–19.

———. "What Really Makes Professional Morality Different: Response to Martin." *Ethics* 91 (1981): 626–30.

Frey, R. G. *Interests and Rights: The Case Against Animals.* Oxford: Clarendon Press, 1980.

Gauthier, David. "Reason and Maximization." *Canadian Journal of Philosophy* 4 (1975): 411–33.

Gert, Heather J. "Rights and Rights Violators: A New Approach to the Nature of Rights." *The Journal of Philosophy* 87 (1990): 688–94.

Gibbard, Allan. "Hare's Analysis of 'Ought' and its Implications." In *Hare and Critics: Essays on* Moral Thinking, edited by Douglas Seanor and N. Fotion, 57–72. Oxford: Clarendon Press, 1988.

Gilbert, Joseph. "Neutrality and Universalizability." *Personalist* 53 (1972): 438–41.

Goldman, Alan H. *The Moral Foundations of Professional Ethics.* Totowa, N.J.: Rowman and Littlefield, 1980.

Gorr, Michael. "Reason, Impartiality and Utilitarianism." In *Morality and Universality*, edited by Nelson T. Potter and Mark Timmons, 115–38. Dordrecht, Netherlands: D. Reidel Publishing Company, 1985.

Grice, Geoffrey Russell. *The Grounds of Moral Judgement.* Cambridge: Cambridge University Press, 1967.

Hajdin, Mane. "External and Now-For-Then Preferences in Hare's Theory." *Dialogue* 29 (1990): 305–10.

———. "External Reasons and the Foundations of Morality: Mother Teresa vs. Thrasymachus." *The Journal of Value Inquiry* 26 (1992): 433–41.

———. "Is There More to Speech Acts Than Illocutionary Force and Propositional Content?" *Noûs* 25 (1991): 353–57.

Hare, R. M. "Abortion and the Golden Rule." *Philosophy & Public Affairs* 4 (1975): 201–22.

———. "Amoralism: Reply to Peter Sandøe." *Theoria* 55 (1989): 205–10.

———. "Comments." In *Hare and Critics: Essays on* Moral Thinking, edited by Douglas Seanor and N. Fotion, 199–293. Oxford: Clarendon Press, 1988.

———. *Essays in Ethical Theory.* Oxford: Clarendon Press, 1989.

———. *Essays on the Moral Concepts.* London: Macmillan, 1972.

———. *Freedom and Reason.* Oxford: Clarendon Press, 1963.

———. *The Language of Morals.* Oxford: Clarendon Press, 1952.

———. "Moral Reasoning about the Environment." *Journal of Applied Philosophy* 4 (1987): 3–14.

———. *Moral Thinking: Its Levels, Method, and Point.* Oxford: Clarendon Press, 1981.

———. "Prudence and Past Preferences: Reply to Wlodzimierz Rabinowicz." *Theoria* 55 (1989): 152–58.

———. "A Rejoinder." In *The Domain of Moral Education,* edited by Donald B. Cochrane, Cornel M. Hamm, and Anatasios C. Kazepides, 115–19. New York: Paulist Press, 1979.

———. "Relevance." In *Values and Morals,* edited by Alvin I. Goldman and Jaegwon Kim, 73–90. Dordrecht, Netherlands: D. Reidel Publishing Company, 1978.

———. Review of *Contemporary Moral Philosophy,* by G. J. Warnock. *Mind* 77 (1968): 436–40.

———. Review of *The Object of Morality,* by G. J. Warnock. *Ratio* 14 (1972): 199–205.

———. "Some Reasoning about Preferences: A Response to Essays by Persson, Feldman, and Schueler." *Ethics* 95 (1984): 81–85.

———. "Universalizability and the Summing of Desires: A Reply to Ingmar Persson." *Theoria* 55 (1989): 171–77.

Harris, John. *The Value of Life.* London: Routledge & Kegan Paul, 1985.

Harsanyi, John C. *Essays on Ethics, Social Behavior, and Scientific Explanation.* Dordrecht, Netherlands: D. Reidel Publishing Company, 1976.

Hart, H. L. A. "Are There Any Natural Rights?" *The Philosophical Review* 64 (1955): 175–91.

———. *Bentham.* London: British Academy, 1962.

———. "Bentham on Legal Rights." In *Rights,* edited by David Lyons, 125–48. Belmont, Calif.: Wadsworth, 1979.

———. *The Concept of Law.* Oxford: Clarendon Press, 1961.

Kant, Immanuel. *Kant's Critique of Practical Reason and Other Works on the Theory of Ethics.* Translated by Thomas Kingsmill Abbott. 6th ed. London: Longmans, 1909.

———. *Lectures on Ethics.* Indianapolis: Hackett, 1980.

Kekes, John. "On There Being Some Limits to Morality." *Social Philosophy & Policy* 9, no. 2 (1992): 63–80.

Kelsen, Hans. *General Theory of Law and State.* Translated by Anders Wedberg. New York: Russell & Russell, 1961.

Khatchadourian, Haig. "The Human Right to Be Treated as a Person." *The Journal of Value Inquiry* 19 (1985): 183–95.

Kripke, Saul A. *Naming and Necessity.* Cambridge, Mass.: Harvard University Press, 1980. First published in *Semantics of Natural Language,* edited by Donald Davidson and Gilbert Harman, 253–355. Dordrecht, Netherlands: D. Reidel Publishing Company, 1972.

Lappin, Shalom. "Moral Judgments and Identity across Possible Worlds." *Ratio* 20 (1978): 69–74.

Levin, David S. "Abortion, Personhood, and Vagueness." *The Journal of Value Inquiry* 19 (1985): 197–209.

Lewis, Clarence Irving. *An Analysis of Knowledge and Valuation.* La Salle, Ill.: Open Court, 1946.

———. *The Ground and Nature of the Right.* New York: Columbia University Press, 1955.

Lewis, David. "Attitudes *De Dicto* and *De Se.*" *The Philosophical Review* 88 (1979): 513–43.

———. "Individuation by Acquaintance and by Stipulation." *The Philosophical Review* 92 (1983): 3–32.

———. *On the Plurality of Worlds.* Oxford: Basil Blackwell, 1986.

———. "Survival and Identity." In *The Identities of Persons,* edited by Amélie Oksenberg Rorty, 17–40. Berkeley: University of California Press, 1976.

Lyons, David. "The Correlativity of Rights and Duties." *Noûs* 4 (1970): 45–55.

———. "Rights, Claimants, and Beneficiaries." In *Rights,* edited by David Lyons, 58–77. Belmont, Calif.: Wadsworth, 1979.

MacKay, Alfred F. "Extended Sympathy and Interpersonal Utility Comparisons." *The Journal of Philosophy* 83 (1986): 305–22.

Mackie, J. L. "*De* What *Re* Is *De Re* Modality?" *The Journal of Philosophy* 71 (1974): 551–61.

———. *Ethics: Inventing Right and Wrong.* Harmondsworth, England: Penguin Books, 1977.

Martin, Mike W. "Professional and Ordinary Morality: A Reply to Freedman." *Ethics* 91 (1981): 631–33.

———. "Rights and the Meta-Ethics of Professional Morality." *Ethics* 91 (1981): 619–25.

McCloskey, H. J. "The Complexity of the Concepts of Punishment." *Philosophy* 37 (1962): 307–25.

———. "Rights." *The Philosophical Quarterly* 15 (1965): 115–27.

McDonald, Michael. "Collective Rights and Tyranny." *University of Ottawa Quarterly* 56 (1986): 115–23.

McGilvray, James. Review of *The Matter of Minds*, by Zeno Vendler. *Canadian Philosophical Reviews* 6 (1986): 250–54.

McPherson, Thomas. "The Moral Patient." *Philosophy* 59 (1984): 171–83.

Mill, John Stuart. *Utilitarianism.* Glasgow: Collins, 1962.

Morris, Christopher W. "Punishment and Loss of Moral Standing." *Canadian Journal of Philosophy* 21 (1991): 53–80.

Murphy, Jeffrie G. "Moral Death: A Kantian Essay on Psychopathy." *Ethics* 82 (1972): 284–98.

Murphy, Jeffrie G., and Jean Hampton. *Forgiveness and Mercy.* Cambridge: Cambridge University Press, 1988.

Nagel, Thomas. *The Possibility of Altruism.* Oxford: Clarendon Press, 1970.

———. *The View from Nowhere.* New York: Oxford University Press, 1986.

Narveson, Jan. "Animal Rights." *Canadian Journal of Philosophy* 7 (1977): 161–78.

———. "Animal Rights Revisited." In *Ethics and Animals*, edited by Harlan B. Miller and William H. Williams, 45–59. Clifton, N.J.: Humana Press, 1983.

———. "Commentary." *The Journal of Value Inquiry* 4 (1970): 258–60.

———. "Comment on Hajdin on Sanctions and Morals." *Dialogue* 32 (1993): 761–65.

———. "The How and Why of Universalizability." In *Morality and Universality*, edited by Nelson T. Potter and Mark Timmons, 3–44. Dordrecht, Netherlands: D. Reidel Publishing Company, 1985.

———. *The Libertarian Idea.* Philadelphia: Temple University Press, 1988.

Nelson, William. "On the Alleged Importance of Moral Rights." *Ratio* 18 (1976): 145–55.

Nielsen, Kai. *Equality and Liberty: A Defense of Radical Egalitarianism.* Totowa, N.J.: Rowman and Allanheld, 1985.

Nozick, Robert. *Philosophical Explanations.* Cambridge, Mass.: Harvard University Press, 1981.

Oldenquist, Andrew. "Rules and Consequences." *Mind* 75 (1966): 180–92.

Parfit, Derek. "Lewis, Perry, and What Matters." In *The Identities of Persons*, edited by Amélie Oksenberg Rorty, 91–107. Berkeley: University of California Press, 1976.

———. "Personal Identity." *The Philosophical Review* 80 (1971): 3–27.

———. *Reasons and Persons.* Oxford: Oxford University Press, 1984.

Perry, John. "The Importance of Being Identical." In *The Identities of Persons*, edited by Amélie Oksenberg Rorty, 67–90. Berkeley: University of California Press, 1976.

———. "The Problem of the Essential Indexical." *Noûs* 13 (1979): 3–21.

Persson, Ingmar. "Hare on Universal Prescriptivism and Utilitarianism." *Analysis* 43 (1983): 43–49.

———. "Universalizability and the Summing of Desires." *Theoria* 55 (1989): 159–70.

Pojman, Louis P. "Is Contemporary Moral Theory Founded on a Misunderstanding?" *Journal of Social Philosophy* 22, no. 2 (Fall 1991): 49–59.

Price, M. S. "On the Non-Necessity of Origin." *Canadian Journal of Philosophy* 12 (1982): 33–45.

Putnam, Hilary. "Robots: Machines or Artificially Created Life?" *The Journal of Philosophy* 61 (1964): 668–91.

Raz, J. "On the Nature of Rights." *Mind* 93 (1984): 194–214.

———. "Principles of Equality." *Mind* 87 (1978): 321–42.

Regan, Tom. *All That Dwell Therein.* Berkeley: University of California Press, 1982.

———. *The Case for Animal Rights.* Berkeley: University of California Press, 1983.

———. "Narveson on Egoism and the Rights of Animals." *Canadian Journal of Philosophy* 7 (1977): 179–86.

Rodman, John. "Animal Justice: The Counter-Revolution in Natural Right and Law." *Inquiry* 22 (1979): 3–22.

———. "The Liberation of Nature?" *Inquiry* 20 (1977): 83–131.

Rorty, Amélie O. "Slaves and Machines." *Analysis* 22 (1962): 118–20.

Rorty, Richard. *Philosophy and the Mirror of Nature.* Princeton: Princeton University Press, 1979.

Ross, W. D. *The Right and the Good.* Oxford: Clarendon Press, 1930.

Roxbee Cox, J. W. "From Universal Prescriptivism to Utilitarianism." *The Philosophical Quarterly* 36 (1986): 1–15.

Sandøe, Peter. "Amoralism—On the Limits of Moral Thinking." *Theoria* 55 (1989): 191–204.

Schueler, G. F. "Some Reasoning about Preferences." *Ethics* 95 (1984): 78–80.

Searle, John R. *Intentionality: An Essay in the Philosophy of Mind.* Cambridge: Cambridge University Press, 1983.

Sher, George. "Compensation and Transworld Personal Identity." *The Monist* 62 (1979): 378–91.

———. "Hare, Abortion, and the Golden Rule." *Philosophy & Public Affairs* 6 (1977): 185–90.

Silverstein, Harry S. "Universality and Treating Persons as Persons." *The Journal of Philosophy* 71 (1974): 57–71.

Singer, Peter. *Animal Liberation: A New Ethics for Our Treatment of Animals.* New York: New York Review, 1975.

————. "Reasoning towards Utilitarianism." In *Hare and Critics: Essays on* Moral Thinking, edited by Douglas Seanor and N. Fotion, 147–59. Oxford: Clarendon Press, 1988.

Slote, Michael. *Goods and Virtues.* Oxford: Clarendon Press, 1983.

Sommers, Christina Hoff. "Filial Morality." *The Journal of Philosophy* 83 (1986): 439–56.

Sprigge, T. L. S. "Definition of a Moral Judgement." In *The Definition of Morality,* edited by G. Wallace and A. D. M. Walker, 119–45. London: Methuen, 1970.

Stone, Christopher D. *Should Trees Have Standing?: Toward Legal Rights for Natural Objects.* Los Altos, Calif.: William Kaufmann, 1974.

Strawson, P. F. "Social Morality and Individual Ideal." *Philosophy* 36 (1961): 1–17.

Thomson, Judith Jarvis. "A Defense of Abortion." *Philosophy & Public Affairs* 1 (1971): 47–66.

Tooley, Michael. *Abortion and Infanticide.* Oxford: Clarendon Press, 1983.

Vendler, Zeno. "Changing Places?" In *Hare and Critics: Essays on* Moral Thinking, edited by Douglas Seanor and N. Fotion, 171–83. Oxford: Clarendon Press, 1988.

————. *The Matter of Minds.* Oxford: Clarendon Press, 1984.

————. "A Note to the Paralogisms." In *Contemporary Aspects of Philosophy,* edited by Gilbert Ryle, 111–21. Stocksfield, England: Oriel Press, 1976.

Vlastos, Gregory. "Justice and Equality." In *Human Rights,* edited by A. I. Melden, 76–95. Belmont, Calif.: Wadsworth, 1970.

Waldron, Jeremy. "A Right to Do Wrong." *Ethics* 92 (1981): 21–39.

Walker, Owen S. "Why Should Irresponsible Offenders Be Excused?" *The Journal of Philosophy* 66 (1969): 279–90.

Warnock, G. J. *Contemporary Moral Philosophy.* London: Macmillan, 1967.

———. *Morality and Language.* Oxford: Basil Blackwell, 1983.

———. "Morality and Language: A Reply to R. M. Hare." In *The Domain of Moral Education,* edited by Donald B. Cochrane, Cornel M. Hamm, and Anastasios C. Kazepides, 107–14. New York: Paulist Press, 1979.

———. *The Object of Morality.* London: Methuen, 1971.

Warren, Mary Anne. "On the Moral and Legal Status of Abortion." *The Monist* 57 (1973): 43–61.

Wellman, Carl. *A Theory of Rights: Persons Under Laws, Institutions, and Morals.* Totowa, N.J.: Rowman & Allanheld, 1985.

White, Alan R. *Rights.* Oxford: Clarendon Press, 1984.

Williams, Bernard. "The Idea of Equality." In *Philosophy, Politics and Society,* 2nd series, edited by Peter Laslett and W. G. Runciman, 110–31. Oxford: Basil Blackwell, 1962.

Wiseman, Mary Bittner. "Empathetic Identification." *American Philosophical Quarterly* 15 (1978): 107–13.

Wittgenstein, Ludwig. *Philosophical Investigations.* Translated by G. E. M. Anscombe. Oxford: Basil Blackwell, 1958.

Wolf, Susan. "Moral Saints." *The Journal of Philosophy* 79 (1982): 419–39.

Wright, Georg Henrik von, *Practical Reason.* Oxford: Basil Blackwell, 1983.

Yochelson, Samuel, and Stanton E. Samenow. *The Criminal Personality,* vol 1. New York: Jason Aronson, 1976.

Index

A

Abortion, 90, 153, 158–59, 194
Accessibility between anchors to
    subjectivity, 143
Action-rules (Fotion), 53, 99
Adams, Robert Merrihew, 170
Admirability, claims of, as not
    subject to arguments based
    on shoehorn maneuver, 28
    of immoral person, 5–6
    and morality, 3–7
    of people serving as models in
        real life, 4–5
Adultery, justification of claim of
    wrongness of, 46–47
Aesthetic discourse, 1
Agent-oriented maneuver, 35
Agent-range rule, 187
Ambiguity of agents and patients
    in moral claims, 46–48
Animals, duties to, 72, 77, 191
    equality between humans and,
        105
    as members in the moral com-
        munity, 150–51, 154–57, 213
    mental life of, 211–12
    as moral agents and patients,
        155–57
    as moral patients, 90
Anticorrelativism, correlativism
    versus, 65–67, 189
    radical, 189–90
    refutations of theories of,
        76–86
Antirelativism combined with
    noncognitivism, *xii*
Archimedean point, 11

Argument-place(s), for moral
    agents, 22, 34–35, 37, 43–46,
    56
    for moral patients, 22, 36–37,
        43–46, 56
    multiple, 43–46
    for prudential agents, 32, 36
Argumentation, methods of, *xi*
Aristotle, view of ethics of, 188
Arrington, Robert L., 169–70
Ascriptions of duties. *See* Duty-
    ascriptions
Ascriptions of rights. *See* Right-
    ascriptions
Ayre, Alfred Jules, *xii*

B

Barnes, Jonathan, 188
Bentham, Jeremy, 66, 111
Bentham's theory of rights, 66,
    111
Berkeley, George, 198
Bittner Wiseman, Mary, 176, 204
Boundaries of moral discourse,
    types of, xi

C

Carter, Randy, 203
Castes, 53
Character traits of moral agents,
    59–62
Charity, duty of, 72–75
Churchill, Winston, 170
Claims, 79–80. *See also* Legal
    claims *and* Moral claims
Coercion, justification of, 79

Computers as members of
moral community, 160–61
Consciousness, analysis of
notion of, 95–96
Consequences, of behavior,
Kantians claim of disre-
garding, 57–58
of correlativism, 66
diffused, 58
of the general account of
boundaries of moral com-
munity, 145–67
Content of rules for respectful
behavior toward others,
109–10
Contractarianism, 152–53, 210
Correlativism, alleged counterexamples to, 71–76
anticorrelativism versus,
65–67, 189
consequence of, 66
Correlativity, 189
Counterpart theory, 138–39
Criminals, as insane, 214
as members of the moral
community, 162–65
Criteria for evaluating functioning of moral discourse,
balance of neatness and
correspondence with
actual behavior one of, *xviii*
expressive power one of, *xviii*
neat structure of account as
one of, *xvii*
use of, *xix–xx*

D

Deontological ethics, 57–58
Designated argument-places, *xiv*
in moral and prudential
claims, 30–36
types of, 22
universalizability and, 36–41

Discourse, evaluating functioning of, *xvii–xx*
Discourse of admirability, 6–7, 18
Discourse of etiquette, 28
Distinguishing characteristics of
moral discourse, analysis
of, *xxiii*
assumptions about, *xx*
Hare's three, *xiii–xiv*
presence of two types of designated argument-places
in moral claims as, 36, 89
Divine punishments and
rewards, 171
Dogs as members of the moral
community, 155–57. *See
also* Animals
Donnellan, Keith S., 178
Duties, to abstain from tax evasion, 75–76
to animals, 72, 76–77
to babies, 76–77
of charity, 72–75
conditional, 184
as dispensable term, 86
to oneself, 56–57
rights as grounds of, 85–86,
189
to someone, 76–77
Duty-ascriptions, *xv*
discourse of, 61–62
moving between right-ascriptions and, 66
qualifying, 67
virtue-ascriptions not analyzable in terms of, 61, 189
Dworkin, Ronald, 107, 196

E

Empathetic identification, 175
English, Jane, 208
Equal consideration, principles
of, 105–7

Equality, 103–5
Essential properties, 122–27,
 130–32, 144–45
Ethics, ancient Greek, 188
 deontological, 57–58
 medical, 50–52, 186–87
 nonutilitarian, *xv*
 specialized branches of,
 50–52, 102
Evaluative discourse, 115

F

Feinberg, Joel, 79–83, 192
Fetuses as members of the
 moral community, 157–58,
 208
Fotion, N., 53, 99, 187, 194, 200
Fox, Michael, 211
Frankena, W. K., 15–16, 171,
 173, 194
Freedman, Benjamin, 186
Freedom, limiting others',
 76–79
Freedom and Reason, Hare's the-
 ory in, *xi,* 169, 177
Future generations as members
 of the moral community,
 160, 212

G

Gert, Heather J., 190
"Golden-rule" arguments, 27,
 194
Goldman, Alan, 186
Gorr, Michael, 181
Grice, Geoffrey Russell, 190
Groups as members of the
 moral community, 162

H

Hare, R. M., *xi–xiv,* 1

Hare's theory, on abortion,
 158–59, 194
 assumptions of other possible
 worlds of, 206
 defined, *xi*
 definition of overridingness
 in, 7
 departure of author's analysis
 from, 36–37, 182
 Frankena's criticism of, 171
 "golden-rule" arguments of,
 27
 insistence on universalizability on every argument-
 place of, 40
 limitlessness of arguments
 based on shoehorn
 maneuver for, 126
 moral relativism refuted by,
 94
 for morality versus other
 forms of prescriptive discourse, 1–3
 prudential principles coincid-
 ing with moral principles
 in, 171
 relation between morality
 and people's interests in,
 177
 relation between prudence
 and intuitive-level moral
 thinking in, 171–72
 right in, 183
 universalization on argument-places in, 38–39, 169
 view of essential properties
 of, 125–26
Hart, L. A., 76–79, 179, 190–92
Hepburn, Katharine, 4–6

I

Impersonality of reasons for acting, 58–59

Inanimate nature as member of the moral community, 157, 185
Individual variables, 33–34
to represent moral arguments, 49–50
Infants as members of the moral community, 158–60
Injury to another, 193
Insane as members of the moral community, 164–67
Institution of moral claiming, nonexistence of, 82

J

Jarvis Thomson, Judith, 158

K

Kant, Immanuel, 173, 191, 197
Kantians, 57–58, 207
Kekes, John, 172
Kelsen, Hans, 12, 173–75
Kripke, Saul A., 131, 200
Kripke's theory of identity across possible worlds, 131–34, 201–4

L

Language-game, *xx*
Language of Morals, The, xi–xii, 183
Language, Truth and Logic, xii
Lappin, Shalom, 206
Laws of physics, 98–99
Legal claims, 80–82
Legal discourse, 28, 174–75
Legal rights, 191–92
Levin, David S., 208
Lewis, David, 135, 201, 205–6
Liberties, protection of, 83–85

Liberty-rights, 67, 83–85
Linguistic minorities, education for, 213–14

M

McCloskey, H. J., 18, 174, 190
McDonald, Michael, 213–14
MacKay, Alfred F., 175, 197
Martin, Mike W., 186
Medical ethics, 50–52, 186–87
Membership in the moral community, ability to use language as criterion for, 152
applications of understanding, 102–15, 153–67
being member of *Homo sapiens* and, 194
changes over time in prevailing views about, 102
contractarianism and, 152
controversy about, 90, 101
general theory of, 127–30, 145
independence of questions about, 89–95, 97
methods of moral argumentation and, 95–99
moral discourse between people with varying views on, 92
percentages of membership in, 62–64
proving qualification for, 166
questions about membership in, 89–115
racist attitudes and, 91–92
relativism about, 94–95, 129, 146, 208
stable and unstable, 150–54, 209–10, 212
Mentally retarded people as members of the moral community, 164–67

Metalanguage, 51
Mill, John Stuart, 111
Moral agency, *xiv*
   alternative way of discussing,
     99–102
   moral patiency together with,
     212
Moral agents, *xiv*, 43–64
   ambiguities about, 46–48
   argument-places for, 22,
     34–35, 37, 43–46, 56
   character traits (virtue-ascrip-
     tions) of, 59–62
   defined, 33–34
   individual variables that
     occupy argument-places
     for, 50
   limits to the realm of, 99
   membership in the set of,
     xv–xvi, 62, 89
   in moral community, 55
   participants in moral dis-
     course as both moral
     patients and, 128
   rationality of, 194
   specifying domains of, 95
Moral argumentation, methods
   of, 95–99
Moral claims, ambiguity of
   agents and patients in,
     46–48
   analysis by illocutionary force
     and propositional content
     of, 185
   belief of derivability of,
     177–78
   conditional, 184
   conflicts between legal claims
     and, *xxii–xxiii*
   designated argument-places
     in, 30–36
   domains of variables for,
     99–101

   failure to make valid, 80
   formulation of substantive,
     103–4
   inconsistency among easy-to-
     remember formulations
     of, 185–86
   individual constant or indi-
     vidual variable required
     for, 33–34, 49–50
   made in moral discourse, *xxi*
   paradigms of, 61
   phrastic part of (Hare), 49
   properties of, *xxi*
   putative versus basic, 55
   simple versus complex, 184
   as singular and universal, *xxii*
   standard form of, 48–49
Moral community, 49–55
   boundaries of, *xi*, *xvi*
   conclusions about, 127–30
   defined, 55
   membership in. *See*
     Membership in the moral
     community
   properties belonging to
     members of, 193–94
   references in moral discourse
     to, *xi*
   union of sets of moral agents
     and moral patients as, 55
Moral discourse, action-rules
   and range-rules in, 53
   analytic notion of, *xxiv*
   anthropological notion of,
     xxiii–xxiv
   distinguishing characteristics
     of. *See* Distinguishing char-
     acteristics of moral dis-
     course
   Hare's theory of functioning
     of. *See* Hare's theory
   as moral thinking at the criti-
     cal level, *xxiv*

overridingness of. *See*
Overridingness of moral
discourse
participant in, as both moral
agent and patient, 128
prescriptivity of, *xiii*, 7–14
with radical racists, 149–50
references to members of the
moral community in, *xi*
shoehorn maneuver and,
21–22, 28–30
universalizability of, *xiii*
Moral judgment, *xxi–xxii*
Moral opportunity, 187
Moral patiency, *xiv*
alternative way of discussing,
99–102
moral agency together with,
212
radical racist's view of questions of, 148
Moral patients, 43–64
ambiguities about, 46–48
animals as, 90
argument-places for, 22,
36–37, 43–46, 56
claim for, *xiv*
defined, 35
domains of, 95
of the duty of charity, 74
identical with right-holders, *xv*
individuals intended as, 54
limits to the realm of, 99
membership in the set of,
xv–xvi, 62, 89
moral claim required to contain a term for, 56
morally wrong treatment of
individuals who are not,
160
in moral community, 55
participants in moral discourse as both moral
agents and, 128

permitting moral agent's
behavior by, 83
right-holder as, 66
role of, 59
sense of use of, 180
variables that occupy argument-places for, 50
Moral realism, attraction of, *xii*
Moral relativism refuted by
Hare, 94
Moral right, 79
Moral rules, equality in applying, 105
obeying, 183–84
questions about content of,
xvi, 93–94, 97, 101
same set of variables for
agents and patients for, 55
as set of rules that specify
respectful behavior toward
others, 109–10
Moral sanctions, 17–20
Moral system, contradictions
within, *xxii–xxiii*
of society divided into castes,
53
Moral view. *See* Moral system
*Moral Thinking: Its Levels,
Method, and Point,* Hare's
theory in, *xi*, 199–200
Morality, admirability and, 3–7
agents and patients for
branches of, 50
conceptual connection
between nonmoral pre-
scriptions and, 174
contractarianism's view of,
152
harmony of happiness with,
173
matters of degree in, 62–64
other prescriptive discourse
versus, 1–20
prudence and, 1–3, 15–17

right-based, 87
wider sense of, 15–17
Morally perfect people, unap-
pealing characters of, 3–4
Mother Teresa, 4–5
Myself, 117–44, 131, 135–39
Myself-in-*W* (other possible
world), 136–37
Myself$_c$ (continuant), 135–37, 205
Myself$_p$ (present temporal
stage), 135–39, 159, 206

N

Naming and Necessity, 131,
200–201
Narveson, Jan, 17, 173–74, 210
Naturalistic fallacy, 96
Nelson, William, 79, 192
Noncognitivism combined with
antirelativism, *xii*
Notion of morality, *xxiii. See also*
Moral discourse

O

Oldenquist, Andrew, 187
Organizations as members of
the moral community, 162
Ought, moral, 112
Overridingness of moral discourse, *xiii,* 2, 7–14
criticism of, 15–17
defined by Hare, 7
establishing, 8
ought built into, 7, 11

P

Parfit, Derek, 58–59, 135, 172,
187–88, 201, 205
Past generations as unstable
members of the moral
community, 212

Personal identity, across possible worlds, 130–39
over time, 132–33, 135–36, 159
Parfit's theory of, 201
sperm-and-egg essence of,
133–35, 201–3, 205
use of term, 205
Pojman, Louis, 172
Prescriptive discourse, *xiii*
conflicts within, 7–14
morality versus, 1–20
other names for, 12
Principles of equal consideration, 105–7
"Prisoner's Dilemma," 8, 149
Protection of the self, 172
Prudence and morality, 1–3,
15–17
Prudential agents, argument-
places for, 32, 36, 179
Prudential claims, designated
argument-places in, 30–36
Prudential discourse, 1–2
in arguments with radical
racists, 148–50
delegation of authority of,
8–11, 209
discourse of admirability distinct from, 6–7
features of, 33
shoehorn maneuver and, 26,
29–30
Prudential judgements, 170
Prudential prescription, 176

R

Racist, ordinary, 146–47
radical, 146–50
Radical racism, 146–50
Range-rules (Fotion), 53, 99,
187
Rape, justification of claim of
wrongness of, 46–47

Reasons and Persons, 172, 187–88,
  205–6
Reflective equilibrium (Rawls),
  xx
Regan, Tom, 180, 197
Relativism, about membership
  in sets of moral agents and
  moral patients, *xvi*
  about questions concerning
    membership in the moral
    community, 146, 208
Respect for persons, 107–11,
  197
Retarded people as members of
  the moral community,
  164–67
Right to do wrong, 190–91
Right to life, 70–71
Right-ascriptions, *xv,* 65
  canonical form of, 70
  form of expression for, 68–70
  moving between duty-ascrip-
    tion and, 66
  qualifying, 67
Right-holders, 65–88
  animals as, 72
  for charity, 72–75
  control over freedom of
    another of, 191
  defined, 65
  membership in the set of, 89
  as moral patient, 66
Rights, 65–88
  Bentham's theory of, 66, 111
  as dispensable term, 86–88
  dynamic aspect of, 190
  Feinberg's analysis of, 79–83
  as grounds of duties, 85–86
  Hart's analysis of, 77–79
  infringing on or violating,
    68–69, 78–79
  legal, 191–92
  model of, 67–68

natural, 85, 191–92
respecting, 68–69
waiving, 83
Rights-duties correlativism, *xv*
Ross' paradox, 184

S

Samenow, Stanton E., 164
Sanctions, moral, 17–20
Science, criteria of moral
  agency or patiency nondis-
  coverable by, 96–97
Seanor, Douglas, 194, 200
Shoehorn maneuver, 21–41
  agent-oriented and patient-
    oriented, 180–81
  application of arguments
    based on, *xv–xvi*
  arguments about personal
    identification and, 136–39,
    159
  arguments for moral dis-
    course and prudential dis-
    course based on, 22, 37,
    94, 97, 136
  contingent limitations on use
    of, 117–22
  examples of, 23, 25–26,
    29–30, 33
  importance of, 21
  limitations associated with
    problems of transworld
    identification on use of,
    140–41
  limitlessness for Hare of
    applicability of arguments
    based on, 126
  moral discourse not distin-
    guished from other forms
    by use of, 21–22, 28–30
  prudential discourse and, 26,
    29–30

role of, *xiv*, 24
stages of, 23–24, 27, 30–32, 37, 176, 178
statistical methods for, 198
universalizability and, 23–28
Singer, Peter, 194
Slote, Michael, 170–71
Spencer, Herbert, 111
Sprigge, T. L. S., 17, 173
Standard view of virtues, 59–60

T

Tax evasion, duty to abstain from, 75–76
Taxes, other taxpayers as beneficiaries of paying, 75–76
Theory of personal identity (Parfit), 59
Tooley, Michael, 53–54, 187, 195
Transcendental self, 207
Transfer of consciousness, 139–44
Transference of consciousness, 175
Transworld identification, general theory of, 130–39, 203, 205

U

Universal instantiation, 31
Universalizability of moral discourse, *xiii*, 177–78
consequences of, 169
designated argument-places and, 36–41
for every argument-place, 40
notions of, 194
prudential judgements and, 170
restricting the requirement of, 39–40

shoehorn maneuver and, 23–28
trivial consequence of, 104
Universalization performed on every argument-place occupied by individual constant, 38
Universalizing a claim, 31
Utilitarians, commitment to equal right to happiness of, 111
disputes between Kantians and, 58
disrespectfulness of value by, 112–13
moral code for, 112
respect for individuals and, 197

V

Value, defining, 114–15
in general, 114
moral, 115
treatment that respects a person's, 112
Vegetarianism, 211–12
Vendler, Zeno, 139, 175, 199–200, 206–8
Vendler's theory of transfer of consciousness within a single world, 141–44
accessibility in, 143–44
anchors to subjectivity in, 142–44
transcendental self in, 143–44
Virtue-ascriptions not analyzable in terms of duty-ascriptions, 61, 188–89
Virtue-ethics, 60
Virtues, 59–62, 188

W

Waiver of rights, power of, 83
Waldron, Jeremy, 192
Warnock, G. J., 176
Warren, Mary Anne, 187
Wellman, Carl, 192
Wider sense of morality, 15–17
Williams, Bernard, 195
Wittgenstein, Ludwig, 195
Wolf, Susan, 3–7, 170

Y

Yochelson, Samuel, 164